SPIRITUAL JUDAISM

SPIRITUAL JUDAISM

Restoring Heart and Soul to Jewish Life

DAVID S. ARIEL, Ph.D.

HYPERION • NEW YORK

Library of Congress Cataloging-in-Publication Data
Ariel, David S.
Spiritual Judaism / David S. Ariel.—1st ed.
p.   cm.
Includes bibliographical references.
ISBN 0-7868-6306-4
1. Judaism—Essence, genius, nature. 2. Spiritual life—Judaism.
3. Jewish way of life. 4. Prayer—Judaism. I. Title.
BM565.A76 1998
296.3—dc21   98-12594
CIP

FIRST EDITION
10 9 8 7 6 5 4 3 2 1

To my parents

LENORE AND MILTON FEIERSTEIN

"What can you give them like that which they have given you?"
—The Wisdom of Ben Sira

ACKNOWLEDGMENTS

I wish to thank the students in my seminars on Jewish spirituality who read early drafts of the book and offered challenging and thoughtful contributions: Barbara Beder, Sue Cahn, Judy Deutchman, Shirley Feldesman, Melanie Ferstman, Sherri Feuer, Loren Frieder, Miriam Friedlander, Joan Fry, Paul Gellman, Helen Goldenberg, Julie Handler, Nancy Kay, Sheila Lash, Bob Lev, Linda Ludwig, Wendy Mittelman, Lynn Rosen, Lee Rosenberg, Susan Rzepka, Elaine Saferin, Charlyne Schreck, Sam Schulman, Deeda Shubert, Henry Simon, Myrna Spira, Karal Stern, Lora Swartz, Carol Tuschman, Jonathan Wilson, and Dick Wooley.

Several close friends and colleagues read various versions of the book and offered many useful criticisms and suggestions. These include Ron Horvat, Arthur Lavin, Diane Lavin, Lifsa Schachter, Kyla Schneider, Mitchell Schneider, and Rob Spira.

I also appreciate the support of the Board of Governors of the Cleveland College of Jewish Studies, who have encouraged me to pursue my writing alongside my college work. I owe a great debt of gratitude to the officers: Jim Spira, Margery Kohrman, Marc Silverstein, Mort Weisberg, Shelly Brodsky, Ilana Horowitz Ratner, and Marc Saltzberg. Other college leaders have also provided exceptional support along the way: Bob Apple, Micki Becker, Larry Bell, Ernie Benchell, Rina Frankel, Marie Genshaft, Saul Gottlieb, Joe Horwitz, Fran Immerman, Jon Joseph, Irv Konigsberg, Alan Krause, Ray Leventhal, Marcia Levine, Fred Livingstone, Herb Marcus, Allen Miller, Ron Moskowitz, Michael Penzner, Dan Aaron Polster, Jim Reich, Eli Reshotko, Mitchell Schneider, Alan Schonberg, David Shifrin, Alvin Siegal, Michael Siegal, Naomi Singer, Muriel Weber, Erwin Weiss, Judith Weiss, and Donna Yanowitz.

My colleagues at the Cleveland College of Jewish Studies have made it possible for me to devote precious time to writing while managing the day-to-day affairs of an exciting institution. In particular, I wish to thank the members of the administration, especially Nili Adler, Lance Colie, Allan Feldman, Ron Horvat, Jean Lettofsky, Nancy Lurie, Linda Rosen, Lifsa Schachter, and Sue Tishkoff. Members of the Faculty Senate who have often influenced my thinking include Moshe Berger, Ron Brauner, Roger Klein, Alan Levenson, Jeffrey Schein, and Jane West Walsh. My assistant, Ronna Leubitz, has been helpful on a daily basis.

Since the beginning of the project, Jill Grinberg, my literary agent, has been a close confidante, a strong advocate, and an engaged reader of the book.

Laurie Abkemeier, Senior Editor at Hyperion, has made my dream of writing this book a reality.

From the day that I began this book, it has become a family project. My wife, Kay, and my children—Judah, Micah, and Aviva—have survived another one of my periodic literary hibernations. I thank them, yet again, for their patience.

CONTENTS

xi

Contents

xii

A NOTE TO THE READER

All biblical passages are quoted from the Jewish Publication Society's *Tanakh: A New Translation of the Holy Scriptures According to the Traditional Hebrew Text*. In transliterating Hebrew words, I have used the common Hebrew phonetic spellings instead of the less familiar, scholarly rules of transliteration.

In Hebrew, there is no neutral gender—every noun and pronoun is either male or female even if the subject is gender-neutral. English, of course, has the neutral gender, and, increasingly, English speakers employ the gender-neutral pronoun "It" when referring to God. However, this practice would not be faithful to the Hebrew and might sound confusing to the reader. Therefore, I have generally surrendered to the use of gender-specific language when talking about God, even though I would prefer not to use it at all.

STARTING AT
THE BEGINNING AGAIN

Every renewal is nothing less than a return to first principles.
—*Chayyim Nachman Bialik*

THE CLEARING, THE FIRE, AND
THE MELODY

My teacher, Gershom Scholem, quoting Shmuel Yosef Agnon, the Hebrew writer who won the 1966 Nobel Prize for Literature, tells the following tale in *Major Trends in Jewish Mysticism*: When the great spiritual master of Hasidism, the Baal Shem Tov, set out on his spiritual quest, he went to a special clearing in the forest outside the village where he lived. In the clearing he lit a fire in a special way, then sang a *niggun*, a Hebrew melody without words. And that was sufficient for him to reach the heights. When his disciple, the Maggid of Mezritch, came to him for guidance, he had already forgotten the instructions for lighting the fire, but he remembered the location of the clearing and how to sing the melody. And for the Maggid to reach the heights, that was sufficient. When the Maggid's student, Rabbi Moshe Leib of Sassov, arrived at the

1

clearing, he would say: "Not only have we forgotten the instructions for lighting the fire, but the melody, too, has been lost. All we have is the clearing in the forest, and that is enough." Finally, Rabbi Israel of Rizhin sought guidance, noting with sadness: "We no longer know how to light the fire or how to sing the melody, and we do not know the place. All we have is the story of how it was done." And, for him, that was enough.

What is our spiritual situation? Our generation never knew the location of the clearing, never learned how to light the fire, and never sang the melody. We cannot easily answer the question for ourselves: Why be Jewish? The problem for Jews today is the very meaning of Judaism. Many of us do not find our faith to be a significant factor in our lives or a compelling guide to life today. We search, often in vain, for a spiritual home in Judaism. Our spiritual aspirations are often quite high, but Judaism does not seem to be sufficiently spiritual. Many of us have turned outside Judaism—to New Age religions, Buddhism, and elsewhere—in our search. We value our own inner experience and look for a spirituality that can be expressed in how we live our lives. We have little regard for tradition unless it speaks to our own experience. We feel Jewish, but we find it difficult to put that feeling into words.

We look for groups that provide us with a community of shared concerns, that make us feel connected to others, and that give expression to our deepest feelings. While congregations often provide valuable services to their members, many of us still do not feel at home in our synagogues. We see Jewish institutions, especially synagogues and temples, as too preoccupied with institutional rather than spiritual concerns. We miss a sense of intimacy and connectedness if we are not part of the inner circle. Many younger Jews do not find synagogues to be places that touch their hearts. As one of my students said, "The basic thing isn't there yet in congregations— the acceptance, the quality of human interconnectedness, the relationships, true community." Because the liturgy is strange to many

2

people, the words of the religious services seem foreign and empty. We need to turn our synagogues into palaces of the heart once again.

THE SPIRITUAL CONFUSION OF MODERN JUDAISM

It might not matter that we cannot find the clearing in the forest, do not know how to light the fire, or cannot sing the melody of Judaism. But we cannot even tell the story anymore. We must start at the beginning again. What has happened to lead so many of us to feel that we cannot find a spiritual home in Judaism even if we desperately want to find one? Why do we find ourselves in this spiritual condition today? The answer lies in understanding the dynamics of modern Jewish history. In the last two centuries, Jews in many Western societies have moved from exclusion to acceptance, and Judaism has been modernized as the result of advances in knowledge, science, technology, and culture. As our people moved from the ghettoes into the mainstream, however, we paid a high price. The price of admission into the non-Jewish world has been the surrender of our spiritual integrity as Jews. As we sought to become integrated within gentile societies, we adopted many of the ways of thinking and living of our non-Jewish neighbors. We had to do this if we were to move into modern society. In the process, we surrendered what was unique about our own heritage. We diluted Judaism, buried our spiritual heritage, and made ourselves over in the image of what might be acceptable to the gentile world. In choosing between isolation and acceptance, we sacrificed the spiritual heart of Judaism that once held us in its powerful grip.

I have written this book to help us restore "heart and soul" to Jewish life through bringing the best of the spiritual traditions of Judaism from the periphery to the center. As the historian Lucy

3

Dawidowicz explained in *The Jewish Presence*, Jewishness for us is no longer a matter of fate, but of choice. The problem for earlier generations was anti-Semitism, but the challenge for us is preserving Judaism and Jewish souls. We must bring our own spiritual search back to Judaism, to move from the outside back to the center through rediscovering the spiritual dimensions of Judaism that we have lost. Judaism is a regular renewable resource, a source of psychic energy that reappears in unlikely ways. The voluntary choice of being Jewish now requires a thoughtful decision about what kind of Jew to be. I wrote this book to help you in reaching that decision.

A SECOND INNOCENCE

Is the past a useful guide to us today? While we do not want to live as our ancestors did, we still sense there is something engaging about the path our ancestors followed. We wish we could have the innocence that allowed them to lead a traditional Jewish life. We long for a world where not everything is ambiguous, relative, and subjective. We often tend to idealize and romanticize the Orthodox way of life for its apparent authenticity, purity, and precision. At the same time, we are not willing to surrender our independent judgment, critical thinking, and personal autonomy and embrace a binding system of behavior. We cannot easily accept divine law as the basis of faith when we know that it was developed by people like ourselves. We could only accept the law if we surrendered our modern outlook, our individuality, and our autonomy. We know too much to slip back into the innocent faith of our ancestors. Still, we long for that innocent faith and spiritual certainty, regretting that our own path is far less clearly marked.

Paul Mendes-Flohr, a contemporary Jewish thinker, describes this longing as the dilemma of the modern Jew: How can we retrieve the Jewish past and innocent faith without forfeiting our modern knowledge? We yearn for what the philosopher Ernst Simon calls a "second innocence" through a renewal of religious faith. Our ancestors never needed to look outside of Judaism to satisfy their spiritual needs. Their original innocence led them to assume that Judaism provided all the answers. Because we do not share their innocent faith and have lost our own spiritual way, we do not easily assume that Judaism can provide the necessary guidance. The yearning for a second innocence through a regained faith leads us to ask: How can I incorporate Judaism into my own spiritual life? According to Mendes-Flohr, the renewal of Judaism depends on a return to religiosity, a spiritual process of spontaneous and expressive manifestation of faith, shared with other Jews.

Rather than assuming we should return to traditional Judaism, we should explore how we can integrate Judaism into our own spirituality. We can learn from the experience of those who came before us and decide how much of the wisdom of the past addresses the questions we have today. We can learn from the accumulated wisdom of the one hundred generations that preceded us but not accept the past blindly. At the same time, we have a great responsibility, because the spiritual teachings and practices that we retrieve from the past will determine what we transmit to the next generations. As the twentieth-century Jewish philosopher Franz Rosenzweig said, "we are the children of our own ancestors and the ancestors of our own children." We need to find the proper balance between the traditions of the past and our duty to our own spiritual selves. This is how the Baal Shem Tov understood the opening phrase of the prayer, "Blessed are you, our God and God of our fathers." We praise God as both "our God" and "God of our fathers" because we must develop spiritually according to our own personal path as well as the path of tradition.

What is spirituality? Spirituality is a highly personal outlook about what is sacred to us, it is the expression of our most deeply held values, and it is that sense of higher purpose that guides our daily lives. Spirituality is not an otherworldly approach or a retreat into the occult. It is what you know in your heart to be true—"heart-knowledge." We are called as Jews to search for the tradition of heart-knowledge in Judaism.

We can integrate Judaism into our own spirituality and incorporate our own spirituality back into Judaism if we think of Judaism as a journey rather than as law. Judaism provides the spiritual teachings that can guide our hearts and enables us to apply those teachings to our life in the world. The Jewish journey is the expression of our spiritual aspirations and the embodiment of our spiritual teachings. The Jewish journey unites us with Jews of different generations through shared symbols that shield us from spiritual isolation.

We can draw upon all the traditions of Judaism to shape our own Jewish journey even if we do not follow any one Jewish denomination in particular. Jewish spirituality is not limited to the recipes of Orthodox, Conservative, Reconstructionist, or Reform Judaism. We should embrace the best of each of them while understanding that each denomination is a limited construct within a Jewish totality that is much greater than any one of its parts. Each denomination is a modern interpretation of Judaism, even Orthodoxy. The Jewish journey should explore all of Judaism, not only the modern varieties.

A PERSONAL JOURNEY

My own Jewish journey began in 1967 when I discovered the writings of the two leading Jewish philosophers, Abraham Joshua Heschel and Martin Buber. Heschel taught at the Jewish Theological Seminary and was famous not only for his writings about Judaism but equally for his involvement in the Civil Rights movement and his outspoken views against the war in Vietnam. Heschel's critique of contemporary Judaism spoke to me in a very personal way. He put into words the contradiction I felt between my Jewish ideals and my disappointment with the organized Jewish community. In his essay "The Insecurity of Freedom," he observed that the Jewish community has preserved the people at the expense of preserving the soul of the individual Jew. He explained that we have focused on strengthening Jewish philanthropy, fighting anti-Semitism, preserving the State of Israel, building self-defense and welfare organizations, and protecting Jewish rights. He said that we have emphasized identity and community but have not made Judaism compelling as a living religion. He called for a greater emphasis on Jewish meaning, spirituality, and values. Heschel's words spoke to the very alienation from synagogue Judaism that I and many other searching Jews felt at the time.

Heschel had become a legend for his pioneering stance as a Civil Rights leader who marched with Dr. Martin Luther King, Jr., in Selma, Alabama, and, later, gave voice and leadership to the Jewish peace movement, a nonviolent anti–Vietnam War effort. He energized many young Jews in those days to see Jewish spirituality, the Civil Rights movement, and antiwar activism as interconnected. I remember the spring night in 1968 when Heschel introduced Martin Luther King to a conference of Conservative rabbis. Heschel, who had helped found an antiwar group called "Individuals Against the Crime of Silence," spoke of the Jewish imperative to end the war in Vietnam. Dr. King spoke that evening about the connection between the Civil Rights movement and the antiwar effort. Before leaving that night, he autographed my "Individuals Against the Crime of Silence" membership card. One week later, King was assassinated, but the moral message that he and Heschel conveyed continued to influence me and many other Jews politically and spiritually.

Also of profound inspiration to me were the works of Martin Buber, the Israeli philosopher, who introduced Hasidism, the eighteenth-century Jewish mystical movement, to non-Hasidic readers through his many writings. He found in Hasidism the inspiration for his own Jewish philosophy. Hasidism was both a teaching and a way that provided its followers with an "intuition of eternity"—the awareness of the enduring presence of God within each of us—which

Buber regarded as the most remarkable of human achievements. Buber taught that there is nothing unholy, only that which is waiting for the holiness within to be uncovered. Buber, who stressed that ultimate human fulfillment occurs in the immediacy of human relationships, inspired many of us in the late sixties and early seventies to delve deeper into the Jewish spiritual legacy.

THE JEWISH JOURNEY

What are the teachings we hope to rediscover as seekers wishing to rediscover the spiritual teachings and practices of Judaism? How can we recapture the spiritual dimensions of Judaism in a way that is appropriate to modern Jews? How can we restore heart and soul to Judaism without resorting to static and rigid denominational labels? How can we make Judaism a living source of inspiration that draws faithfully on the past but looks boldly to the future? How can we learn the location of the clearing in the forest, the instructions for lighting the fire, and the melody that once inspired the souls of our ancestors?

We can begin by rediscovering the spiritual teachings of Judaism and by asking, *What do we believe?* We believe in a God who does not diminish the power of human beings. We, not God, have the power to guide our lives and shape the world. We believe that God speaks through our deeds and that His language is the human experience. We believe that human empowerment, the greatest fulfillment of the human potential of each individual, is a sacred, holy, and religious duty. We believe that we are created in the image of God and that a divine spark is planted in each of us. We believe that the divine spark within us allows us to fully appreciate the here and now.

We believe that our soul is the ladder that allows us to rise higher and higher toward the divine and thus strengthen the divine image within us throughout our lives. We have a great deal of control over the course of our lives through the exercise of our moral judgment. But we are also subject to forces in our imperfect universe that are beyond our control. Our world is naught but broken vessels and scattered light. To the extent that we have control, we can raise the sparks scattered and hidden in the shattered vessels all around us.

Our soul lifts us above our merely physical selves. We believe in a moral code that recognizes our freedom and our autonomy. When we become the master of our own lives and enjoy all that the world offers, we have brought out the divinity within us. When we help another person to ascend the ladder, we finish the work of creation. When we help bring out the human potential of each individual, we have brought God into the world. God stands in need of us because only we can perfect the world.

We believe that Judaism is a compelling system of belief and practice that leads to realizing God in the everyday world. It teaches us that we live within God, within a divine universe, and that we ourselves are infused with divinity. We believe that we are a unique and distinct people while acknowledging the equality and uniqueness of others. We believe that the Torah can guide our spiritual path today even as we find wisdom in many quarters. We believe that the spiritual experience behind the Jewish customs and practices can help direct our path through the world. And we believe in a soul that allows God to sing within us.

Judaism is a spiritual discipline that guides us to create a heaven on earth. The Jewish ideal is not left to the future; it is the imperative of today. There is no greater purpose for a Jew than to recognize the possibilities within the present moment, to raise the holy sparks in the everyday world around us, and to bring the divine ideal into the world. Our spirituality is not about transcending or rising above the everyday. Rather, it leads us to dignify and sanctify the everyday by bringing God into our world. We do not seek heaven; we seek to create heaven on earth without ever leaving home.

What is our mission, our calling, our purpose on earth today? The

9

Jewish people is a spiritual nation with a unique mission and calling to see the world not as it is but as it can be. Before we can begin to see the world in ideal terms, we need to develop a vision of what a revitalized Jewish life can be. We do not need to surrender our modern way of life or change who we are in order to bring about Jewish renewal. On the contrary, renewal will occur when we bring who we are and all that we know in our hearts to be true into the heart of Judaism. Jewish renewal occurs through our infusing life with our distinctive, modern outlook while allowing ourselves to be touched and revitalized by Judaism.

In order to imagine a better world, we have drawn upon the American tradition of voluntarism, which vests the responsibility of transforming society in the citizens, not just the government. We draw upon the American tradition of egalitarianism to remove the distinctions that prevent women from achieving full participation in society. We are inspired by the American respect for diversity that allows us to recognize that there are multiple paths to common goals. And we are influenced by the spirit of American individualism, which respects, above all, the individual journey. The Judaism emerging in North America might yet make a symphony out of all the songs of the different peoples of the world.

The challenge of "raising the sparks" does not lead us to spiritual narcissism or religious extremism. While Judaism promotes our spiritual journey, we are not only focused on ourselves. We do not retreat from society but advance into the world in order to reach our spiritual goals. Spiritual Judaism promotes self-fulfillment within the context of family and community. Indeed, we sacrifice some spiritual height for the stability that is provided by the fixed structures of family and society.

A GUIDE TO THE JEWISH JOURNEY

This book is a resource for those who, like me, are Jewish seekers engaged on a lifelong journey. I have written it to assist you in your own Jewish spiritual quest. Throughout the book, I have included explanations about the inward path of Judaism based on the experience and wisdom of those who came before us and what we understand today. But I have also included with each explanation a guide to the outward path, the way we turn our spiritual values into concrete expression in our daily lives. I hope the book will serve as a companion on your journey by elucidating the Jewish spiritual outlook and offering pointers to your own further exploration.

The first chapter, "God Speaks in Deeds and His Vocabulary Is the Universe," explains the Jewish understanding of God. The title is taken from Isaac Bashevis Singer's Nobel Prize acceptance speech, in which he defined his God as the being who expresses Himself through the universe and everything within it. This chapter will help you go beyond the simplistic and paternalistic view of God to a personal belief that can satisfy the seeker in each one of us: God is an infinite, unknowable being who encompasses the universe and fills each one of us with His being. The divine presence can be experienced within our lives. Realizing that God is within us leads us to the belief that our own self-fulfillment is a sacred, holy, and religious duty. Recognizing the divinity in others leads us to understand our connection and responsibility to other people. In this chapter, we explore how the God within manifests itself in ourselves, our relationships, and our approach to life.

The second chapter, "A Human Being Is a Ladder Placed on Earth Whose Top Reaches Heaven," explores the Jewish spiritual idea of what it means to be a human being created in the image of God. We are each a divine vessel striving to recognize the God within while accepting the responsibility to realize the divine in other people. The human challenge consists of the daily routine of cultivating the divine image within ourselves and within others. We struggle to

11

rise higher and higher on the ladder and to help others up the rungs. We explore how we can turn this belief into a guide to our own behavior. We also explore how we, as individuals, can nurture the divine spark within ourselves by listening to what the voice of the universe is saying to us. In this chapter, we examine the nature of the human soul, the decisive role of the inner voice, and the spiritual responsibilities of human life as we move through the different stages of our life's journey. These stages include love, relationships, and how we face our own mortality.

The third chapter, "A Person Is Called a *Mentsh* Because He Struggles," plays on the double meaning of the Yiddish word *mentsh*. The term refers to a morally developed human, but it also means "to struggle," implying that to be human is to be engaged in a struggle for human goodness. Life, however, also involves moments of loss, suffering, and pain. In this chapter we learn how to make sense of our own suffering and how to help heal ourselves through rituals and through the support of family, friends, and community. After an examination of suffering that happens to us with no apparent reason, we turn to the question of why people inflict cruelty on others. We will look at the Holocaust as a case study in human cruelty, but we will also explore other examples of human cruelty drawn from my experiences in the former Soviet Union and the Middle East. Finally, I discuss *mentshlichkeyt*, the Jewish code of goodness, and the ways we wrestle with our own goodness and humanity throughout our lives through self-awareness and the cultivation of human character.

The fourth chapter, "The Inward and Outward Path," moves into a discussion of how we can restore heart and soul to modern Judaism. In this chapter, I explore how the past can be useful as a spiritual guide to the present even as we continue to introduce new approaches and practices within Judaism. Judaism is an inward and outward spiritual path that guides us through life. The Jewish rituals are steps along the path, not laws to be blindly followed. In this chapter, we learn from the accumulated wisdom of those who came before us how to walk lightly in their footsteps as we create a new spiritual path for those who will come after us. In order to illustrate this, we explore several important areas of human spirituality from a Jewish perspective, including time, food, and family. We look at the meaning and practice of the Sabbath, the spirituality of food, the spiritual dimensions of Jewish holidays, and Jewish spiritual practices for the home.

In the fifth chapter, "Become an Ear That Hears What the Universe Is Saying," I discuss how we can connect our own personal spirituality to the Torah. Moses and our ancestors heard the voice of God and translated the message into the Torah. We too can become an ear that hears what the universe is saying to us through finding the voice of God in the sacred texts of Judaism. When we discover how others heard the voice of God, we can learn how to discover our own inner voice. We can be aided by learned interpretation, but we must also make Torah our own through finding our own voice in the text. In this chapter, I explain how we can take part in this process of discovering our own voice through Torah. We will explore how we can create a spiritual Jewish education for ourselves and our families. This chapter also provides a guide to how we can rebuild Jewish life through creating more spiritual Jewish congregations and communities.

The sixth chapter, "God Sings Within Us," presents a spiritual approach to personal prayer. Prayer is God's song within our own hearts, the voice we hear when we listen to what the universe is saying to us. In this chapter, we explore how to nurture our deep inner sense, our inner voice, by letting God sing within us through techniques that help ready us for prayer. This chapter explores how to use the prayer book as the record of what our ancestors heard when God sang within them and offers some alternatives to the traditional prayers that allow for a meaningful connection with Jewish prayer. I also provide a guide to how we can create our own prayer groups and find our way back home to Judaism.

In the seventh chapter, "Israel Sings All the Melodies of the

13

World," I explain that there is a spark of holiness within every people and that each culture has its own unique melody. The Jewish
task is to create a symphony from all the melodies of the different
cultures of the world. The purpose of the Jewish people is to bring
together the divine aspirations of every people and culture and elevate them by helping to create the ideal society in the real world.
The Jewish challenge is to raise the sparks, repair the world, and
close the gap between the divine ideal and the earthly reality. The
Jewish people must struggle to create heaven on earth and to see the
world not as it is but as it can be.

The epilogue, "Heaven on Earth," guides us to go beyond this
book to find our own unique Jewish path as we seek to realize
heaven on earth. The book ends with a section on resources and
with further suggestions for our individual, spiritual search.

As we set out together, the key to our spiritual quest is this: We
can draw from the Jewish spiritual tradition without falling into the
trap of fundamentalism. We can have a spiritually rich Jewish life
without returning to the antiquated ways of the *shtetl*. We can move
beyond the denominational fragmentation of Judaism today into a
new era of spiritual Judaism. We can find in Judaism the very principles by which to guide our lives and the answers to our deepest
personal questions. We can incorporate the best spiritual traditions
of the past into the Judaism of today. We can immerse ourselves in
the resources of the Jewish tradition by going back to the sources.
We can realize our vision of Jewish renewal through promoting the
spiritual teachings and practices of Judaism. And, in this way, we
can find the location of the clearing, learn how to light the fire, and
sing the enduring melody of Judaism once again.

Chapter One

GOD SPEAKS IN DEEDS AND HIS VOCABULARY IS THE UNIVERSE

The wisdom which a person requires is, first, to know
and contemplate the mystery of God and, second,
to know yourself.
—*Zohar Chadash*

THE ETERNAL MYSTERY

God is an unfathomable mystery beyond any conception of which we are capable. Yet, it is only human that we are drawn to try to understand the great mystery. Our souls yearn for a higher purpose, for expanses sublime, for the unity beyond diversity. We yearn to know: Is there a guiding hand to the universe? Did a creator bring the world into existence by design, or is it the result of blind forces? Did God create humanity, and is there a destiny and meaning to our lives, or do we just pass through time without purpose?

It is a great irony that while we truly know nothing about God, we say so much about Him. Although our sacred texts teach that God created the world, led our ancestors out of Egypt, gave our people the Torah, brought us into the Land of Israel, has watched over us throughout history, and now judges our actions, we do not actually know anything about God Himself. We attribute many things to God, but all these expressions are mere figures of speech and do not convey anything about who God actually is. We cannot truly know whether God is male or female, strict in judgment or merciful, prone to anger or quick to forgive. Our descriptions of God may be only our own limited and misguided impressions based on what we have experienced. But they are the intuitive guesses we make when we try to describe that which we can never truly know.

The Torah depicts how our ancestors understood the truths conveyed to them but does not convey who God truly is. That knowledge is not given to mortals and was denied even to Moses. Although we use the proper noun "Him" to refer to God, God is not of the male gender. When asked to explain why the Torah depicts God in human terms, our commentators explained that "Torah speaks in the language of humankind," meaning that Torah expresses indescribable truths in the everyday language accessible to human beings.

We can be guided in our search for the unknowable by the wisdom of those who came before us. Judaism is helpful in our search because it is the longest continuous human effort to seek answers to the fundamental questions about God and humanity. We can also be aided in our quest by the growing body of humanistic and scientific knowledge that we have gained in the last century. We recognize that other dimensions exist beneath, above, and beyond the visible realm. The heart stirred by feeling and emotion, the soul soothed by music or lifted by art, the mind moved by imagination, and the spirit touched by another human being all tell us that what we experience of the visible universe is only a pale reflection of what exists. Our feelings exist, although it is difficult for us to understand and define them. We know that different kinds of music and art have an effect on us, although it takes a connoisseur to explain why. We use our imagination even though we do not know what stimulates our consciousness. And there is no more powerful yet mysterious enigma than human relationships. Yet, we know that these dimensions of experience have as much of an effect on us as do our genes, our physique, our education, and our experience.

The discoveries of modern psychiatry, physics, and genetics have shown us that the invisible reality is more powerful than the visible forces in the world. Our lives are often shaped by our unconscious, which causes us to act in often inexplicable ways. The sciences teach us that the forces of energy, electricity, and magnetism are the unseen powers that mold our physical universe. Genetic discoveries show that human traits, predispositions, and even our very history may be deeply embedded in our genes.

The existence of these invisible realities has only recently been discovered. For centuries, religions paved the way for believing in the possibility of other dimensions of reality that shape every aspect of life. Now, we take it for granted that the invisible is the ultimate reality. We know now that invisible reality includes the emotions, consciousness, the psyche, energy, and genetics. We can only sense that there is an irreducible, unfathomable, ineffable, infinite mystery of all mysteries, which we call God. Even physicists such as Paul Davies now claim that "the Infinite is the mysterious source of every physical thing that exists."

Just as there is still no scientific proof for God's existence, there was no proof of the existence of these other invisible realities until the last century. Religious understanding often precedes scientific knowledge. Religion is perhaps the spontaneous, wondrous, intuitive sense of the eternal source of all the mysteries. The spiritually sensitive men and women of the past expressed their understanding of God in the best way they could. As we learn more about the invisible realities that we can know, we need to bring our new understanding back to religion and the continuous quest for answers.

The infinite source of all being will always remain beyond our knowledge. If we knew the Infinite, we would be the Infinite. We must content ourselves with the understanding that we will never know the eternal, unknowable, inconceivable, and indescribable God. But we will not stop seeking to penetrate deeper and deeper into the mystery.

"YOU CANNOT SEE MY FACE AND LIVE"

The divine mystery unfolded for our ancestors thirty-two hundred years ago when more than 600,000 former Israelite slaves stood on a broad, harsh, sandy plain in the Sinai Wilderness at the foot of a cragged mountain peak. This mountain was as rough as if the earth had simply pushed all the rock deep within it upwards, leaving it split, creviced, and bare. The days were sweltering and the nights were bone-chilling cold. The Israelites' memory of their slavery in Egypt, the plagues that had led to their release, and their rapid exodus were all fresh in their minds. They believed that their God, who had created the world, spoken to their ancestors, and guided Moses with a firm hand, was responsible for bringing them to this place. Several months after their departure, the mass of Israelites spread out across this plain as their leader, Moses, disappeared up the mountain and, over the course of three days, came back down with messages that he had received from their God.

On the third day, as dawn was breaking, the entire camp woke up to a terrifying noise. Without warning, the weather changed: The skies were covered with dark clouds, the heavens crackled with lightning, and the overwhelming sound of thunder and a high-pitched trumpetlike sound pierced the air. No rain fell. The mountaintop was covered in a dense smoke as if a fire were burning unseen, out of control. Moses disappeared up the mountain again. Gradually, at first, but then growing louder, another sound was heard as if coming deep out of the throat of God, a full guttural roar too indistinct to be identified as a specific word. The rolling, rumbling, breathy utterance continued for some minutes, along with the thunder, lightning, and the trumpet, until once again, it all subsided.

The Israelites, stunned, turned to each other with questions: "What is happening?" "Who made those sounds?" "Where is Moses?" The air was left still once again, but the reverberations continued as the people turned to each other in puzzlement and wonder. Their attention was riveted to the mountain where Moses still

18

was, if he had survived at all. And, then, crystal clear for all to see, a lone figure in the distance slowly made his way down the steep path on the mountain until he finally disappeared in the crowd at the base. The air was still, the sky azure blue, and the sun began to rise high in the morning sky.

It took some time for word to spread throughout the camp that Moses had been inside the storm and had spoken with God on top of the mountain. One by one, the leader of each tribe threaded his way to the front of the camp, where he was told what had just occurred. Moses and God have spoken, they were told. And what had God said, everyone wanted to know. Slowly, steadily, each leader was informed about what had taken place. And each returned to his tribe and told them what he knew: At the moment when we all heard the deep throaty roar, God spoke to Moses and told him: "I am *Adonai*, your God who brought you out of the land of Egypt, from a house of slaves. You are not to have any other gods before my presence."

The people were reassured that the thunder, lightning, clouds, and trumpet were signs from their God, who had identified Himself to Moses. They understood that it was their God who had brought them to this point. But they wanted to know what else had happened on the mountain. They pressed their leaders: "What else did God say? What is God like?" Their leaders turned to them and explained the second teaching that God had commanded to Moses: "You are not to make yourself a carved-image or any figure that is in the heavens above, that is on the earth beneath, or that is in the waters beneath the earth." Some of those listening nodded in agreement. They knew their God to be an invisible god who works through deeds and who is never seen by anyone. God is the unseen Creator, the hidden Redeemer from Egypt, the concealed voice of Sinai.

At the same time, some of the others looked puzzled, thinking to themselves: "What sort of God is this who speaks but is not seen? How are we to thank a God who cannot be seen? Where are we to bow down to Him? What kind of God does not want us to dedicate a great monument to Him? What kind of God has no likeness to anything in the heavens, the earth, or the seas?'' Such a God bears no resemblance to anything in the universe. Given their experience in Egypt and their memories of the great temples dedicated to the gods, they wondered whether this was a cruel hoax perpetrated by Moses. For the time being, they kept these doubts to themselves.

Moses spent the next forty days on top of the mountain listening to further instructions from God. When he returned, he brought with him the Ten Commandments that God had chiseled on two slabs of stone. But he immediately faced a challenge from his people, who had grown impatient for him and for more signs from God. He faced a revolt against the second teaching, the commandment against carved-images of God. When Moses saw that they had made a golden calf and were preparing to worship the carved-image, he lost control, smashed the two slabs on which God had written the laws, and killed three thousand rebels.

But apparently, the people were not the only ones troubled by the notion of an invisible, indescribable God. Right after this rebellion, Moses, himself, went back up the mountain and, resting in a crevice in the rock, confronted God, eager to see who this God was who had guided him this far. Moses demanded: ''Show me Your Glory!'' Patiently, God responded: ''I show favor to whom I show favor. I show mercy to whom I show mercy. But you cannot see my face, for no human can see me and live!'' Moses saw a dark shadow pass across him and felt the rumbling, moving presence of God on the mountain, but saw nothing. His request to see God was turned down with a firm and stern, ''No!'' From this point on in human history, we have lived with the mystery of the God who reveals Himself in deeds but whose presence cannot be seen.

20 Thus, although we cannot see God's face, we can experience God's presence within the world. The presence of the invisible is everywhere around us. God is present in every moment, every movement, every person. God is present in the majesty of nature, the

inspiration of an artist, the love of a parent, the eyes of a child. We do not look for God only in heaven, in the holy books, or in the synagogue. We look for God in the human soul, in the way we go about our daily lives, and in the way we look at others. God is not out there, He is within. And there is no place where God is not found. As the Kotzker Rebbe said, "Do you know where God is to be found? He is in the place where He is invited to enter."

The attraction of the presence of the invisible is a universal human experience. The Hebrew Psalms tell us that "the heavens speak the glory of God." This means that God speaks to us through nature, not only through the words of Torah. The poet, Judah Halevi, asks: "Lord, where shall I find You? High and hidden is your place. And, where shall I not find You? The whole world is filled with your presence. I have sought Your nearness, With all my heart I called to You. And as I went out to seek You, I found You coming toward me." As the Peasetzna Rebbe said, "All the world is divine, even the particles of earth beneath my feet, as well as the air I breathe within me, and all that exists is filled with divinity. Master of the World! Draw me close to You, surround me with all Your blessings, in complete harmony." Poets such as William Blake capture this sense of the divine in nature for us: "To see a world in a grain of sand, And heaven in a wild flower, Hold infinity in the palm of your hand, And eternity in an hour." And scientists such as Albert Einstein recognize nature's divine mystery when they see infinite energy in the mass of the universe.

THE WORLD WITHIN GOD

Judaism tells us that more than we seek God, God seeks us. The great sage Isaac Luria (1534–1572), known as "the Ari" (meaning "the Holy Lion")—an acronym based on his Hebrew name, _Ado-neinu_ ("Our Master") _Rabbi Isaac_—was one of the most original and influential Jewish thinkers since antiquity. He resided, at the end of his short life, in the Galilean town of Safed, where he developed his teachings. The Ari's works, which relate perhaps the greatest spiritual story ever told in Judaism, are both a legitimate interpretation of traditional Jewish theology and a revolutionary departure from it. He expressed his ideas in the idiom of the Kabbalah, the Jewish mystical tradition, and medieval Jewish mythology. Lurianic Kabbalah eventually became the most widely accepted formulation of Jewish spiritual belief until the modern era. The Ari's teachings were adopted by Jews of all persuasions throughout the Jewish world. Among the spiritual foundations of Judaism, his teachings were discarded, however, in the process of modernization. They are largely unknown to all but a few scholars today.

Although the Ari's language is incomprehensible to us modern Jews, when we translate his works into our vernacular, they have the ring of profound, spiritual truth. Not only did he penetrate the heart of Jewish belief, but he established a clear spiritual path for those who came after him. His teachings counsel us to maintain perspective by not confusing appearance with reality. Our image of God is not the reality of God, and our image of the world is not the reality of the world. What appears as God's indifference to us may only be our mistaken imagination. When things appear to us as flawed, imperfect, or evil, it is only because we have not penetrated deep enough to see the holy spark within every thing. What appears as a "broken vessel" is really a manifestation of divine light. We, however, only see the outward shell, not the hidden light contained within. The Ari teaches us to look at the hidden dimension within all things, the scattered sparks of divine light.

The Ari's teachings can be the basis for understanding the Jewish spiritual approach to God. He taught that all of existence is linked together in one great, continuous chain of being from the eternal, infinite God to the lowest form of matter in the universe. All that exists in the universe, the visible and the invisible dimensions of reality, manifests two characteristics: First, everything contains a spark of the eternal, infinite God that illuminates it and gives it vitality. Because the divine spark pulsates within everything, nothing is inanimate. Everything is alive and energized by the divinity within. Second, everything has its own individual character that defines it as unique and distinct. Even though divinity fills the universe, everything contains divinity in a different way. No two phenomena contain divinity in the same fashion, yet all things share in the essential divine quality. There is nothing that is not endowed with divinity, but there is nothing that does not have its own separate, singular, and particular character. Everything is filled with the divine, but no thing is God Himself.

How can the infinite God fill the entire universe? The Ari teaches that long before creation, the infinite, eternal God was Himself the entire universe, the primal Unity, expansive in every dimension. There was neither time nor space, only the cosmic fullness of God's being. However, something was missing. Even this absolutely self-contained being could not be fully complete except in relation to another being. In order to allow for the existence of something other than Himself, the infinite God limited Himself. The infinite God contracted and withdrew into Himself to allow something else to exist. God created a void, a vacuum, an emptiness within Himself in which He created the universe.

The unique element in this teaching is the idea that creation takes place deep within God, not outside of God. God is all around us, encompassing us on all sides, and we live, as it were, in the womb of God. This is the fundamental difference between the Jewish concept of God and all other Western views of creation. The universe is not set apart from God in a dualistic fashion that defines God as opposite to every other phenomenon. God and the universe are harmoniously linked and differ only in degree. This view differs from Eastern mystical teachings that argue that while God and the universe are a continuum, only God is real and the world is illusion. Jewish teaching asserts that the world we live in is as real as the divinity that breathes within it. Both God and the world are real and

23

share in the same essential energy. This teaching differs also from Christianity, which claims that God and the world are of opposite, and even mutually exclusive, character.

The Ari teaches that God created within Himself a void by contracting away from Himself into Himself. The void is a minuscule point in relation to the infinite God, but it is sufficiently immense for the expansive universe as we know it to exist. At first glance, the void appears to be a vacuum, a bounded empty universe surrounded by God. However, whenever anything withdraws from where it once was, it leaves behind a residue, an impression, a trace of its presence. The withdrawal of God away from the emptiness within did not leave a total vacuum within the universe. On the contrary, faint traces of God fill every dimension of this void. The "empty" universe is encompassed by God, who is beyond, unknowable, and impenetrable. At the same moment, even before the universe was formed, it was lavished with divinity. Our universe was formed in the residue of God's infinite presence.

Within this paradoxically God-filled vacuum, the Infinite began to create. God radiated His infinite light into the void in order to create the universe. The divine residue collected the light that God directed within the void. The universe was formed by the intersection of the radiating divine light and the residue of God's former presence within the void. Thus, the universe is made up of the divine energy and divine matter together.

As God set about to order the universe, He still could not radiate directly. Once again, He contracted into Himself, reduced Himself, before emanating out into the void. God wanted to create a form of existence lower and denser than His own infinite being. Therefore, He condensed Himself and, in the process, created a vacuum within which the world could be formed. This vacuum, however, was inherently unstable because it was in a state of disequilibrium: It was both an emptiness and an entity that contained divinity. The instability caused by the coexistence of two inherently opposite states of being—infinite divinity and limited divinity—could not be maintained. The condensed form of divinity within the vacuum, the divine residue, was highly volatile. Then, as God began to create within this unstable environment, the pressure on this system increased dangerously. The more that God created, the more the universe became supersaturated with divinity and, consequently, more unstable.

The universe that God was radiating consisted of divine light contained within subtle vessels. The light came directly from God, while the vessels took shape within the void created out of the residue of God's own being. The more that God directed His light into the light-vessels, the more the strain upon them increased. Just when God was forming the universe from Himself and within Himself, the entire system imploded. The vessels He had created from the residue within the void were too weak to contain the infinite divine light, and they collapsed under its power.

As a result, the vessels formed by the two constituent elements of the universe—direct light and the divine residue—were shattered, scattered, and exiled throughout the cosmos. Traces of the light stuck to the shells of the vessels. The collapse resulted in the chaotic scattering of divine light and broken vessels. God then set about to create order out of chaos. This time, He could only create a balance between the chaotic forces of the universe. The direct light and the residual light appear not as elements on a continuum but, rather, as two distinct polarities—divine energy and divine matter. The broken vessels were now doubly removed from God, first, through His contraction, and, now, through the rupture. The shards of these vessels now served as the matter that God acted upon in creation. The sparks of light, the traces of divinity, provided the energy that illuminated matter. God began to redirect His light within the mire and, ultimately, created the world that we inhabit. The broken vessels and the scattered sparks of divine light formed our world. Our world is not an ideal world but rather a reordering out of the chaos. It is an amalgam of divine light—albeit diluted and scattered—and broken vessels.

RAISING THE SPARKS

The universe that lay before God was not what He had intended, although it was the only possible outcome. God failed to create His ideal world; He could not create the perfect world of unity and harmony that He had intended. He freed the world from Himself and untethered the world from His being. The universe was in a state of chaos, but it was now independent of God, who now had little control over its final shape. This leads to another of the fixed laws of the universe: The world exists within God, is linked to God, but is independent from Him, and is filled throughout with sparks of divinity that can be restored to their intended unity only by us.

The broken vessels and sparks of light fell deep into the abyss created by the rupture. The rupture took place in the divine world and the scattered light and shards of vessels landed, finally, in our universe, forming the world as we know it. Ours is the last in the stages of unfolding of God's light and, paradoxically, His absence. Our world is all hidden light and broken vessel, presence and absence. God's power only extends to the realm of the radiated light and the vessels before the rupture. After the rupture, the sparks of light became part of our domain and essentially our responsibility.

The Ari explains that the chaos, disorder, and confusion apparent in our world do not mean that God has created a bad world or that He has abandoned it. On the contrary, the universe is filled with divinity even if it is not at first apparent. The world that we inhabit has two appearances: The outward appearance is that of a chaotic, disrupted world that seems far from ideal. But the outward appearance only conceals the inward vitality that comes from the hidden sparks of light within the vessels. Nothing is one-dimensional, nothing is black or white, nothing is absolute. Everything is relative, everything has two dimensions, everything oscillates from black to white, white to black, and back again. Everything has an outward appearance, a vessel or shell, and an inward essence, a spark of divine light.

The Ari described the outward appearance, the shell, the vessel, as the "back," and the inward essence, the spark, the light, as the "face." Because everything in the world has these two aspects, things can appear differently at different moments. Sometimes we see the shell, the "back" of something, and confuse it with the light within, the "face." We often confuse the vessel for the light, the outward appearance with the inward character. Because everything depends on our perspective, we must be careful in drawing conclusions about the "face" when all we see is the "back." This is how we can understand Moses' request to God, "Show me Your Glory!" Moses wanted to know God directly. But God responded: "You cannot see my face, for no human can see me and live!" We can rarely see the face of things directly. Mostly, we see the dark shadows that pass across our lives and confuse them with the living face of reality. We cannot know God directly, although we can see the traces of God in the world.

The Ari's teaching did not end with disruption, but with the unfinished task of creation. After the cataclysm, God's ability to shape our universe was limited. The work of uniting the scattered light and the broken vessel is beyond God's capacity. God could create order out of chaos, but now the world was independent of Him, beyond His reach. The universe appeared to go along its own course. Only we who live in the realm of the scattered light and the broken vessels can repair the tear. As human individuals, alone and in concert with each other, we can repair the tear that is not of our own making. Only we can complete the task of creation.

This is the Ari's teaching of repairing the world (*tikkun olam*) through raising the sparks. There is nothing that is devoid of divinity; everything is hidden light waiting to be revealed and reunited with its vessel into a harmonious whole. As Rabbi Abraham Isaac Cook has noted, there is nothing in the universe devoid of God's presence. There is no object, no event, no emotion, no person, no group, nothing at all, that is not filled with the divine: "One feels the divine

27

force coursing the pathways of existence, through all desires, all worlds, all thoughts, all nations, all creatures."

This becomes a challenge that calls on us to find the hidden sparks of light everywhere and to reunite them with the broken vessels. As the Kabbalist Israel Sarug said, "It should be the aim of every Jew to raise these sparks from where they are in this world and to elevate them to holiness by the power of his soul!" This process depends not on God but on us. Because God is incapable of creating the ideal world, the potential for true perfection of the world rests with us. By raising the sparks, recognizing the divine within the world, and finding the sparks wherever they are hidden, we can bring about repair of the world. We are both the last stage in the great chain of being and the very source of the world's own salvation. Everything depends on us. As the seventeenth-century Kabbalist Rabbi Isaiah Horowitz said in *The Two Tablets of the Covenant*: "The ultimate repair can be performed by man alone, for only he is created in the divine image."

In its final form, the world is composed of light and vessel. God presides over a fractured universe and is known to us through His appearances in the world. Our knowledge is both a partial knowledge of God and knowledge of a partial God. When we know God in His relation to the world, we know God's appearance, not His being. God has different "appearances," each of which is one of the partial and different ways in which we perceive God. The infinite God is not the same as any one of His "appearances." Each one is a manifestation of the true God just as the world is a lesser manifestation of God.

28 CREATING GOD IN OUR IMAGE

For many of us, it is difficult to believe in, let alone to feel a personal connection with, God. We are raised to believe in a supernatural being who has created life and presides over the universe and humanity as a benign, moral, and watchful ruler who is accessible to us at special moments like a caring parent who provides reassurance and comfort when we are in distress. But when it comes to believing that God is both our moral guide and a demanding judge, belief often fails us. If God truly watches over us, why does He allow terrible things to happen to us? How can God allow the death of those we love—our parents, children, or siblings? If God is good, how can He permit the brutal murder of so many innocent victims throughout the world? If God is transcendent, how can we even call God "He"?

We often find it difficult to accept how the Jewish prayer book describes God. Many of us cannot easily call God "the God of Abraham, Isaac, and Jacob, Great, mighty, revered God . . . You are the king who helps, saves, and protects." We might object to the omission of the "God of Sarah, Rebecca, Rachel, and Leah," or to the notion of a God who saves and protects us. When we attend *Rosh Hashanah* services, we often stumble over calling God "our Father, our King," language that reinforces a male stereotype of God. The language of the prayer book can easily strike us as grandiose and impersonal. It can make us feel that our own concept of God does not find expression in the written words of the prayer book.

The Yiddish poet Jacob Glatstein wrote that the God of his unbelief is magnificent. Glatstein was raised in eastern Europe and came to America before World War I. He had lost his faith early on, but the faith he had lost was one that revered the loving, caring, listening God of all the universe. The faith he had lost was the belief in the God who weeps when a child suffers, who answers the prayers of the broken-hearted, who judges the actions of His people. He could no longer believe, certainly not after Auschwitz, yet the God in whom he no longer believed was still the magnificent God who parted the Red Sea and who spoke at Sinai. His image of God was of a being as great as He ought to be, even if He no longer existed.

Many of us have been taught since childhood that these images are, in fact, God. But when we begin to consider what we ourselves believe, this God fails us. Not this God, Himself, but our belief in this God fails to persuade us. Our experience tells us that God is not a demanding judge or a father figure. The great, powerful God is one in whom we have difficulty believing. Such a God is indeed so awesome that He may be worthy of our unbelief. The God "out there" may be magnificent, but He is not the God with whom we are personally involved. Repelled by belief in such a God, we might conclude that God is neither magnificent nor real.

But we might also look at this problem from another perspective. When we no longer believe in God, it may be a certain image of God in which we cannot believe. The problem may be one of perception. Perhaps our image of God is based on a limited understanding or a misconception that we have adopted as a result of our own education and upbringing. Most of us hold an image of God in our minds as a personal being whom we expect to listen to us when we call to Him, who should reward us when we are good and punish us if we are bad. This is the childhood image of God as parent that many of us never outgrow because we rarely have the opportunity to examine our beliefs from an adult perspective.

This God is not in fact the God of Judaism. Our ancestors understood God according to the best information and understanding they had available to them. But our view of God has developed and has become more sophisticated over time. Each generation adds a little to the understanding of the previous one. As our understanding unfolds, we can sense that God is an unknowable mystery who is manifested in various "appearances." What if we were to understand these appearances not as truths but as metaphors that express the various ways in which we sense the presence of the invisible in our lives? For example, we praise God, "who forms light and creates darkness," "whose word brings on the evening twilight," and "who rolls away light before the darkness and darkness before the light." But God does not form, create, speak, or roll away anything, as we might. We cannot know how, or even why, day and night came to be. But we know they reflect the presence of the invisible. How fortunate we are that poets can turn our wonder into speech so that we do not stand in stunned silence. As soon as we begin to speak, however vivid our metaphors might be, we probably say more than we really should. We often take our metaphors too literally. When our tradition describes God as sitting on a throne in heaven, it means only to convey God's supremacy. When God is described in masculine and fatherly terms, it is only to convey divine power in terms that are familiar to a patriarchal society.

What if we were to rely more on metaphors, images, and appearances that are not meant to literally describe God? If we took the descriptions of God as metaphors, we might not find ourselves alienated by some of the language in the prayer book. We are often troubled today by the predominance of the king and father images. If we understood these as metaphors, we might be less troubled by some of the paternalistic descriptions of God. If we grasp that God is neither male nor female, father or mother, king or ruler, we could move beyond the childish images to a more spiritually satisfying and empowering understanding. While some of the traditional images seem to suggest a paternalistic, judgmental God, there are also feminine metaphors in Judaism that describe God as the divine mother, bride, and queen. Each metaphor is one of the ways in which we perceive God in the world. Because of the difficulty in truly comprehending God, all we have are metaphors and images, inadequate as they may be.

KING, FATHER, MOTHER

Our tradition portrays God in three basic images or appearances: the king, the father, and the mother. God appears to each of us, and to each age in human history, through one or another of these images. They are the predominant images that appear in the Torah, the rabbinic tradition, the prayer book, the Kabbalah, and in the consciousness of modern Jews. Each of these images or archetypes recurs in every stage of Jewish civilization. They are the product of the Jewish collective consciousness. They are primordial images whose meaning and purpose always remain the same.

The king image is the ultimate archetype of the watchful "King over all the earth," the "King enthroned supreme," the Creator God, who brings the world into being by His command. This is the image to which we offer our prayers on the High Holy Days of *Rosh Hashanah* and *Yom Kippur*. The king establishes the reality of the world and generates the energy and goodness that flows into the world as blessing. The king creates humanity by invoking in the royal plural, "Let us make man in our image." The king is the calm steward, the source of unity, the transmitter of wisdom, the mysterious, heavenly deity called in Hebrew *Ehyeh* ("I Am"). This is the God of the more sublime passages of the Hebrew Bible, the God of the first of the Ten Commandments on Mount Sinai, the highest level of human awareness of God. The king image, however, is not rooted in gender but is intended to convey the transcendent power of the hidden, unknowable God.

The father image is the masculine archetype of God, the stern yet compassionate judge, the wise and knowing parent who regards His children mercifully. "Have we not all one father? Did not one God create us?" (Malachi 2:10). God is "as a father who has compassion for his children" (Psalms 103:13). The Talmud refers to "Our Father in heaven" to describe the personal, caring, and protective image of God. Many of the Hebrew prayers are directed to the father image: "O Father, merciful Father, ever compassionate, have mercy upon us." We ask God that He forgive us as a father forgives his children: "Forgive us, O Father, for we have sinned." The father image is also the voice heard at Sinai, the heavenly Father called in Hebrew *YHVH* ("Being"), and the Holy One, Blessed be He. He is the warrior God who brought us out of the land of Egypt, the strategist God who led us through the Sinai Desert to the Land of Israel. This is also the image of God the Father on the High Holy Days with their emphasis on judgment and repentance.

The mother image is the feminine archetype of the caring, nurturing God with whom we feel deeply intimate in those moments of heightened religious fulfillment. The female image of God is the one with whom we have a relationship, to whom we pray and who answers our prayers. The tradition refers to this image of God as the *Shechinah* ("Divine Presence"). We recognize the presence of the divine within the world because the *Shechinah* is in every place. Whenever God feels the suffering of an individual, the *Shechinah* is present. Whenever the presence of God is experienced within the world, the *Shechinah* is among us. Whenever we reach out to God, we ought to imagine that the *Shechinah* is before us, and "enjoy the radiance of the *Shechinah*." This is the God who hears and answers our prayers, and the nurturing, maternal God who protects us when we are in distress, when we are gathered "under the wings of the *Shechinah*." This is the God who is moved by our distress, whose presence we might recognize in the world. This is the Sabbath bride, the patroness of the Sabbath, the moment in time when all the daily conflicts are settled, the struggles of the week are resolved, and the contradictions of life are harmonized.

When we pray to "our Father, our King" on the High Holy Days, we invoke the patriarchal images that are dominant on these holidays. In doing so, we acknowledge our mortality, our frailty, our creature consciousness within a vast and sometimes frightening universe. We do not literally believe that God is male or that God decides our fate. We feel as if we are being judged even though it is we who are judging ourselves. And since we associate judgment with fatherly traits, we call God "the Father." On the Sabbath, we describe the presence of God as the Sabbath Queen, in order to express our sense of relief from the stress and routine of the six days of the week. We describe the God who brings us this day of soul-nurturing as feminine. But again, this is an archetype or metaphor, and we should not confuse it with the reality of God.

At times, we resort to simple explanations. When things happen to us, we sometimes attribute the cause to God. When we need something, we might believe that God will answer us. When we look to God for solutions to our problems, we create God in the image of a father. When we need care and nurturing, we recreate God in the image of mother. If we would take these images literally, we would violate the second commandment that warns us against making graven images. We cannot make God conform to our images of what God should be. Yet, as humans, we cannot avoid trying to make the infinite real. This the divine paradox: God is the unfathomable mystery who cannot be known, yet His presence can be experienced in the world. As we seek God, we find Him coming toward us.

What are the relevant images of God that serve us today? All the images that we have of God are based on our ideas of relationships. Too many of the images from the past are based on parental images of God that emphasize our dependence, inadequacy, and need for protection. These images are inadequate for many of us today because our understanding of relationships has changed as we have grown and society has evolved. The conventional images of God that are prevalent in Judaism and that reflect a parent–child model are not spiritually compelling today. We can use a new imagery of God based on a mature understanding of relationships. We can replace the parent–child model for our relationship with God with a new model of father to adult and mother to adult. We can find new images from within the tradition that reflect these more appealing notions of our relationship with God.

The new images can preserve the mystery of God as the unknowable, infinite God of the universe. We can turn to those images in the Jewish tradition that highlight the God within us that ennobles and empowers us. The tradition is redolent with images that go beyond the king–subject and parent–child models. These images include God within nature, God within the human heart, God as concealed yet revealed, and God as a fire that is not quenched. Our

34

imagery could also emphasize God as partner, God as the object of our soul's desire, God as artist of the creation, and God as teacher. These and many other images from within the tradition may yet help us to create a more spiritually rewarding connection with the Jewish tradition.

AN INTUITION OF ETERNITY

We are each created in the image of God, in the likeness of the unlimited source of all being. The hidden, unknowable God of the universe is within us. The divine image is the soul that gives us life, consciousness, and personality. It is the individuality, the uniqueness, that each one of us possesses and that we spend our lifetimes trying to cultivate. It is the voice that we can hear within ourselves when we listen attentively to our deepest thoughts. It is what Martin Buber called the "intuition of eternity," the awareness of the enduring presence of the God within. It is the oceanic consciousness that we are an integral yet infinitesimal part of the great, expansive universe. It is the hidden spark within each of us that comes from the Infinite.

The most difficult challenge we face is to recognize the divine spark within ourselves and within others. Yet, if we truly believe that everything ultimately derives from the mystery of God, we must accept the fact that everything has the spark of the divine within. This statement is more than an explanation of how things come to be. It is actually the theory that makes self-understanding a religious duty. To know ourselves, our true selves, and to listen to the true voice within, is to trace the stages back to where our soul, our consciousness, our inner divine voice come from. As a medieval Jewish philosopher, Shem Tov ibn Falaquera, said, "If you know yourself, you know God."

Although we can never fully understand how the world came to be from the infinite source, we know that everything comes from the Infinite, shares in the Infinite, and returns to the Infinite. So, we can say that God speaks through the orderliness of the universe that causes the sun to shine each morning, the goodness of a world that provides us with food in good season, and the miracle of life that is renewed each day. The infinite God does not usually speak in words, although, at times, we experience being spoken to by God. God speaks to us through every thing that exists, through the world that has come to be, the energy that gives life to matter, the divine spark that fills each human soul. As Isaac Bashevis Singer said in his Nobel Prize acceptance speech, "God speaks in deeds and His vocabulary is the universe."

My father is fond of telling me about his boyhood walks with his father on the Sabbath. My grandfather, who spoke only Yiddish, would often mumble to himself incomprehensibly. Finally, my father asked him what was he mumbling. He explained that he was saying to himself, *"Baruch Hashem Yom Yom"*—"Day by day, praise God." Every day a Jew says to himself, "Day by day, praise God." This is the essential Jewish outlook on the world. Abraham Joshua Heschel taught that to be Jewish is to stand in radical amazement at the goodness of all life, to feel awe at the wonders of life. Every day that we wake up, we thank God for the renewal of life. When we look at the beauty of nature, we are astonished. When we look at the incredibly complex variety of chemical and neurological processes that are necessary to maintain a healthy organism, we stand in awe. When we truly love another person, we are touched on a very deep level. Day by day, we praise the infinite, unknowable God who speaks in deeds and whose vocabulary is the universe.

THE SPIRITUALITY OF RADICAL AMAZEMENT

How can these teachings be applied to our lives? We experience God by understanding that the divine spark illuminates the world in which we live. We can find in Judaism a discipline that teaches us how to concentrate intensely on particular moments as having deeper significance than surface appearance. We can do this through simple blessings and other attentive exercises. We can pause before every action that we take throughout our day, to think about the divinity within everything we enjoy, and to consider the impact of everything we do. For example, right now, we can look around and take pleasure in our surroundings, savor the moment, and appreciate the divinity all around us. That moment is a form of blessing.

In Judaism, there is a blessing for everything, including eating, the most basic of human activities. Eating is not just a physical action but a spiritual one as well. As the Ari himself said, "You can mend the cosmos by anything you do—even eating. Do not imagine that God wants you to eat for mere pleasure or to fill your belly. No, the purpose is mending. Sparks of holiness intermingle with everything in the world, even seemingly inanimate objects."

The spirituality of eating is central to Judaism. As one Jewish mystic said, "When you eat and drink, you experience enjoyment and pleasure. You must remind yourself to ask in wonder at every moment: What is this enjoyment and pleasure? Then, you will answer yourself: This is nothing but the holy sparks within food and drink!" Of course it is difficult to maintain on a daily basis a spiritual outlook with regard to mundane actions like eating. That is why Judaism asks us to stop for a moment before most daily routine tasks to pause and be aware. We have different Jewish blessings for bread, fruit, vegetables, grapes, and other foods:

- When we eat bread, we thank "God, our Lord and King of the universe, who brings forth bread from the earth."

- When we eat a fruit, we say: "Blessed are You, God, our Lord and King of the universe, who creates the fruit of the tree."
- When we see a natural wonder, we say: "Blessed are You, God, our Lord and King of the universe, whose deed is Creation."
- When we see the ocean: "Blessed are You, God, our Lord and King of the universe, who made the great ocean."
- When we see a shooting star, hear thunder, or see lightning: "Blessed are You, God, our Lord and King of the universe, whose power and strength fill the universe."
- When a rainbow appears, reminding us of the biblical sign of God's covenant with Noah after the Flood: "Blessed are You, God, our Lord and King of the universe, who remembers the covenant, remains faithful to it, and keeps His word."
- When we see a tree in bloom: "Blessed are You, God, our Lord and King of the universe, who left nothing out of His world, who created beautiful creatures and fine trees for people to enjoy."
- When we see a man-made wonder: "Blessed are You, God, our Lord and King of the universe, whose universe has this."
- When we are in the presence of a Jewish scholar: "Blessed are You, God, our Lord and King of the universe, who gave of His wisdom to those who stand in awe of Him."
- When we see a non-Jewish scholar, we say: "Blessed are You, God, our Lord and King of the universe, who gave of His wisdom to flesh and blood."

Other blessings praise God when we put on new clothes, when we hear good news or bad news, when we escape from danger, when we are sick, and when we are healed.

It would be a useful exercise to devote one day to those moments when we might stop and offer a silent blessing. Just think of how many moments like these make up our day. We do not always need to vocalize our awareness of them. These moments of blessing, however, help us to realize how our lives are filled with countless opportunities to raise the divine sparks scattered all around us.

A DWELLING PLACE FOR GOD

Because each of us possesses the divine spark, we are the dwelling place for God. Our spiritual task is to see each individual as containing the divine light and to help bring out the hidden spark. We have to help allow that light to shine in all its brilliance. As Martin Buber said, in every person, there is a hidden spark, something precious that is in no one else—our own individuality. And so we should honor each person for what is hidden within him or her, for what only that individual has. At the same time, we each share a common humanity that unites all of us.

In Yiddish, Jews are called *Yiddin*, the same name as the *yod*, the tenth letter of the Hebrew alphabet. Two *yods*—one next to the other—spell the name of God. If one *yod* is higher than the other, this is not God's name. Likewise, if two Jews relate on an equal basis, they create God's holy name. But when one sets himself up as superior to the other, God is not there. The relationship between two people is one of spiritual equality and of facilitating what is yet-to-be brought out from within us. There is no difference among us—other than the degree to which the light shines within us.

We are each like a diamond in the rough that cannot show its brilliance until it is polished. There is light, as from a diamond, in each one of us. Each one of us possesses the holy spark, but we do not always express it to its fullest. The challenge is to help ourselves and those individuals within our midst whose spark is hidden or whose light is dim. We believe that there is no one in whom the light does not shine. The sparks may be less evident in some people, but that only means that we must work harder to find the light.

Raising the sparks is both a spiritual and a practical, worldly task. We must recognize, respect, and cultivate the divinity within ourselves and others. We can find the light and raise the sparks by recognizing the divine quality within ourselves and in others. In practical terms, this means imitating the "appearances" of God. We believe that God's "appearances" are the hidden ideals to which we aspire. The rabbis tell us: "Just as God is gracious, so you must be gracious." But we can only reach the ideal through self-improvement, through our relationships, and through the communities that we create. Touching the Infinite and reaching the perfect is the spiritual goal of Judaism. But this aspiration can only be achieved through our relationships with other people.

The practical implication of the belief that God is within each of us is the importance of an ethic of self-realization. We must bring out the God-qualities in ourselves and bring God into our lives. We must also recognize that the God whom we imitate in the world is usually one or another of the "appearances" of the unknowable God. When we "impersonate" one of the hidden ideals that we call God's "appearances," we become partially complete vessels. When, finally, we balance all the partial qualities of God, we become whole people. Neither the king, the father, nor the mother is the complete God but only partial qualities of God. We must integrate all the qualities into a complete unified whole within ourselves before we become complete.

Our spiritual tradition counsels practical goals and specific steps necessary to actualize the divine qualities within ourselves. Maimonides' principle of the "golden path" can serve as a guide for our path. He tells us that the ideal human quality is the middle path between two extremes. He explains that the right approach is not to go to an extreme in impersonating the divine qualities but, rather, to follow a path of balance. However, if we tend to one extreme by virtue of our own inclination or past habits, we might overcompensate temporarily in the other direction. We might need to be excessive in our impersonation of one divine quality in order to compensate for a tendency in the opposite direction. When we have reached that balance, we can move back toward the golden path, the secure middle.

How could we follow this course in our own lives? If, for example, we tend to be too judgmental of other people, we might make a corrective effort, for a time, to be completely accepting of them, even if it does not come easily. Over time, we might find the proper balance between judgment and acceptance. If we are inclined to speak harshly about others or to share rumors or gossip with other people, what Judaism calls *lashon ha-ra* (immoral language), we might pursue a course in which we make a conscious effort to say only good things about people. If we overindulge in some personal habit, we can try to give it up until we can find a balance between indulgence and abstinence. We cannot expect ourselves to be saints, but we can correct our excesses and find a comfortable middle ground.

HARMONY OF THE MALE AND THE FEMALE

Each human quality is connected to the ways in which God appears to us. The first quality of the king, for example, is quietism, indifference to the negative emotions that often drive our lives. This ability not to react excitedly to the little disturbances that we face every day is called "imitating the king." A king presides and does not let others control him or his reactions regardless of how much disruption there is in his kingdom. The king understands that a true leader does not act precipitously during a crisis. A king is at his strongest in a crisis if he acts according to a clearly formulated value system and knows what is strategically important and what is a mere distraction or provocation. A king is able to make decisions in difficult situations because his principles guide him and he is not swayed by his own private preferences. To achieve the status of the king, we need to stand above our emotions and gain perspective. To act on the basis of the highest divine qualities is an awesome challenge. It is difficult to achieve this level without cultivating humility and love of other people through practice, patience, and forgiveness when we fail to achieve these goals.

For example, when someone criticizes or provokes us, as in an argument with a lover or spouse, we can be kingly by not reacting

41

or responding emotionally or vindictively. A relationship cannot work if we try to win an argument with our partner. For there to be a winner, there has to be a loser, so the necessity to predominate leads to a power struggle and conflict. As long as we operate with categories of winning and losing, we are functioning from the lower rungs of the ladder. A king does not need to use his power, because he is powerful. He does not need to react to every challenge as a threat to his power, because he feels secure. Therefore, we can be kingly in our relationships by not reacting defensively or with hostility to challenges. If we react to the provocation, we cannot listen to the challenge fairly and without feeling threatened.

The king is also altruistic and generous toward other people. The king does not lack for anything, because he is satisfied with what he has. Because he views other people generously, he does not want what they have. As the *Mishnah* says, "Who is wealthy? The one who is satisfied with his own portion." The king is so confident in his own accomplishment that he welcomes the achievements of others. Because the king is certain of his own power, he is not threatened by the power of others. While we may ordinarily feel jealousy at another person's success or achievement, the king turns jealousy into love by appreciating others' success. The king has confidence in his own stature so that he can let another person's honor be as precious to him as his own.

The king acts with compassion and forgiveness to those who hurt him. When he sees another person suffering, he does whatever he can to ease his trouble. He understands that other people's cruelty derives not from strength but from their own sense of weakness. He wants to see the weak become strong, and he wants even the cruel person to become so strong within himself that he no longer expresses his powerlessness inappropriately. When another person tries to hurt the king, he understands it as a reflection upon the other person and does not take it personally. He is understanding of the offending party and forgives him for the shortcoming that causes him to hurt another person. Just as God forgives us, we should find the spark of passion in our desire for revenge, and turn it into forgiveness. When he is faced with another person who is reacting angrily, a true king soothes him and helps him become calm. He welcomes each person with cheerfulness, maintains his equilibrium, and does not react to provocation.

The king is genuinely humble and does not elevate his own stature. He knows that there is always someone higher than him. He knows that just as God contracted Himself to create the universe, so must we each constantly bring ourselves down a level to keep perspective on our self-importance. The king is a positive listener who listens for the good about other people, not the bad. He is also a positive speaker, who speaks only about the good in others.

The father quality, the masculine archetype of God, is the ability to be strict yet compassionate with ourselves and with others. It is the ability to take the appropriate reaction at a given moment according to the requirements of the situation and not act in the heat of the moment. It is the quality that requires thoughtful aggression when the situation demands it and honorable retreat at other times. Even though it is best to be kingly and avoid anger or aggression, sometimes these qualities are necessary. For example, there are times when our children, friends, colleagues, or people with whom we have business act irrationally and do not respond to reason. There are times when we need to use firmness, anger, or even our physical strength to control a situation. The key is not to lose control ourselves, but to use our emotions—even anger—as a controlled technique to achieve a solution and restore calm. The key is to govern the expression of our emotions in a way that is appropriate to the situation rather than to be governed by them. Thoughtful aggression does not mean using physical force but, rather, wielding power in a moral way when no other method works. It is the strategic quality that allows us to pass over momentary rewards in favor of long-term goals. It comes from our capacity to listen to the divine voice within that can guide us in facing life's challenges.

The mother quality, the feminine archetype of God, is immediacy and presence, the ability to enter into a relationship on an equal basis with another person. It is the ability to see another person as he truly is, to see in him the same measure of human dignity as oneself, and the capacity to feel what he is experiencing. It is the ability to love, to give, to feel, to empathize. It is the quality of passionate knowledge that brings enthusiasm to our experience. It is the ability to retreat from activity, to turn inward, to be quiet, to appreciate harmony and stillness.

That God has a feminine dimension that must be incorporated fully into ourselves, just like the masculine dimension, is an age-old Jewish principle, but in practice Judaism has not done full justice to the rights of women until recently. The exclusion of women from equal status and participation in Judaism is the one area in which Judaism has failed to follow through on its own original spiritual precepts. Now that this lapse is finally being corrected, modern Jews are seeking to restore the feminine aspects of God into their own lives.

The ideal appearance of God is neither that of the king, the father, nor the mother by itself. The ultimate personification of the divine qualities is not restricted to inwardness, altruism, compassion, humility, positive speech, aggressiveness, presence, or passion, but is the cohesion of all these qualities in one integrated whole person. True imitation of God occurs when we impersonate God in all His appearances at once. The whole person is then greater than the sum of his or her parts. When all the kingly, fatherly, and motherly qualities are found in harmony within one person, the person is complete.

The Kabbalists who followed the Ari described their goal as uniting the masculine and feminine aspects of God. They meant that the only true quality of God resided in the reconciliation of contradictions, the harmony of opposites, which they described as the synthesis of the masculine and feminine qualities of God. God is neither male nor female, but the harmony that comes with the balance of the characteristics of each gender. Likewise, we human beings are most complete when we balance the different and conflicting tendencies in our own character, when we soften the "masculine" part of our personalities with our "feminine" qualities, and vice versa. When we see ourselves as a unity, we see God as the unity of different qualities as well. A person who rises above the appearances of God and the appearances of his own self raises the divine sparks all the way back to their roots in God.

The Kabbalists called this process of uniting the contradictions within ourselves and of knowing God as a unity beyond male and female *devekut* ("bonding"). Bonding is essential to both the internal coherence of a fully realized human being and the spiritual awareness and connection with God. The dual tasks of balancing the conflicting human tendencies within ourselves and rising above a narrow understanding of God as male or female is a fundamental Jewish principle. It is so central to Judaism that one Hasidic rabbi pronounced that "Judaism without *devekut* is idolatry!"

This way of thinking about God can help us in our daily lives. Such an approach moves away from the notion that God is powerful and we are subservient. It avoids the devaluing of human beings that is implicit in some religious teachings. Rather, it says that God is the ideal to which we strive, the source of the different qualities we hope to emulate. This approach to God empowers us to have an adult-to-adult relationship with God. It rejects the immature notion that God is a father and king figure and discards the idea of male and female stereotypes.

Judaism teaches that true spirituality consists in the daily routine of building a better world. We express ourselves in our own deeds. Our spiritual vocabulary is the self we become. Our attention is devoted to the work of realizing the divine in the everyday world. We do not seek God in the heavens but in the way we go about our daily lives. We must be engaged in the holy task of finding the sparks, uncovering and removing the obstacles, and letting the light of the soul shine. A Jew must be a spiritual harvester—nourishing and bringing forth fruit from the seed of the human soul. Our responsibility to living in the here and now is one of the unique features of Judaism.

Jewish spirituality is realized in the way we lead our daily lives, not by a retreat from the everyday. Our task is not to look to heaven for solutions, but to build the kingdom of God within the human heart and within society. There is an ancient story about Rabbi Yochanan ben Zakkai, who lived in the first century, right after the destruction of the Temple, a time of national calamity and messianic expectation. One day, this great leader was planting trees in his garden when a neighbor came up to him, very agitated, and said: "Stop your work, come with me, up to Jerusalem, for I have heard that the Messiah has arrived." The planter said, "No, first I must finish my planting. When I am done, then I can go out to greet the Messiah."

Chapter Two

A HUMAN BEING IS A LADDER PLACED ON EARTH WHOSE TOP REACHES HEAVEN

> As the hand held before the eye conceals the greatest
> mountain, so the little earthly life hides from the glance the
> enormous lights and mysteries of which the world is full, and
> he who can draw it away from before his eyes, as one draws
> away a hand, beholds a great radiance of the inner worlds.
> —*Martin Buber*

JACOB'S LADDER

Yaakov Yosef of Polnoye, the disciple of the Baal Shem Tov, said that a human being is a ladder placed on earth whose top reaches heaven. The great moment of this awareness occurred nearly four thousand years ago when Jacob, Abraham's grandson, made this discovery. The Torah tells us that Jacob set out from his home in the land of Israel at the threshold of adulthood on a journey to his grandfather Abraham's ancestral home to find a wife. He arrives at an ancient holy site and camps there. That night, he has a dream. He dreams that a ladder is set up on the earth, its top reaching the heavens. Messengers of God are going up and down on it. In the dream, God, standing in front of Jacob, speaks to him, promising him that He will watch over him, give the land of Israel to his descendants, and make the people of Israel a great nation. When Jacob wakes from the dream, he is awestruck and says to himself: "God is in this place, and I did not know it!" He calls this place Beth El, the house of God.

This is one of the pivotal moments in Jacob's life and in the spiritual history of humanity. For what actually happened was that the dream was not an event that occurred outside of Jacob but rather something that occurred within himself. He recognized that he himself was the ladder and the messengers of God the stages of his own spiritual development. Jacob's ladder is the Jewish metaphor used to describe a human being: a ladder placed on earth whose top reaches heaven. At the top of the ladder is true human fulfillment, the recognition of the divinity inherent within each of us. At the bottom is the human being struggling with all the difficulties and complexities of life. These are the rungs within each of us, some higher and some lower. But we are each Beth El, the house of God.

The narrative of Jacob's ladder also suggests that we achieve awareness of the divine within through attentiveness and wakefulness. While Jacob slept, he thought he saw divine messengers. But when he awoke from the dream, he realized that it was more than a dream. He recognized that "God is in this place, and [he] did not know it!" He became conscious in that moment that the dream was not a voyage outside himself but rather a voyage within himself. The ladder is not outside us, it is within. Jacob's ladder is the human soul. The messengers climbing up and down the ladder are facets of Jacob himself. The dream is really about the life of his own soul as he prepares for the responsibilities of adulthood. And just as the place where the dream occurred is Beth El, "the house of God, the gateway to heaven," in Judaism, our soul is "the house of God, the gateway to heaven."

The soul is the image of God, the infinite within us. The soul is our true self, who we are when we strip away every transitory identity, pose, and posture. The soul is the seeker within us that guides us higher and higher on the path of our lives. The soul is the expressiveness within us that reaches out to create, to verbalize, to connect with others. The soul is our awareness, the conscious mind within us that listens on the deepest level. The soul is the seat of the emotions, that part of our being that is capable of love, deep feeling, and passion. The soul is our strength, the deep well that we draw from when we think we cannot go forward, the endless reserve of energy and resilience. The soul is timeless and eternal, that infinite part of us that existed before we were born and that will endure after we die.

It is difficult for us to find the soul within ourselves. The soul in us is like God in the world, paradoxically hidden but present. The Talmud contains a hymn that describes the soul as analogous to God: "As God fills the entire world, so the soul fills the body. As God sees but is not seen, so the soul sees but is not seen. As God is pure, so the soul is pure. As God is deeply hidden, so the soul is deeply hidden." The infinite soul fills us, gives us life, and is the most authentic part of who we are. But we cannot grasp it, we cannot identify it, we cannot even find the words adequate to express it. In Hebrew, we call the soul the *neshamah*, the breath.

THE IMAGE OF GOD

It is a basic axiom of Judaism that God created the first human being in His own image. Each individual is the earthly representation of God. All people participate equally in this noble stature and each person is unique. However, it is impossible to define the image of God precisely because God Himself is beyond our understanding. God Himself cannot be imagined in likeness to anything in our world of experience. We are not created as a replica of God, but in the image of God. Any image is a representation of something that cannot be faithfully replicated. God could not even replicate Himself, but could only create a world in which His perfection is conveyed in hidden ways. The scattered sparks of light are hidden within the vessels that we call human beings. If we are created in the image of

49

God, we are not true replicas but only passable representations. As such, we represent the appearances of God as king, father, and mother. We strive to approximate God's characteristics as best we know them, but we can never be God. We try to live up to the image of God by holding up God's appearances as virtues that we incorporate into our daily lives.

We try to know God in order to understand ourselves. The more that we uncover the reality behind the appearances, the better we understand the ideal to which we aspire. The more we understand God, the better we know what it means to be a human being created in the image of God. We want to look behind the veil not in order to reach an unreachable truth, but in order to attain the essence of humanity. We cannot reach the mysterious source of all being, but we can know the scattered sparks trapped within the human vessel. The image of God is the hidden spark and the light of God within us. Through uplifting the sparks, we nurture and cultivate the divine image. We raise the image up, rung by rung, on the ladder.

The belief that a human being is a ladder shapes and determines our approach to understanding the nature and purpose of human life—to refine the image of God within us. Anything that strengthens the divine image is called "holy," anything that detracts from it is "unholy." This requires that we look at other people as "holy" and at our own lives as opportunities to strengthen the divine image. The spiritual dimension of Judaism is the emphasis on strengthening the image of God, the divine spark, wherever it might be found. All human actions, behaviors, habits, and attitudes are directed toward bringing the divine into the world. When we fail to seek the holy dimension in life, we weaken the bond between ourselves and God.

Judaism is the call to recognize, respect, and cultivate the divinity within ourselves and within others. Judaism challenges us to nurture and cultivate the divine image implanted within each one of us. We accept a universal principle of equality that accepts no inherent distinction in ultimate worth between religions, races, and genders in theory or in practice. We can have only one standard by which we act in relation to other human beings, because all people are created in the image of God. The Sabbath law, for example, specifies that we may not work on the Sabbath, but it also states that the Jewish employer should follow the same practice for his non-Jewish employees. The Torah reiterates that, in matters affecting human dignity, one universal law applies. As the Talmud says, God created one original human being so that no one may later claim greater stature, worth, or nobility of ancestry. We accept no innate distinctions among individuals.

This affirmation of equality is the core Jewish value that propels so many Jews into social and political activism. It is also what I understood the Jewish moral imperative to be as a teenager growing up in the sixties. In the summer of 1964, one year after the assassination of President Kennedy and during the height of the Civil Rights movement and the Cold War, I became aware of the absurdity of war and bigotry as a violation of the essential oneness of humanity. That summer was "Freedom Summer," the turning point in the Civil Rights movement. I had been taught to believe that human equality was universal. In the segregated South, however, brutal racism was directed against blacks and their white allies in the Civil Rights movement. Two Jewish Civil Rights workers, Mickey Schwerner and Andrew Goodman, were murdered, along with James Chaney, a black activist, in Philadelphia, Mississippi, by the local sheriff and the Ku Klux Klan. I could not fathom the kind of hatred that ran so deep in this country that it could spill out in such hideous form. The only way I could make sense of this was to compare it to the Nazi hatred of Jews. And, yet, I saw these events as an attack upon the very principles of universal human equality and my own religion. This was a pivotal moment in my life and it shaped my understanding of what it means to be a Jew.

Many of us who grew up after the sixties came to believe that Judaism compels us to work toward social and political justice. Some of my friends have devoted their lives to education, medicine, social work, the mental health professions, and human rights advocacy. In our youth, we shared a common belief that all people are created equal in the image of God. But we also recognized that our society was still a long way from helping each of its members live on the highest rung of the ladder. We saw our calling as helping others to gain their basic rights as human beings created in the image of God. Long after the Civil Rights movement, we still struggle with the challenge of how to promote equality among people of different races, gender, and national origin.

THE TREASURE IN OUR OWN HOUSE

In order to fulfill the hopes for ourselves and our society, we must see each human being as an unfinished work in progress who may require help in moving from stage to stage and rung to rung. The Torah explains that after creating the sun, the moon, the stars, the reptiles, the fish, and the cattle, God says "behold, it is good." But after creating man and woman, God says nothing at all. One sage explains this puzzling omission thus: All the reptiles, fish, and cattle were created as fully developed as they would ever be. Only human beings are unfinished at creation, but they are endowed with the capacity for self-improvement. Therefore, God cannot yet say that, "behold it is good." God withholds comment because the work of human growth and development is not yet complete. Its completion rests with us, not God. As the Kotzker Rebbe said: "God created only the beginning. The rest is up to us!"

While there are no fundamental differences among people, we make different meanings out of our own lives. In Judaism, human empowerment, the fulfillment of the human potential of each individual, is a sacred, holy, and religious duty. The Baal Shem Tov taught that each person contains the spark of divinity but that no two persons have the same spark. Each one of us must look inside to find our own unique abilities. He stressed the importance of each

52

of us finding our own unique original place in the world. Although we are influenced by many forces, including heredity and environment, we must struggle to find our way. We must forge our own road, a new road that has not yet been traveled.

Martin Buber, in *Hasidism and Modern Man*, told the story of Rabbi Eizik, son of Rabbi Yekel of Cracow. After many years of great poverty that had never shaken his faith in God, he dreamed that someone told him to look for a treasure in Prague, under the bridge that leads to the king's palace. When the dream occurred a third time, Rabbi Eizik set out for Prague. But the bridge was guarded day and night and he did not dare to start digging. Nevertheless, he went to the bridge every morning and kept walking around it until evening. Finally the guard, who had been watching him, asked in a kindly way whether he was looking for something or waiting for somebody. Rabbi Eizik told him of the dream that had brought him here from a faraway country. The guard laughed: "And so because of a dream, you wore out your shoes to come here! As for having faith in dreams, if I had had it, I once had a dream that told me to go to Cracow and dig for treasure under the stove in the room of a Jew—Eizik, son of Yekel, that was the name! Eizik, son of Yekel! I can just imagine what it would be like, how I should have to try every house over there, where one half of the Jews are named Eizik and the other Yekel." And he laughed again. Rabbi Eizik excused himself, traveled home, dug up the treasure from under his own stove, and used the treasure to build the House of Prayer that is called "Reb Eizik Reb Yekel's Shul." "Take this story to heart," added Buber, and make what it says your own: "There is something you cannot find anywhere out there in the world, and there is, nevertheless, a place within yourself where you can find it." We must each help others find what is uniquely theirs, and the place within them where they can find their own treasure.

Although "each person must raise himself," people are also interdependent. We must rely on others and allow others to lean on us. The Kotzker Rebbe noted that "there is nothing straighter than

53

a slanted ladder." For a ladder to be stable, it must sacrifice vertical height by leaning diagonally against a fixed structure. Likewise, spiritual growth is achieved by sacrificing height for stability. It is impossible to take a direct route to the top of the ladder placed on earth. None of us can reach our goals without relying on others. Interdependence requires some sacrifice of our own time and some loss of control over the conduct of our daily lives. But, unless we lean the ladder placed on earth against fixed structures like family, friends, and society, we remain a ladder with no support.

As a writer, I am constantly aware that writing requires countless hours of withdrawal and retreat into the sanctuary of my study. At the same time, the true test of the truth of my writing is in the next room with my wife and children. If I cannot live my ideals with them as a husband and father, my writing means nothing. Yet, to be with my family often requires sacrificing time for writing. I know that I must sacrifice some of my spiritual freedom to write in order to achieve spiritual stability—the harmony between my theories and my practice—by turning to my family. As I give them support, they return support to me.

There are surprises in store for us when we reach outside of ourselves to others. One of my students announced at the first session of a course on Jewish spirituality that he belongs to Alcoholics Anonymous. I could tell that his personal revelation made many people in class, including me, uncomfortable by crossing over the line of what is appropriate to share about yourself with strangers. Our fear was that he might be overly personal, or preoccupied with his own need to talk about himself. In fact, he turned out to be one of the most valuable members of the group because he helped the rest of us to break down our barriers of caution and stop hiding behind the polite rule that says we should not risk being too personal with strangers. We all came to appreciate his courage in opening up to others, because it made it possible for the rest of us, including me, to reveal more about ourselves. And because we did, we were able to dig deeper into the personal dimensions of spirituality. By relying on others, we risk sacrificing our privacy and autonomy, but we gain more by strengthening our bonds with other people.

THE INNER VOICE

Each one of us is born with the ability to raise the sparks within and to become a complete person. An ancient teaching explains that we are each spiritually unique and complete beings from birth. Before we are born, our souls are filled with all the goodness, wisdom, and perfection possible. Before we are born, the Talmud says, we know the entire Torah. This means that we possess all the wisdom and enlightenment the world has to offer. According to this tradition, when we are born, an angel comes and smacks us on the philtrum, the upper lip, and we forget everything we know. We then start from scratch to regain the goodness, wisdom, and perfection we once had. This means that everything we need to know, we knew before we were born. Life is not a process of learning life's wisdom from nothing, but rather the process of remembering what is buried deep inside us. We are not a blank slate. Learning is not a process of filling an empty vessel with something it lacks. Learning is the process of bringing out the inherent wisdom that exists in different ways within each and every one of us.

How do we rediscover the wisdom within us? We begin with listening to what our souls are telling us at every moment throughout our lives. This inner voice is the divine voice, the divine spark, the image of God within us. Rabbi Pinchas of Koretz was famous for telling people who came to him for advice: "Your own soul will teach you! Every person is constantly being taught by his own soul." One of his students once asked him, "If this is so, why don't we follow what our souls teach us?" Rabbi Pinchas answered, "The soul teaches constantly, but it never repeats." The inner voice speaks incessantly to us, but we are not always ready to hear it. Other voices within us often get in the way. We often listen to the wrong voices, the voices of other people's expectations, the voice of criticism, the voice of competition.

Listening is a great responsibility. The inner voice can be heard in a dream, such as Reb Eizik's about finding the treasure in our own house. It can also be heard when we are awake, sitting quietly, listening to the inner voice that speaks to us constantly. It can be heard at any moment when we look for the divine spark and allow ourselves to recognize it. As Rabbi Abraham Isaac Cook said: "When you train yourself to hear the voice of God in everything, you attain the essence of the human spirit." In Judaism, we become "a holy person" (*tzaddik*) when we train ourselves to such an extent that we make listening to the inner voice automatic within us.

How do we train ourselves to listen to the divine voice? The Kotzker Rebbe advised his followers: "Never stop looking inside yourselves!" That is where God is truly to be found. He also counseled that, in every situation, we must ask ourselves, "what do I really want?" The inner voice responds to us when we ask ourselves what we really want and when we are prepared to listen to the answer. The intense focus on listening to the inner voice can help us discover the truth that exists in the deepest reaches of our soul. The search for truth leads us not to heaven but to the human heart. As the Kotzker Rebbe said: "One should not look to heaven before one looks into oneself."

This task is not an easy one, because we are not trained to listen to the inner voice. For too many of us, education has meant learning that goes against the grain of our inner voice. We are not taught to discover and to internalize but rather to master and memorize. We often treat children, to use an automobile analogy, as empty fuel tanks waiting to be filled with high-octane educational gasoline. At the same time, we teach them *not* to rely on their instincts, *not* to trust themselves, *not* to rely on their own authority. But we should approach children, to use a spaceship analogy, as self-contained orbiting stations with a crew that has a natural inquisitiveness and wonder about the universe, equipped to conduct experiments using teamwork and ingenuity, and supported by a talented ground crew.

Our culture often discourages us from listening to our inner voice. We are told that people who listen to their inner voice are often eccentric misfits. That is how we often portray our poets, artists, and mystics. Sometimes we are told that if we follow the inner voice, we might follow it down the wrong path. We often associate sociopathic and psychopathic behavior with people who listen to their inner voice. However, listening to the inner voice does not mean listening to "voices" that compel us to act in strange ways. The person who thinks he or she is being directed to act by a higher power or invisible force that has power over them is listening to "voices," not the inner voice.

Many of us find that learning to hear our inner voice requires special training. Psychotherapists often bring a deep spiritual approach to the task of guiding people who have lost the ability to know their own feelings. It may be difficult to rediscover the inner voice, that absolutely honest voice within our souls that often tells us what we do not want to hear. It tells us that we might need to act in a different way from that to which we are accustomed. It tells us truths that can be uncomfortable. It is the voice that Abraham heard four thousand years ago that told him: "Go-you-forth from your land, from your kindred, from your father's house, to the land that I will let you see" (Genesis 12:1). We usually understand the voice that Abraham heard as the voice of God at the moment when a human being first became conscious of the presence of God. But the author of the *Zohar*, who wondered about the curious phrase, "Go-you-forth," explained that the commanding voice was Abraham's inner voice telling him to journey within himself, to turn inward toward his own soul, to discover the divinity within himself.

The inner voice always tells us what we need to know, even if it is not what we want to hear. It always tells us what is best and right for us and never leads us astray. So why is it so difficult for us to listen to the inner voice? Why do we have difficulty trusting the voice of our own soul? The inner voice whispers, the other voices shout. At some times the voices of habit, conditioning, criticism, fear, uncertainty, and insecurity prevent us from hearing the quiet inner voice that encourages us to break the old habit, to try something new, to be independent, to take a risk, to trust our own instinct, to move ahead with confidence. At other times, the inner voice often tells us what is right and that is not necessarily what we want to hear. We sometimes think instant gratification is more important than what is good for us in the long run. The voice of instant gratification often tries to drown out the inner urgings of wise moderation. We let ourselves fall prey to our impulses, to our appetites, to our desire for immediate pleasure. We need to develop the ability to listen a while longer to what our impulses tell us, what needs our appetites want to satisfy, and what causes us to act precipitously— before we act. We should wait an extra moment before we act impulsively so that we hear our inner voice clearly. Sometimes all that is required is the patience to listen to what these other voices are saying, to let them have their say without acting on them, and to say to ourselves that we are stronger than they are. We need to cut through the noise that too often governs us and listen to the soft voice of truth within.

The inner voice often gets buried under other voices that we hear. We often go about our lives guided by those other voices that we have learned to listen to. Too often education becomes a process in which children are taught to ignore their own inner voice and listen to the other voices. As a parent, I worry that some traditional educational institutions stifle a child's ability to listen to his or her inner voice. When we are young, we encounter parents and teachers who encourage our inventiveness, creativity, and self-expression. As we grow up, however, we are often taught to produce according to a teacher's or employer's expectations and to conform to a set of impersonal school or work requirements. Schools and employers are too often interested only in our work output, not our spiritual life. The price of conformity may be that we learn to listen less to our own inner voice and more to the voice of outer authority, be it that of a teacher, a professor, or a boss. In growing up, we each need to find a balance that allows us to hold on to our spiritual side as we take on the responsibilities of adulthood.

CULTIVATING THE DEEP INNER SENSE

The person who listens to the inner voice still has to evaluate what the inner voice is saying. Although the inner voice always speaks the truth, we cannot always act on what it tells us. We often have to compromise about what we know to be true because it is not always socially appropriate or acceptable to act on the basis of absolute truth. For example, if our inner voice tells us that something about a particular relationship or work responsibility is not really right for us, it is not always appropriate to come right out and act upon the message. Sometimes we have to take the knowledge that the inner voice offers us and find indirect and roundabout ways of applying it, because other values, such as relationships and employment, are at stake.

We can avoid listening to the wrong voices by learning to rely on certain external guides. Until we develop confidence in our ability to hear our own inner voice, we must rely on the checks and balances that others provide. For example, children are not always well-behaved and moral and they sometimes show callous disregard of the feelings for other children. We adults guide them by educating them about moral behavior and social responsibility. We tell them to treat others as they want to be treated, to consider how they would feel if they were treated a certain way, to think about their actions, and to learn how to develop empathy. Since these qualities are not readily accessible to children, we adults must instill in them certain moral rules.

Similarly, the teachings of the Torah can train us to become moral

59

individuals. The Torah and the way in which its teachings have been interpreted over time are thorough and comprehensive guides to ethical practice. There is no better source for moral education than Torah and no secular guide to ethics has ever replaced it. Through Torah, we can educate our soul in the ethical guidelines that govern and regulate how we operate in the world. Through continuous and regular moral education, we can train the inner voice to truly be a moral voice. The inner voice eventually becomes our guide to instinctive moral behavior.

Our goal is to cultivate the soul so that it guides us through life instead of allowing other forces to guide us. The soul, however, does not develop within us without effort. It requires attention and, above all, discipline. There is an old story told by S. Ansky, the author of *The Dybbuk*, about a troupe of German acrobats who gave their performance in the streets of a Jewish town in eastern Europe. They stretched a rope across the river and one of them walked along the rope to the opposite bank. People came from everywhere around to see this amazing feat, and in the midst of the crowd of onlookers stood the famous rabbi, the Baal Shem Tov himself. His students were astonished, and asked him what he was doing there. The holy man answered them thus: "I came to see how a man might cross the chasm between two heights as this man did. And as I watched him I realized that if we humans would submit our souls to such discipline as that to which the acrobat submitted his body, what deep abysses might we not cross upon the tenuous cord of life!"

Constant attention to developing the proper character in ourselves is an essential precondition to spirituality. One of the oldest Jewish spiritual practices is a technique called "self-accounting" (*cheshbon nefesh*). This is the practice of listening to the inner voice and of taking note on a daily basis of our life's balance sheet, of all the good that we have achieved, and the faults that we must continue to correct. In fact, Rabbi Simcha Bunim suggested that we need to carry around with us two small ledgers, one in each pocket. On one, we write at the top, "For my sake the world was created," on which we list all the good things in our lives. In the other, we write at the top, "I am but dust and ashes." On this we list all the things we still need to improve.

Self-accounting helps us to become more careful in the choices that we make. We make critical choices about our lives, our careers, our mates, our friends. The right choice allows our soul to shine, the wrong choice clouds the light within us. Placing ourselves in the right environment has an influence on the condition of our soul. The Rabbi of Rizhin explained that the soul is like a diamond that does not show its luster until it is polished and placed in the right setting. When we place ourselves, our souls, in the right setting, the diamond-light in each of us will shine. So we must learn to be as careful as a chess player with every move we make in life. Before we take any action, we should think in advance if we will have any cause to regret it.

The rabbis talk about the "deep inner sense" that guides the morally and spiritually developed human being through life. They describe the purpose of education as cultivating this "deep inner sense" within a person so that ultimately he or she becomes a complete human being. Isaiah Horowitz, author of *Two Tablets of the Covenant*, described the ideal person as having "proper behavior, great modesty, high moral character, all sweet attributes; who loves people and is loved by them, a person of peace, a complete person, one who strengthens the world in his holy words and daily conversations."

The path to becoming a complete person is to become self-aware. Self-awareness begins by understanding our place within the universe, by knowing that the mysterious God is within us, and by realizing that our task is to raise the scattered sparks of divinity within our fragmented world. When we understand this, we are able to know ourselves and to listen to the divine voice within our soul. As the *Zohar* says: "The wisdom which a person requires is, first, to know and contemplate the mystery of God and, second, to know yourself." And, when we know ourselves, we become more deeply aware of God.

Self-knowledge is redemptive and healing, whereas a lack of self-awareness causes suffering. Most, but certainly not all, of the diffi-

61

culties we face in life result from our own ignorance, which leads us to repeat the same patterns of self-destructive behavior. The enlightenment of self-knowledge comes through looking inside ourselves and listening clearly to our inner voice.

TECHNIQUES FOR ACHIEVING SELF-KNOWLEDGE

What are the techniques that can help us to achieve self-knowledge? The first is the practice of solitude or retreat called "isolation" (*hitbodedut*). Since ancient times, groups within Judaism have practiced a form of solitary meditation to achieve attentiveness to the inner voice. The holy men of long ago would sit for one hour before beginning their morning prayers, meditating and listening to the voice of God within them. True meditation is the cultivation of solitude and the exclusion of all outside distractions. In solitude, we can listen to the inner voice that speaks but does not repeat. It is that true voice, the voice that reveals itself to our minds when we are ready to discover it. This is what the prophets call the voice of God and what others call divine revelation. It is not something limited to Moses and the great prophets. It is an entirely natural phenomenon that can be achieved by each of us through training and practice.

The practice of taking time to be by yourself in order to listen, in a concentrated fashion, to the inner voice is an old Jewish custom. One of the best techniques is to retreat to nature in order to eliminate all the extraneous voices and to attune our ears to the immediacy of God's creation. Another technique is to retreat to a particular room or place devoted just to the purpose of solitude away from where we live and work.

Some people find the technique of choosing a particular verse or passage as their own personal excerpt to be helpful, one from the prayer book, Torah, or Book of Psalms that has some particular allusion or reference to their own character or goals. What often works best is to select a verse that reminds us of our personal goal or a desire for character improvement. We can memorize, recall, or invoke this personal passage as we go through the day, or during certain moments in our life when its mention could be useful. Other people find the practice of writing personal resolutions in a journal to be useful reminders in the process of increasing self-knowledge. These are called *kabbalot* because they are written resolutions that usually begin with a phrase such as "I take responsibility" (*kibbel*) to correct a particular character flaw or behavior. The advantage of keeping a spiritual journal is that it allows us to remember the specific goals of character improvement and permits us to monitor our progress along the way.

A variation on this practice is writing an ethical will (*tzavaah*). The ethical will has its origins in Isaac's blessing of his sons, Jacob and Esau, and Jacob's subsequent blessing of his own sons. Later on, the ethical will developed as a literary form in which parents express their ideals and aspirations in the form of a letter to their children. These are private prayers that complement the blessings of formal, public prayer. Bahya ibn Pakuda, the medieval Jewish philosopher, encouraged this practice. He advised us to observe the following practice: "Judge your soul every day. If you have previously neglected this, you ought to take account of yourself now, for no one knows when death might strike. Do not add failure to failure, negligence to negligence. Life is like a book. Write in it what you wish to be known of you."

While there are many examples of ethical wills, one of the most moving is the one written by a dying young wife and mother and published in Jack Riemer and Nathaniel Stampfer's *Ethical Wills: A Modern Treasury*. Her poignant words remind us of the vulnerability of life and the sense of urgency with which we must face our responsibilities each day. In the last days before she died, she wrote to her young children:

I can't really tell you what I want for you because, even now, I don't know what I want for myself. What is important is to make each day good, and not to say "tomorrow" or "in the future, it will be better." Happiness is a goal, but not something we must have every moment. That is not life. I want you to be good Jews. It's something I've always been proud of. I would like to be able to help you and enjoy you, just as my parents did with me. But that is not possible. I wish you had more memories of me to help you know me. The saddest part is leaving you and not knowing how you will develop. I would like to think you will be good, honest people, who have enough self-esteem to stand up for yourselves and not be afraid to say what you think. You are as good as anyone. Every person is special and so is each of you. Not just to me but to yourselves.

Who cannot be moved by the lost promise of a mother not seeing her children grow up? Such reminders of the unpredictable upheavals in life prod us to experience each moment thoughtfully.

Another technique is to adopt a spiritual mentor who can guide us through the process of spiritual growth. An ancient Jewish text, *Avot de-Rabbi Natan*, tells us to "acquire a friend with whom you share food, drink, and learning; with whom you share your home, explain the mysteries of Torah, and the secrets of your heart." Other people can help point us in the direction of the inner voice and help us understand how to listen to it, but ultimately we must learn how to listen to it on our own. We learn from other people, whether the rabbi, the *tzaddik*, the teacher, the therapist, or a peer counselor. They can help us look for the divine spark within us, but they can never find it for us. Each one of us must discover the treasure within our own house for ourselves. Consider the old Yiddish phrase that says, "What a man does not work out for himself, he does not have."

Another way to hear the inner voice is to step back and consider the consequences, implications, and goals of any action before we take it. One tradition tells us that we should only act with full awareness and true attentiveness and intentionality. Rabbi Isaiah Horowitz recommends that we take a moment to recite the following formula to ourselves before acting: "Lord of the world—Your holy words declare, 'He who trusts in the Lord will be surrounded with favor' (Psalm 32:10), and 'You keep the heavens, earth, and everything in them alive' (Nehemiah 9:6). Grant me a portion of Your love and bless the work of my hands as I undertake this activity."

Judaism is a path to help us navigate our way through the world. Rather than understanding it as a system that tells us what we should do, we would be better served to see Judaism as a time-tested system of pointers, guideposts, and directional signs on the spiritual path. Each person is different, so we must each find our own way within Judaism. There is no one right spiritual path that works for everybody. The path is different for each of us. When one learned rabbi said that he wished that he had the mind of a certain great sage, the heart of another, and the personal qualities of a third, his teacher told him: "No! With your own mind, your own heart, your own qualities!"

THE COMPLETE PERSON

Judaism is a discipline that guides us on the ascent up the rungs of the ladder. At the top of the ladder is "the complete person" (*ha-adam ha-shalem*), who rises from rung to rung through training and effort to become a fully developed human being. Such a rare holy person is called a *tzaddik*. The Baal Shem Tov defined a *tzaddik* as someone who makes God his unconscious. He means that true holiness is reached when we make listening to the inner voice such a regular part of our lives that it no longer requires a conscious effort.

While we are all created equally in the image of God, we cannot stop there. It is not sufficient to be fragments of vessels containing the divine light; we must each make the vessels whole and raise the

65

sparks. We are each born with the potential to rise from rung to rung on the ladder, but only we can do that for ourselves. Our goal is to reach the highest rung on the ladder, but we can only achieve heaven on earth by ourselves. In order to reach this goal, we must master each rung on the ladder, we must learn how to climb, and we must learn how to recover when we slip to a lower rung. As with rock climbing, this task requires the right tools, individual training and effort, and the support of others.

Although we are each born with a pure soul, we also live in an incomplete, fragmented world. We are subject to drives and impulses that cause us to slip to the lower rungs of the ladder. The slippage, however, is not failure but the natural ebb and flow of a growing, changing, and vibrant individual. Judaism has always tended to view human character as complex and difficult to categorize. Human frailty and inadequacy are taken for granted, as is the possibility of perpetual improvement.

Judaism is unique, however, in teaching that all human drives and impulses are holy—even the impulse to do evil. Some Jewish thinkers describe the good impulse as weaker and less potent in us than the evil impulse. They describe the good impulse as like a man confined in a prison cell, whereas the evil impulse is energetic and dynamic. When faced with moral choices, a human being is more likely to be drawn to the immoral.

How can we choose the right course of action if the evil impulse is a more powerful force than the good impulse? The Hasidim explained that it was impossible to conquer our evil impulse. It is too strong and potent a factor in our lives. However, since the sparks of divinity are found everywhere, they must even be present in the evil impulse. The temptation of succumbing to our evil impulses cannot be resisted by a sheer act of will. Human willpower is notoriously weak. The only solution is to raise the sparks of divinity that are hidden within the evil impulse. When it confronts us, it excites and arouses us. We do not have control over the emotion that it stirs up in us. We do have control, however, over whether we follow through on the urge that inflamed us in the first place. We can choose to substitute another more appropriate or acceptable action and carry it out with the same passion and excitement that we felt in the first place. This is what the Hasidim call "worshiping God with the evil inclination." What matters is to preserve the passion, to fan the flames, and to raise the sparks by becoming passionate in doing the right thing.

There is no such thing as truly evil thoughts. When a student asked the Kotzker Rebbe about why evil thoughts are called "alien thoughts," the Kotzker chided him: "How can you call your own thoughts alien?" If we are each created in the divine image, filled with sparks of life, how can any thought be alien if it is ours? It may be rooted in the hidden sparks, waiting to be raised, but no thought can be evil. Only actions can be judged, evaluated, and categorized as good or evil. Thoughts, feelings, and emotions are all internal and contain the spark of holiness waiting to be raised.

The path toward realizing our full human potential involves accepting responsibility toward ourselves and others. While we can often determine what those responsibilities are for ourselves, we can also benefit from the wisdom of the past. The wisdom of our tradition defines our responsibilities to other people as obligations. When we talk about our obligations, we are describing moral obligations based on our spiritual principles, not legislation blindly based on the authority of our ancestors. We, in turn, scrutinize the inherited wisdom of the past in light of our own knowledge and experience.

SPIRITUAL RESPONSIBILITIES

Our spiritual responsibilities are called "duties of the heart" (*chovot ha-levavot*). We call them that to indicate the collective wisdom that our ancestors have left to guide and point us in the right direction.

They are the steps that we must take to raise ourselves from rung to rung up the ladder. The prophet Micah identified the primary spiritual responsibilities of every human: "He has told you, O man, what is good, and what the Lord requires of you: Only to do justice, and to love goodness, and to walk modestly with your God" (Micah 6:8). Of course, we cannot obligate another person to follow the duties of the heart, to be moral, or to have kindness and compassion. But we can take seriously our obligation to constantly strive to live according to these virtues in our personal lives and in the public arena. For many of us, Judaism is inseparable from the high moral and spiritual expectations we impose on ourselves.

What are the other duties of the heart that we learn from our tradition and that we can embrace today? The first duty of the heart is justice (*tsedakah*). Justice is necessary to enable every person to have equal opportunity in rising up the steps of the ladder. Justice does not give someone an advantage, only an opportunity. The earliest laws of social justice in the Torah specify that farmers must leave a corner of the fields unplowed so that the poor can harvest the unpicked corners for themselves. If the reaper forgets to pick up a harvested sheaf of wheat, he may not return later to collect it but must leave it for the poor to collect. Nor may he return to gather the wheat that has fallen on the ground during the harvest, because that, too, belongs to the poor. The Torah states that we have the responsibility to sustain poor people and others regardless of whether they belong to our ethnic or religious community: "You shall leave them for the poor and the stranger" (Leviticus 19:10).

Justice also requires that we treat all people equally. Jewish concern for the needs of others is not limited to Jews. We have responsibility toward non-Jews because divine goodness is universal. As Torah says, "The Lord is good to *all* and His tender mercies are over *all* His works" (Psalm 145:9). We have seen the results in this century of what happens when a tribal mentality prevails. Jews have been the victims of anti-Semitism, which denied our humanity. We continue to see the destructive power of tribal hatred directed against neighbors and countrymen of different religion, ethnicity, or race. We know what it is to be strangers and aliens in a land not our own, and to have felt the murderous sting of tribalism. That is why it is so important for Jews to struggle against all forms of discrimination, tribalism, and dehumanization when we see it in ourselves and in others.

Rabbi Israel Salanter once said that "spiritual needs are more important than material needs, but another person's material needs are my own spiritual obligations." The spiritual obligations toward other people do not always mean that we have to solve other people's problems for them. Our responsibility is to help another person develop the capacity for helping himself. Maimonides, in his statement about charitable support, *Laws Regarding the Poor*, explained that the most effective help we can give to another person is to provide a gift, a loan, a business partnership, or a job that allows the person in financial straits to become financially self-sufficient. The more we enable him to solve his own problems, the more we facilitate his ability to climb higher and higher up the ladder.

The duty of justice toward others requires that we find peace (*shalom*) within ourselves. This is because unless we find peace within ourselves, we never create harmony with other people. The way to find inner peace is to be true to our own inner self, to find the treasure within our own house. Each person has a unique destiny and no person can live out the destiny of another. Only by turning within ourselves, to know ourselves, to find our true inner voice, can we find peace. The Talmud says: "Seek peace within your own place." This means that we cannot find peace except within ourselves. And when we make peace within ourselves, we will be able to pursue peace in our relationships and, ultimately, within the world. There can be no peace between people unless there is peace first within each person. As Martin Buber said, all conflict between people is the result of conflict within a person. Finding peace within ourselves is the first step to peace in our relationships, in our families, and in the world.

Justice also requires absolute uncompromised truth (*emet*). We must be honest, above all, with ourselves. For, unless we are honest with ourselves, we cannot be honest with other people. We must be honest even if it means offering unwelcome criticism to another person. Criticism, however, should only be offered with care, compassion, and concern for helping the other person grow. Criticism offered to hurt, diminish, or punish another person is not truthful. The Torah commands us: "You are not to hate your brother in your heart; rebuke, yes, rebuke your fellow, that you not bear sin because of him." Our responsibility toward justice includes the obligation to persuade others of their duties.

The second duty of the heart is to love goodness (*chesed*). The Torah teaches us that we should "love the stranger, for you were strangers in the land of Egypt" (Deuteronomy 10:19). This basic principle establishes that we should feel empathy for others just as God showed compassion for us. The *Alter* ("Sage") of Slobodka, one of the founders of the Mussar ("Morals") movement, explained that God plants kindness (*chesed*) in the heart of the Jewish people. Judaism is absolutely inseparable from the virtue of kindness. The Jewish people are called "compassionate children of compassionate parents." In practice, however, we often fall short of the goal. Therefore, we speak about spiritual obligations to remind us of the importance of nurturing the goodness in ourselves through our treatment of other people. That is why we have developed a code of goodness that includes the responsibilities of

- showing "compassion" (*rachmanut*) toward others
- shunning "improper speech" (*lashon ha-ra*), the duty to avoid gossip and speaking harshly of others
- not causing humiliation, or "making a person's face turn white" (*malbin pnei chavero*), the duty never to shame or embarrass another person
- "returning the lost item" (*hashavat aveidah*), the duty to return property to its rightful owner

- "respecting seniority" (*mipnei seivah takum*), when standing in the presence of old age, the obligation to respect older adults
- "granting hospitality" (*hachnasat orchim*), that is, extending gracious hospitality to guests and strangers
- "visiting the sick" (*bikkur cholim*), the duty to visit and care for the sick and infirm
- "kindness to living things" (*tzaar baalei chayyim*), the obligation not to inflict pain on animals

The third duty of the heart, modesty or humility (*shiflut*), is illustrated in how we relate to others. Rabbi Israel Salanter noticed that his teacher would disappear from the *Bet Midrash*, the house of study, every day at the same time. One day, he followed his teacher secretly. His teacher walked to the hill at the edge of town and waited until a peddler passed by with his wagon. Then, he helped the peddler push the wagon up the hill and returned to the *Bet Midrash*. His actions showed humility, the ideal of service to others, and indifference to stature. In the Chelm yeshivah, an important Mussar school, there were no janitors. All the students performed the custodial services as a responsibility that was not beneath their dignity.

The Kotzker Rebbe said: "Just as your task in the world is to repair yourself and reach perfection spiritually and ethically, so you are obligated to love your neighbor, to raise him higher and higher, to repair him, perfect him, and raise him onto the same spiritual path as yourself." How do we help those who turn to us for assistance? The duties of the heart include helping other people move from rung to rung up the ladder. We develop empathy for those who are stuck on the lower rungs because there are times when we have been there too. When we make a meaningful contribution to others—a friend, a parent, a child, a family member, an immigrant family struggling to create a new life, an elderly person weakened by age, a person restricted by physical or mental disabilities, a displaced mother struggling to preserve her dignity, a person in personal or

71

family crisis, a medical patient, a person in recovery, an unemployed worker, or a child in day care—we help them move from rung to rung on the ladder. We reach down to those who are stuck on the lower rungs and hoist them up with all our strength. But we do not see ourselves as different from those we help. We are only on a different rung on the same ladder, at a different stage in the process of completing the work of our own creation.

We are also obligated to be especially gracious to individuals who convert to Judaism. The daily prayer book includes a plea that God should "arouse His tender mercies on behalf of righteous converts." Other sources command us "to love the converts to Judaism," to help them, and to treat them with respect and with kindness because they have surrendered their connection to their own past. Maimonides explained that there is absolutely no difference between a native-born Jew and a sincere convert to Judaism. He did not accept the notion that Judaism is a fact of birth alone. A convert has no different legal status than a born Jew. Furthermore, "we are commanded to have great love in our hearts toward converts; God, in His glory, loves converts." Maimonides also ruled that converts have the identical religious obligations as other Jews. This includes the obligation that converts recite such blessings as "Blessed are You, O Lord, our God and God of our fathers" even though their forefathers were not Jews.

The corollary of the view that the spiritual task of a Jew is to help himself and others is the conviction that we are all interconnected as part of the great fabric of humanity. Every member of the Jewish people is responsible for helping every other Jew and non-Jews as well. The Talmud tells us that only one Adam was created so that no one might say "My father is greater than yours." We all have one common father in order to establish equality among all people, regardless of their race, creed, or national origins. To be Jewish is to balance concern for ourselves with concern for others. We are all our brother's and sister's keepers. As the Torah tells us, "You should love your neighbor as yourself" (Leviticus 19:18).

72

Some years ago, when I was living in Israel, I was an assistant director on a film being produced for Israeli television about American students in Israel. One of the most memorable scenes in the film is a conversation between several students and David Ben-Gurion, the first Prime Minister of Israel, at Sdeh Boker, his kibbutz in the Negev Desert. Our small crew spent two days filming this great man, the leader of the Jewish struggle for national independence, the founding father of the State of Israel, who, against all odds, led his nation through the war of independence and the early, decisive years of statehood. He created the democratic institutions of the young state, shaped its foreign relations, and was Israel's spokesman to the world.

When we, the members of the film crew, met Ben-Gurion, he had retired to the kibbutz, where he was writing his memoirs. We joined him on his two daily walks as he reminisced about his childhood in Russia, his life as a pioneer in Palestine, and his relations with world leaders such as John F. Kennedy, Charles de Gaulle, and King Hussein of Jordan. When we finally began to film him talking with the American students, he appeared not as the Zionist revolutionary and hardened state-builder, but as an endearing Jewish grandfather teaching his young students the lessons of his life. He turned to us and said, "You know, the most important lesson in life is that you should love your neighbor as yourself; that is the whole basis of the Torah!" We sat there astounded not only by his sentimentality, but even more so by the fact that no other world leader would have chosen to convey a moral legacy as noble as this.

THE LIFE OF THE SOUL

Judaism regards the earthly stage of the life of the soul as a continuation of the journey that begins before birth. Before birth, our soul lives within the realm of the sparks of divine light. At birth, the soul enters the world of the broken vessels and the scattered light. Although the soul enters the world of chaos, the body serves as a vessel for the holy soul and as the vehicle by which the soul navigates through the world. The body is an extension of the soul and through it the soul acts to raise the sparks. Judaism views the body with reverence as the agent by which the soul acts in the world. As Rabbi Isaac Scher, a leader of the Mussar movement, said, "The body is inherently spiritual and sacred." Life is the opportunity to raise the sparks that were scattered throughout the universe at the moment of creation and to repair the rupture that only we can repair.

What is the spiritual approach to life? Every human capacity and inclination is potentially holy. We are each born with a pure soul. We are, by nature, good and connected by the root of our soul to God. We are, in fact, an extension of God. Therefore, Jews do not believe that we are sinful by nature or that our bodies are sinful. Among the first blessings that Jews are told to say each morning is the following:

> My God, the soul that You have given me is pure. You created it, You formed it, You breathed it into me, You preserve it within me, someday You will take it from my body, and still You will restore it to me in the time to come. As long as the soul is within me, I thank You my God, and God of my ancestors, Author of all deeds, Master of all souls. Praised are You, Lord, who restores the soul to lifeless bodies.

Our spiritual tradition teaches a developmental approach to life as a progressive ascent up the rungs of the ladder. Every stage in our life is part of the process of nurturing the soul, seeking our own spiritual destiny, and achieving heaven on earth. The process is different for each one of us, but the path is often the same. Life is seen as a circle whereby we return at the end of our lives to the point from which we started. The soul lives a full life before it is born into the human body. Before birth, the divine light shines within our soul, which absorbs wisdom directly from God. God enlightens our soul with all the possible wisdom that we might ever acquire. Our soul grasps the same hidden divine wisdom that is eventually contained within the Torah. Our soul is illuminated by a divine light that allows us to see from one end of the universe to the other. But this state of enlightenment does not last very long. When we are born, our soul forgets everything that we once knew. We begin life not in a state of original sin, but with original wisdom hidden deep within us. When we die, our soul leaves our body and returns to the same pure state of eternal existence.

We enter life with traces of our original wisdom imprinted on our soul and continue the spiritual voyage that we began before birth. Birth is not the beginning of life; it is the first transition from one stage of life to another, from a purely spiritual to an embodied state. In forgetting the wisdom we once had, we are left with a constant striving to remember, to regain the wisdom that was once ours. Our natural inquisitiveness is a yearning to remember, to draw on the deep reservoirs within our souls. Children are natural learners whom we can guide along a path of discovery of the inherent wisdom within themselves. However, we should not see children as empty vessels waiting to be filled with our knowledge. The human life span itself is the process of educating the soul, of helping it to relearn what it knew before it came into the world, and of acquiring wisdom once again.

SOUL MATES

What does Judaism teach about the origin of our individual soul? According to one view, each one of us acquires a particular soul before we are born. There are a finite number of souls that can enter the world. Some souls may be new, created just for us, while other souls may be recycled, having been incarnated one or more times.

Each soul has a particular and unique destiny that it must fulfill before its life is complete. Some souls are thought to be reincarnated over and over until they complete their destiny or correct mistakes from past lives. It is possible that many of us have souls with history. We might add something of our own to the accumulated experience of an old soul heading toward its own destiny.

According to another view, each individual soul is new and is created specifically for the individual, either at the time of conception or forty days or more afterward. Life begins not with the conception of the embryo but with the creation of the soul. The soul is conceived by the father and mother, whose own souls unite to create a new soul. The new soul contains both paternal and maternal characteristics and is androgynous, having both male and female gender in equal measure. Sometime after the soul is conceived, the unified soul divides into a male half and a female half. Only one of these two halves enters into the body, giving it life and determining its gender in the process.

What happens to the unused other half of the soul? Every unused half of the soul has a life of its own. In some mysterious way, it becomes attached to another soul, which enters into another body. Some believe that the other half of the soul goes to another particular male or female person. Others believe that the distribution of souls is random and that the unused halves are scattered as sparks of light among the broken vessels. Nevertheless, each of our souls has an affinity and a relationship with someone else's soul that is established before we are born and without our consent.

From this perspective, love is one of the most important spiritual achievements of the soul during life. Love is the attraction of the two original halves of the soul and their yearning for reunion. The two infants enter the world, each with a soul that was once united with the other. They do not know each other, nor are they aware that they were once united. If they are lucky, as they grow up, their paths in life will cross. If they finally find each other, each one is mysteriously drawn to the other. They feel a deep connection with each other that goes beyond physical attraction. This is the love of two soul mates for their original other half. Their love is the attraction of two souls destined by their unconscious, spiritual bond for each other. This is what we mean by a "marriage made in heaven." Each soul yearns to reunite with its original mate and to recapture the unity they once had. This is the highest form of love.

How do we recognize our soul mate? How can we recognize the difference between this spiritual love and other attractions? Throughout our lives, we feel inner strivings. We often feel a yearning for another person on a physical level as sexual attraction or we enjoy another person's company and wonder whether he or she is our soul mate. We need to recognize the difference between the different kinds of desire. One kind of love for another person is the desire to acquire what we do not have. This is a kind of love based on physical appearance, on resemblance to or difference from our parents, or on finding a characteristic in our mate that we wish to possess ourselves. Another kind of love is based on an inexplicable bond between two people that is all the more powerful because it cannot be put into words. This kind of love, which is not necessarily love at first sight, is the love that stirs deep within us because of a connection between two souls. When this happens, we know that there is a connection on an intuitive level between two people, the kind of love that lifts our soul. This is ultimate love, the love between soul mates.

The only way to differentiate between various kinds of love and desire is to listen closely to our inner voice. Only our deep inner sense can tell us the answer to our deepest questions. True love is soul-knowledge that we can only recognize when it happens. Real life, however, tells us that we can make mistakes and confuse the different kinds of love. Sometimes, we are not ready to meet our soul mate and the opportunity passes. Sometimes, we think we have met our soul mate but it turns out to be another kind of attraction. Sometimes, we have difficulties in our relationship with our soul mate and the relationship ends. We can even have more than one soul mate in a lifetime. Love is a spiritual mystery that constantly challenges and baffles us. That is why our tradition teaches that matching a couple together is more difficult than the parting of the Red Sea!

THE MYSTERY OF DEATH

The other great mystery that we each confront is our own mortality. If there is life before birth, is there life after death? If birth and death are just two points on a circle, what is the spiritual significance of death? Death is the completion of the process that brings with it the return of the soul to its original state of perfection. The end of life is one of the rungs on the ladder, but certainly not the last.

What is the Jewish view on death and the afterlife? Death, in the Jewish tradition, is the completion of the cycle of life. Life is not viewed as a linear progression from birth to death, but as a circle that begins with the enlightened life of the soul before birth and its return to an enlightened state after death. Although the physical body may die, there is no death for the soul. The soul enters the world to be educated. The soul lives in the world only as long as it needs to complete its own education or a portion thereof. When it has achieved all that it will achieve in this world, it is ready to return to its original home. Death is the graduation ceremony from life and the completion of the earthly phase of life.

What happens after we die remains the great mystery. In trying to explain the mystery, Judaism has developed a metaphor to describe the unknown. Because we do not believe that death is the end, we often talk about the afterlife. Judaism uses the metaphor of "the world to come" to explain the afterlife. How we prepare for the world-to-come is Judaism's way of describing how we prepare for death. We do not necessarily believe in a literal world-to-come, but we do believe that whatever it is, it is beyond our understanding.

Once we have reached the end, we have no opportunity to change the past. The *Midrash* says, "In this world, he who is twisted can be

78

made straight, and he who lacks something can have it made good. But in the world-to-come, he who is twisted cannot be made straight, and he who lacks something cannot have it made good." This is the meaning of Hillel's popular aphorism, "If not now, when?" Judaism emphasizes the immediacy of life and action and the danger of deferring change into the future.

While those who care for us in life feel deep grief at our death, the soul experiences joy as it moves on to the next world. Mendele Mocher Seforim, the great Yiddish writer, is reported to have said that while a child's parents are thrilled when their infant is born, it is possible that there is weeping and mourning in some other world that the child has just left. Mendele wondered whether the same thing happens when we die. While we on this earth mourn death, it is possible that in the world into which the departed has been born, its inhabitants celebrate the new arrival with toasts, congratulations, and celebrations. The end may be just a new beginning, depending upon our perspective.

The Talmud describes the afterlife as "the heavenly Garden of Eden," but this does not mean that there is physical place called the afterlife. The afterlife is a spiritual state unlike anything known on earth. It is a timeless place where souls are reunited and freed from the cares of this world and from physical sensations. It is a return to the state of the soul before birth, a time of perfect knowledge and enlightenment. One of the great rabbis of the Talmud had a saying: "The world-to-come is not at all like this world. In the world-to-come, there is no eating, no drinking, no sex, no commerce, no envy, no hatred, no rivalry. The righteous sit with crowns on their heads and enjoy the radiance of the divine Presence." This is his way of saying that the soul is restored to a perfect harmony.

What happens to our souls after death remains the subject of speculation rather than certainty. While it is appealing to try to unravel the mystery and hope to understand what happens after we die, we can never know. Therefore, Judaism emphasizes that we make the most of our lives in this world rather than encourage speculation about the afterlife and reincarnation. Each human being has a particular vocation in life and a specific and unique calling. The Hasidic teacher, Baruch of Medzibozh, said that the world needs each and every human being because every person has the mission to make something perfect in this world. That mission is unique to the individual, who must fulfill his or her own personal destiny. The way we conduct our lives determines how we approach our death. As we face our own mortality, whatever we have accomplished in this world determines how we approach our death. If we are satisfied with the quality of our lives, we can anticipate death agreeably. But if our lives have been filled with regret, we face death with anxiety and fear. But the real importance of our lives is the here and now. Zusya of Hanipol was afraid that when he died and would go to heaven, he would be asked: "Why were you not as great as Moses?" His fear disappeared when he realized that the real question he would face would be: "Why were you not as great as you, yourself, Zusya, could be?"

How do these teachings about life, love, and death deepen our spiritual awareness? They help us understand that life is a developmental process of growth and cultivation of our inner capabilities. When we struggle with all of the challenges of life, these teachings remind us that we have a noble calling and possess the innate abilities that can help guide us through life. They remind us that we can turn within ourselves and to others for support and guidance. Above all, they offer us courage that our lives have meaning and purpose. They challenge us to find our own ideal selves in this world, not in the next. The emphasis on responsibility of the individual is what distinguishes the Jewish belief in human destiny. Rabbi Pinchas of Koretz explained that God created only one Adam to teach us that we should assume responsibility for our lives "as though there were only one person on earth—yourself!"

80

Although we must act at times as if the whole world depends on us, God somehow watches over each one of us and intervenes on our behalf. The Kotzker Rebbe taught that God created a ladder that reaches from heaven to earth and that souls descend on this ladder from the top to the bottom. However, when the soul reaches earth, the ladder is withdrawn and a heavenly voice calls the soul back to heaven. Some souls give up immediately when they discover there is no ladder. Others give up after trying to jump toward heaven several times. The clever souls, however, do not give up but continue to jump higher and higher until, finally, God snatches them and lifts them up the rest of the way.

It is not true that God can save us if only we call out to Him. The infinite God is beyond being concerned with the details of our lives. According to an ancient tradition, "one who seeks to become pure, receives help." This implies that God reaches out to us to the degree to which we extend ourselves to God. When we look to God to fulfill our wishes, we are turning to the father or mother "appearance" of God, not to God Himself. The appearance of God is not the source of genuine help. Only when we rise above our diluted images and false appearances of God can we establish a true relationship with God. When we bind our souls to God, when we reach out to God as complete human beings, God reaches out to us and lifts us up the rest of the way. When we fall on the ladder, we must raise ourselves up. But when we help ourselves up the ladder, God gives us the final boost. God watches over us in proportion to how we watch over ourselves. This discovery is what Jacob experienced at Beth El, "the house of God, the gateway to heaven." He realized that there are no real alternatives to accepting the burden of responsibility and accountability for one's own destiny. And he realized that he, like each of us, is a slanted ladder placed on earth whose top reaches heaven.

Chapter Three

A PERSON IS CALLED A *MENTSH* BECAUSE HE STRUGGLES

The world is a very narrow bridge; the key thing is not to be afraid at all.
—*Nachman of Bratslav*

WHEN OUR WORST FEARS COME TRUE

By nature, I am an optimist who looks at the world with confidence and hope. I was raised in a family where anything was possible, life was good, and the world was a kind place. Growing up, I never confronted death or illness. When one of my closest friends was dying of leukemia in third grade, his family kept his lingering illness well hidden behind excuses for his frequent absences from school. Children were never exposed to bad news. Although my paternal grandparents came from Europe, they never spoke about pogroms or anti-Semitism when I was growing up. Although part of their family had stayed behind in Europe and was murdered by the Nazis, the Holocaust was rarely mentioned. Growing up on Long Island in the 1950s, I believed there were no limits to the possibilities that I could pursue. The world was a kind place, good things happened to good people, and optimism prevailed.

My paternal grandfather came to the United States from Ukraine in 1913. He was a follower of Rabbi Moses Schreiber, known as the Chatam Sofer, the leader of an Orthodox movement that opposed liberal Judaism. He lived by the slogan of the Chatam Sofer: "Everything new is prohibited by Torah!" As Russia prepared for the Great War, pogroms broke out all along the front and many Jews were brutally murdered. My grandfather escaped and settled in Cleveland, where he was a rabbi, Talmud scholar, Torah scribe, and *shochet*, a kosher-meat slaughterer. He never spoke about Europe, although he was thoroughly Old World in his language, behavior, and outlook. He spoke only Yiddish, always wore a high black skull cap, or *yarmulke*, and prayed in a *shtiebel*, a tiny synagogue prayer room. My other grandfather was born in the United States. His own parents had escaped the pogroms that swept Russia in the 1880s. He was a printer who worked for many years for my favorite childhood magazine, *MAD*. He, too, was Orthodox but in a fully American kind of way. He spoke English without an accent, wore his *yarmulke* only in his house, and attended a modern Orthodox synagogue. I grew up enjoying the different worlds my grandfathers inhabited: the world of the Talmud and the world of *MAD*.

My grandparents themselves had escaped the persecution of Europe, but they still knew what it was to be victims. They had lost relatives in the Holocaust. My Judaism, however, was not based on being a victim and, to be honest, I have never experienced victimization in my life. If I had experienced what my grandparents did, I might have come to the same conclusion as did Jean Amery, a Viennese Jewish writer who survived Auschwitz. He said, "Being a Jew not only means that I bear within me a catastrophe that occurred yesterday and cannot be ruled out for tomorrow, it is also a fear." I might have concluded, as did the French Jewish philosopher Robert Misrahi, quoted by Amery, that "from now on, the Nazi Holocaust is the absolute and fundamental reference point for the existence of every Jew." I might agree with the philosopher Emil Fackenheim that "the eleventh commandment is to not give Hitler a posthumous victory."

The Holocaust, although part of my experience as a Jew, did not define my Judaism. The Holocaust, I thought, was only the most recent catastrophe in a long chain of Jewish suffering. While these tragedies have helped to define what it means to be a Jew, they are not the definition itself. It is impossible to imagine Judaism without anti-Semitism, but a Judaism based on victim-consciousness, I thought, is not a Judaism worth preserving.

Because suffering, anti-Semitism, and struggle were never part of my own experience, I could never understand people who saw the world as a hostile, inhospitable place. To be a victim must surely change your place in the world. However, I did not see myself as the heir or descendant of victims. I could not see Jews as victims or anti-Semitism as the defining experience of Jewish existence. I could not understand what it meant to experience pain and be in need of healing.

And then it happened to me. Seven years ago, I discovered that I had cancer. It was while teaching to Jewish groups in Kiev, Ukraine, that I began to experience its terrifying symptoms. I remember the frightening moment of recognition that something was wrong. It was the most profound moment of fear I have ever experienced. Although the cancer was diagnosed and removed by surgery, the experience overwhelmed and frightened me, and I was not able to talk about it or let anyone other than my wife know about it for two years. My inability to look into myself closed me off from those dear to me and nearly cost me my family. I could not understand why this had happened to me and could not face what had happened.

When I finally looked within, I began to examine my own mortality. I began to understand that each of us, at some point in our lives, will suffer and that no one is immune. I began to see that my experience was not unique but actually gave me more in common with other people. It made me more human by binding me closer

85

to other people who have gone through transforming experiences in their lives. It helped me comprehend that suffering is a necessary part of what it means to be human. We are all in need of healing, each in our own unique individual way. When we recognize that we all share private suffering, we are better able to empathize with others and share their sorrows and joys.

The experience also caused me to reevaluate where I was in my life and what was important to me. It gave me a greater sense of urgency in achieving my personal goals. It was a powerful wake-up call for me to examine my life and my values. I now believe it was one of the best things that ever happened to me. While I have not had a recurrence of the cancer, the possibility hangs over me all the time, serving as a constant reminder that life is a gift, every moment is precious, and nothing can be taken for granted. I am grateful that I can no longer be complacent about my life.

HEALING OUR WOUNDS

Eventually we all experience pain and suffering in our lives. We all carry around within us wounds that require healing. Some of us have lost jobs, marriages, or the attachment of families. Some of us have physical wounds or disabilities as a result of an accident, injury, or disease, or care for someone who does. Some of us have experienced the loss or suffering of a parent, a spouse, a sibling, a friend, or even a child. Some of us have experienced the emotional pain of abuse, disability, dependency, or addiction. Others of us have had our dreams shattered and obstacles placed in our paths. No one, in the end, is exempt. What matters is how we respond to the struggles that affect our lives.

For many of us, life is a struggle and we must each provide the resources to help others in their struggle. We must remember that, at the moment when a person turns to us for assistance, we must act as if there were no one else in the world but ourselves who can help. There is a story, perhaps apocryphal, that a university student one day knocked on the front door of Martin Buber's house in Jerusalem and asked to see his teacher. Buber, the leading authority on the sacred character of human relationships, turned the student away because he was too busy with his writing. The next day, Buber learned that the young man had committed suicide. The student's unannounced visit to Buber was clearly a final effort to seek help. The teacher's refusal to put down his pen to help a desperate human soul was a moral failure that contradicted the very principles about which Buber was, at that moment, writing. We can never know the impact of our actions on another person nor can we ever take our responsibilities lightly.

In Yiddish, a person is called a *mentsh,* and we act out of our *mentshlichkeyt,* our humanity. To be a *mentsh,* a compassionate and caring human being, is the highest ideal in Judaism. But as we saw earlier, the Yiddish word *mentsh* also means "to struggle." As Moshe Waldoks has pointed out, there is a phrase in Yiddish: *A mentsh heyst a mentsh veyl er mentsht zikh*: "A person is called a *mentsh* because he or she struggles." The Jewish definition of a *mentsh* is one who struggles with being human and all the difficulties that entails, who works to bring out the best within oneself, who nurtures the divine spark within another person, and who allows each person to find the treasure within his or her own house.

Sometimes it is difficult for us to realize the divine sparks in the world because of the personal suffering and grief we experience. We each need to be healed, but sometimes the pain is so great that we can barely carry it around within us. It is often difficult for us to admit to ourselves that we carry around wounds that go back as early as our childhood. But when we close ourselves off to sharing our burdens with others, we make it even more difficult for us to heal.

How do we heal the wounds that we each suffer? A Yiddish proverb says that the greatest pain is that which you cannot talk about with others. Psychotherapy provides a path for us to open up our hearts to another person, to explore the causes of our personal pain, and to learn to become our own healers. The healing of our own heart must take place within a close relationship in which we know that our burden is never too great for the other person to bear. Emotional healing requires that we expose our souls to another person long enough to find the sparks hidden within our own broken vessel.

The healing rituals in Judaism do not mend all wounds, but they do provide a context for healing within a fellowship of compassion and support. Included among the daily prayers is a prayer for healing. The key to its blessing is the discovery of God's presence within ourselves even at the moment when we feel most empty. When we find the God within, we can heal ourselves: "Heal us, God, and we shall be healed. Rescue us, and we shall be rescued, for You are our triumph. Cover our wounds and heal us of all diseases and pains, and bring us complete recovery from all our grief, for You, God, are a royal, faithful, and compassionate healer. Praised are You, God, the healer of the sick people of Israel." When we have recovered from an illness or escaped serious injury, we are called up to the Torah and recite: "Praised are You, O Lord our God, ruler of the universe, who renders good to the undeserving, for having rendered complete goodness to me."

Personal prayer is an important part of self-healing. The High Holy Day *Selichot* service tells us, "The soul is Yours, the body is your creation; have mercy, God, on your handiwork." When we pray, we open ourselves up to reservoirs of comfort. The ladder placed on earth whose top reaches heaven works in two directions. Just as we rise up on the ladder, God reaches out to us. When we suffer, God's presence suffers along with us.

Poetry can also nourish the hurting heart. When we need healing, the *Book of Psalms* and the Hebrew prayers offer reassurance that we are not alone in our grief. The *Shema Koleinu* prayer speaks of our longing to be heard in our despair:

Hear our voice, O Lord our God, feel for us, pity us, and embrace our prayer with mercy and determination. Turn us to you, O Lord, and we shall be turned. Restore our days to what they once were. Hear our word, God, and understand our thought. Dismiss us not from your view. Don't withdraw Your holy spirit from us. Dismiss us not in our old age. Don't forsake us when our strength fades. Abandon us not, O Lord our God. Don't distance yourself from us. For it is You we seek. Answer us, Lord our God.

But true healing comes from pouring our heart out to God, the healer of shattered hearts. There is nothing more redemptive than the spontaneous emotional outpouring of the human heart. The only way to heal a broken heart is for us to empty it of all its grief. Only when we have cried all the tears that we have in our hearts can we begin to fill the heart again with joy. Rabbi Nachman of Bratslav used to retreat to his own private place of solitude regularly to pour out his heart. He encouraged his followers to "break their own hearts" regularly so that they themselves could be healed.

The healing rituals in Judaism stress the importance of human connections. There is no greater act of kindness in Judaism than *bikkur cholim,* visiting the sick. Judaism teaches that the personal care and comfort of friends and family are indispensable medicine in the healing process. Unfortunately, too many of us now leave this responsibility to professionals. Is it only the rabbi's responsibility to visit congregants in the hospital? Should only the doctor and the nurse tend to the sick? As we have moved healing out of the hands of ordinary people and into the hands of professionals, we have lost an opportunity for spiritual renewal.

GRIEF AND MOURNING

There is a dynamic to the grieving process that is advanced by the Jewish rituals of mourning. Rabbi Joseph Soloveichik described the first two stages of the Jewish mourning process as beginning with despair and ending with confidence. From the moment a loved one dies until the time we recite the *kaddish* at the funeral, the heart is filled with distress. The mourner despairs at his loss, at the cruelty of death, and at the face of oblivion. But at the moment that the first *kaddish* is said at the grave, we start to gather up the debris of our own broken hearts and begin to restore the confidence that we stand before God in a universe that defies death and despair.

The *Yizkor* memorial prayer, recited at the funeral and then several times each year, reminds us of our grief:

> O God, full of compassion, dwelling on high, grant perfect rest under the wings of the Divine Presence, in the company of the holy and pure souls who shine like the splendor of heaven, to [the Hebrew name of the deceased] who has gone on to his world. Master of compassion, shelter him under the shadow of your wings forever, and let his soul be bound up with the bond of life. God is his abode. May he lie in peace upon his resting place. And let us say, "Amen."

The *kaddish* prayer, recited at the end of the funeral, during the mourning period, and on the funeral anniversary each year, speaks only of life, not death:

> Mighty and sacred may His great name be throughout the world that He created according to His plan. May He establish His kingship within your life, within your time, and in the life of the whole house of Israel, quickly and none-too-soon, and let us say, "Amen." May His great name be praised forever and for all time. May the name of the Holy One, Blessed be He, be praised, blessed, honored, adored, extolled, glorified, exalted, and honored. He is beyond all blessing, songs, praises, and words of comfort that are said here in the world. And let us say, "Amen." May there be peace overflowing from heaven, and life for us and for all Israel,

and let us say, "Amen." May He who creates peace in heaven, create peace for us and for all Israel, and let us say, "Amen."

Isolation and loneliness are two of the worst things a person can face. Therefore, we seek healing within our community among those to whom we are connected by bonds of common destiny and shared experience. The *kaddish* prayer is recited only by the person who is in mourning and only when a prayer quorum of ten is present. This practice identifies the mourner to the religious community and offers its support to him or her. Because *kaddish* is never said alone, we are never left alone with our grief. The mourner who stands up in synagogue to recite the *kaddish* is likewise embarked on a public process. He identifies himself publicly as someone who is in mourning. He acknowledges his grief among his community even as the words he recites declare optimistically that life continues. Everyone who sees and hears him must ask "for whom is he saying *kaddish?*" They will come up to him afterwards and offer their comfort. The public act of mourning builds a bridge between the mourner and those who can console him.

We all need a prayer community, a place to turn when we are in need of healing. Providing company and support in the healing process is one of the most important functions of a temple or synagogue. That is why we read the prayer for healing in public at every Sabbath service: "O God who blessed our ancestors, send your blessing upon one who is ill. Have mercy upon him and graciously restore his health and strength. Grant him complete healing, in soul and body, along with all those who are stricken, speedily and let us say, Amen."

There is no greater relief than talking about the pain of our suffering. That is one of the virtues of the Jewish seven-day mourning period, *shivah*, which is interrupted only for the Sabbath and festivals. During *shivah*, the comforters who come to see the mourner are not supposed to initiate the conversation. Their silence allows the mourner to direct the grieving process. Most important, recognizing that nature abhors the vacuum of silence, this observance places the responsibility of speaking on the mourner and prevents him from withdrawing into himself. The path toward overcoming grief is that of remembering and healing through talking.

IS THERE MEANING IN OUR SUFFERING?

But all this brings us back to the question, why do we suffer? How does Judaism understand the problem of human suffering? Does God allow people to suffer? Does God have the power to cause or to prevent our suffering? When bad things happen to good people, is something terribly wrong with God?

We often wonder how God could allow human suffering. A long tradition exists in Judaism that goes back to Abraham and has continued ever since: that of arguing with God, of challenging God, of bringing God to judgment for the suffering of human beings. The Talmud says: "*Chutzpah*—audacity—even against God, is worthwhile!" *Yom Kippur*, the Day of Judgment, was often regarded not only as a day of judgment for us, but also as the day on which we judge God. Rabbi Levi Yitzhak of Berditchev once interrupted *Yom Kippur* services to argue with God: "You wish me to repent of my sins? I have committed only minor sins! But You, God, have committed grievous sins. You have taken babies from their mothers and mothers from their babies. Let us settle our score. You forgive me and I will forgive You!"

Human suffering is not divine punishment for our mistakes. That kind of primitive thinking is not a part of Judaism. It is natural for us to ask whether we have done anything to deserve suffering. When we expect God to protect us, we view suffering as a sign of God's abandonment. But, perhaps the problem is with our expectation, not with God. Suffering is a part of life that is often beyond our control. Certainly, we make choices all the time about issues that affect our lives—health, diet, exercise, and smoking. Our circumstances are in our hands as far as the life choices we have to make. But many people suffer for no reason and neither lifestyle nor genetics can explain why. While one who experiences suffering cannot accept it, one cannot presume that God is the cause of it. Circumstances prevail that are beyond our control, such as heredity, environment, and accidents. Bad things happen to good people for no apparent reason.

For some people, the existence of human suffering is an argument against God's existence. The Holocaust forces us to challenge God and ask, "Where was God during the Holocaust?" The Yiddish poets who survived the Holocaust asked this very question. One poet, Kadya Molodovsky, expresses her contempt for the "God of Mercy" who shows no mercy on His people. She turns the traditional memorial prayer for the dead, *El Male Rachamim*, "God of Mercy," into a protest against God, tradition, Jewish history, and destiny. She writes:

O God of Mercy, choose another people.
We are tired of death, tired of corpses.
We have no more prayers.
For the time being, choose another people.

The biblical book of Job is one of the greatest attempts to wrestle with the question of human suffering. From all appearances, Job suffered for no apparent reason. He was a righteous man who faithfully offered sacrifices to God on behalf of his family. As the narrative explains, the angel Satan argues with God that Job's piety is superficial and that, under duress, Job would abandon his devotion to God. God agrees to the challenge and, in one day, Satan wipes out all of Job's wealth along with his ten children. In the face of such disasters, Job declared stoically: "The Lord has given and the Lord has taken away; blessed be the name of the Lord." Next, Job is inflicted with disease. His wife urges him to curse God. Still, he resists and rebuffs his wife: "Should we accept only good from God and not accept evil?" Only when Job's three friends, who ostensibly come to comfort him, reaffirm their belief that suffering is punishment for sins, does Job begin to protest his innocence.

Job demands to know why God is making him suffer. Could it be that God punishes the righteous for their few sins so that he will ultimately be rewarded or exempted from further punishment? Could it be that God is testing Job's devotion and piety? Neither answer satisfies Job. Then God's voice is heard, addressing Job directly. God reassures Job that his suffering is not due to any sin. Then, God gets angry with Job for daring to think that he can know and judge God's ways. God demands that Job acknowledge how little he knows, how insignificant he is in the scope of the universe. God speaks to Job from within the tempest and chastises him for trying to understand the incomprehensible ways of God. God tells him that the cause of human suffering is beyond our understanding:

The Lord replied to Job out of the tempest and said: Who is this who darkens counsel, speaking without knowledge? Gird your loins like a man; I will ask and you will inform Me. Where were you when I laid the earth's foundations? Speak if you have understanding. Do you know who fixed the earth's dimensions or who measured it with a line? Onto what were its bases sunk? Who set its cornerstone when the morning stars sang together and all the divine beings shouted for joy? Who closed the sea behind doors when it gushed forth out of the womb, when I clothed it in clouds, swaddled it in dense clouds, when I made breakers My limit for it, and set up its bar and doors, and said, "You may come so far and no farther; Here your surging waves will stop"? Have you ever commanded the day to break, assigned the dawn its place . . . Have you penetrated to the sources of the sea, or walked in the recesses of the deep? Have the gates of death been disclosed to you? Have you seen the gates of deep darkness? Have you surveyed the expanses of the earth? If you know of these— tell Me! (Job 38: 1-18)

God's rebuke to Job is the Jewish answer to the question of human suffering. There is no suffering without a purpose, but we as humans cannot know the reason why. God is unknowable and His ways are beyond understanding. Why humans suffer is as much a mystery as is the creation of the world. We can relate to Job's anguish and loneliness. God's silence about the fairness or injustice of his fate leaves Job in a state of despair. Yet, strangely, the voice within the tempest brings Job the desolate comfort of a man who accepts the abyss between human and divine understanding. The only way to make life bearable when we cannot find answers is to recognize that some answers are beyond us. This is also the conclusion of Rabbi Yannai, who said: "The reason why the guilty prosper or the innocent suffer is not within our grasp."

THE WHOLE HEART IS THE ONE THAT HAS BEEN BROKEN

Nothing is accidental and everything happens for a purpose. Sometimes we are subject to the fluctuating rhythms of God's constant contraction and expansion. God's presence is rhythmic, and the ebb and flow of His presence can confuse us because sometimes God withdraws from us and sometimes God reaches out to us. This cycle of withdrawal and expansion occurs as the result of God's own mysterious inner rhythms. The withdrawal phase, called "hiding God's face," is the stage in which God is absent from the world. When God withdraws from the world, the world is vulnerable. In His absence, suffering grows and bad things happen for no apparent reason. The emerging phase is the stage in which God's presence is felt. When God extends His light into our world, He raises the hidden sparks of light and creates a harmony that is felt in our lives and in our world. We should not confuse the momentary phase in the rhythm with the ultimate assurance that God's presence fills the universe. God reaches out, and steps back, only to reach out again.

We can also influence this rhythmic withdrawal and expansion. We have the power to raise the sparks and repair the broken vessels throughout our lives. The more we lift ourselves and assist others in rising higher and higher, the more God helps lift us up. As others in our family, community, and society do their part to help raise the sparks, we reinforce the bond that connects heaven and earth. Individually and collectively, we have the ability to create a strong and stable connection between God and the world. We can concentrate the flow of God's goodness and energy into the world. When we strengthen this bond, we immunize ourselves and the world and draw down divine protection on ourselves and the world.

Conversely, our actions, individually and collectively, can weaken the ties that bind us to God. We can cause an eclipse of God so that the world stands in God's shadow, vulnerable to danger and harm. We can change these conditions through our actions, just as other people's actions can change the conditions that affect us. We are sometimes immunized from harm and sometimes exposed to suffering by our own actions as well as the actions of other people. We may suffer the benefits of other people's actions just as we might suffer their consequences. While we have little control over the consequences of other people's actions, we should strive to do what good we can in our own lives.

What truly matters is how we respond to that which is beyond our control. The Jewish approach to personal suffering is to turn it into an opportunity for self-realization and fulfillment. Even within suffering, we have the opportunity to find the treasure within our own house by maintaining our humanity, our dignity, and our character. Nachmanides says that God only tests those who can stand up to the challenge. A Yiddish proverb says that our burdens are never heavier than our shoulders can bear. Small setbacks in our lives help strengthen our character so that we can better carry heavier burdens later on. Still, we pray that we never have to endure all that we can learn to bear.

God is present even within suffering. The divine spark is hidden even in the pain and provides the basis for self-healing. When we recognize the divine spark hidden in our pain, the suffering itself diminishes. That divine spark may be the reserve of strength that we find even when we think we cannot go on. When we find a deeper personal meaning for our own self in the experience, we no longer see our self as a victim but as an active participant in the healing process. To elevate the divine spark within the suffering can lead us to an even higher rung on the ladder.

Sometimes we suffer deeply or lose something precious in order to achieve something even greater in our lives. Rabbi Levi Isaac of Berditchev said: "When one wishes to transform a small vessel into a large vessel, the small vessel must first be broken. When God wants to see us grow, we are confronted with suffering or illness, which represents the breaking of the small vessel." Sometimes we can grow without crises, while at other times we may grow through suffering. A descent on the rungs of the ladder is sometimes necessary before we can ascend. The rabbi known as the Chofets Chaim said, therefore, that the truly whole heart is the one that has been broken. The deeper suffering in our lives may help us to draw on the deepest reserves of our character. The Talmud teaches that "according to the pain is the gain" (*lefum tzaara agra*). Because suffering is a necessary part of growth, Judaism teaches that God seeks out broken vessels. That is why the *Midrash* calls God "the healer of shattered hearts."

Judaism teaches that we do not always need to turn to God above, but to the God within, for help. Since God is within us, we must find the divine spark within ourselves in order to heal ourselves. When we can find the source of our strength and healing within our own souls, we discover the divinity within us. The reservoir of strength that seems to come from without actually comes from deep within, from the divine within. And since the Infinite is within us, it connects us to the infinite God. We attribute the healing that comes from within us to the infinite source of all healing. Our need for comfort leads us back to the infinite God as the ultimate source of healing. We know, however, that the only road to God passes through the human soul.

At some point in our lives, we each face suffering and loss. When it happens, we react with hurt, anger, and guilt until we are able to transform the experience. Recently, my family returned home one Friday night from synagogue and found an urgent message on our answering machine to call my cousin Ilene. My cousin is an exuberant, outgoing, and successful woman who advises individuals and groups on weight and stress control. People take to her because of her honesty and openness about her own struggle, but she does not see herself as emotionally strong even though she is the center of the family. She has been a devoted mother to her two children, one of whom is raising a child with serious disabilities. Ilene is also the surrogate mother to her younger brother, Richard, who has suffered from a lifelong battle with depression.

We reached Ilene, who told us that her brother Richard had died and that we should come right over. When we arrived, she told us that Richard's friends had been unable to reach him by telephone so she had asked the superintendent at his apartment building to look in on him and call her back. When he did not call back, she sent her husband over to the apartment. When he pulled up, the police told him that Richard was dead, but they would not reveal the cause of his death.

We sat in Ilene's den that evening, waiting for the coroner to contact the family and wondering whether Richard had taken his own life. Later that evening came the horrible news that Richard had shot himself. The next morning, we read his suicide note telling his family and friends that, after years of trying every medical and therapeutic treatment for his depression, he just could not face the desperation he felt every day. He planned his death methodically, calmly, and with complete determination to find the peace that had eluded him in life.

Ilene was devastated by the news. She had nursed and nurtured her brother throughout most of his adult life and had done everything that could be done to help him. In the end, he had kept his intentions secret from the one person who cared most deeply for him. As the news of his suicide began to sink in, Ilene began to have difficulty catching her breath and started to panic. My wife took her out in the fresh air and suggested that it was not panic so much as anger toward Richard that she was feeling. With that, she began to feel the anger and she soon regained her breath. As she began to listen to the inner voice of her emotions, she was no longer at their mercy. That night, and all through the week of *shivah*, my cousin, who did not see herself as a strong person, drew on deep reserves of emotional strength that she never thought she possessed.

There is little comfort in easy explanations of why bad things happen to us. If Richard's death brought him peace, it broke the hearts of those who cared for him. But in her grief, Ilene found the strength she always thought she lacked. Even in the deepest regions of the broken vessels, she found the spark of divine light within. And with that spark, she was able to heal herself with a power that had always been hidden within her.

BEYOND THE MIND'S LIMITS

But other troubling questions challenge and confront us. Having looked at how we can understand our own suffering, we need to ask what causes people to harm and hurt others. If we are all created in the divine image, how can we explain human cruelty and brutality? Perhaps the evidence of human behavior shows that goodness is not in our nature. No event in human history has called into question

God's mercy and human goodness more than the Holocaust. This is beyond what the mind can grasp. The destruction of European Jewry is so vast that it is impossible to comprehend its enormity. Is the murder of six million men, women, and children comprehensible? If I can barely understand the death of one child, how can I grasp the death of so many?

The Holocaust is the fiercest example of abject cruelty in the twentieth century. Who has not been touched by the accounts of the survivors? There is nothing more heartbreaking than to hear the tragedy as it touched even a single life. For example, there is nothing more horrible than the following account that I once heard from a survivor during a visit to Kiev in 1991. She told her story at a meeting of the survivors of the Nazi massacre at Babi Yar, a ravine in the city of Kiev. The Nazi occupation of Ukraine marked the beginning of the Holocaust on Soviet territory. Shortly after conquering Ukraine, the Nazi mobile killing units recruited local Ukrainians to help them with the extermination of the Jews. On the first day of *Rosh Hashanah*—September 29, 1941—German soldiers with the help of Ukrainian guards rounded up the Jews of Kiev. During the next three months, one hundred thousand Jewish men, women, and children were murdered at the Babi Yar ravine. They were marched one by one to the edge of the ravine, shot in the head, and pushed into the ravine below.

One woman testified that she and her three-year-old son were rounded up by the Nazis. She was twenty-four years old at the time and her husband was at the front with the Soviet Army. A Ukrainian policeman marched her to the edge of the ravine and shot her and her child at point-blank range. She fell into the ravine with her baby in her arms. Hours later, she awoke among a pile of corpses, holding her dead child. She passed out and revived several times that night until she crawled across the bodies, out of the pit, and escaped into the dark. After she recovered, she wandered through the city during the day and hid in the forest at night, and somehow managed to survive. She implored, "How could God have let this happen to me and my child?"

But is God to blame for Babi Yar and the other killing sites? The problem of Babi Yar and Auschwitz is not, Where was God, but Where was humanity? Where was the human soul? Where was the soul of the Germans and the Ukrainians? How can we explain what the Nazis did to the Jews, what Stalin did to his own people, what people all over the world are still doing today? If all people contain divinity within them, how do we explain murder at all? Persecution, cruelty, violence, and genocide are the result of the failed moral choices of human beings, not of people who are by nature evil. But can we reconcile the view that no person is evil by nature with the evidence about Hitler, Eichmann, and the ordinary Germans who carried out the extermination of the Jews?

Why do people commit evil? In one of the earliest studies on violence, psychologist Stanley Milgram showed that individuals may commit violence when they are directed to do so by legitimate authority or when they receive social validation and reinforcement for their actions. Milgram conducted a clinical study on volunteer subjects who were instructed to deliver electric shocks to another person. The subjects did not know that their instructors and their supposed victims were all part of the clinical team and that the electric shocks were not real. The subjects thought they were delivering real electric shocks as part of an important scientific experiment. They even heard staged cries of pain. Yet Milgram found that most subjects were willing to deliver increasingly painful and dangerous levels of shock to their victims. Why were otherwise normal people willing to do this? Milgram concluded that the authority and reinforcement of the instructor reassured the subjects that they were behaving properly and contributing to science by their willingness to inflict obvious pain on others. A group, he concluded, can provide moral justification of violence that individuals would otherwise find repugnant.

Many recent studies of the Nazi destruction of the Jews accept Milgram's premise that ordinary people can become brutal killers as a result of social and psychological pressure. Christopher Browning, in *Ordinary Men*, argues that the German killers were drawn not only from the elite SS but also included ordinary policemen who became killers because of group pressure and the fear of being held in contempt by their comrades.

A recent study by social psychologist Roy Baumeister observes that people who commit cruelty and violence are not by nature evil, nor do they see themselves as perpetrating evil. Evil exists in the eye of the beholder because the horror of evil is always measured in terms of its effect on the victim. Most perpetrators see their own actions as less significant than the victims do. Baumeister identifies "threatened egotism," a challenge or attack upon a person or group's inflated self-image, as one of the primary causes of violence. He disagrees with those who see low self-esteem as a major cause of violence. An individual or group that has an extremely high sense of self-esteem may see itself as victimized when its self-esteem is threatened. The greater the gap between one's self-esteem and the perception of one's status by others, the more one is likely to see oneself as an aggrieved victim. The more intense the threat to one's self-esteem, the more violent is likely to be one's reaction against the agent perceived as perpetrating evil. This is true, he finds, in gang violence, domestic violence, and other crimes, including the Nazi genocide.

Baumeister explains that the Germans saw themselves as victims and Jews as their oppressors. His evidence includes the fact that Germans saw themselves as the most cultured nation in Europe, heir to a venerable tradition of philosophy, literature, art, and music. They saw themselves as the most scientifically and technologically capable nation in the world. They saw their own national character as the product of a noble tradition of discipline, hard work, and lofty ideals, including love, appreciation of beauty, and devotion to the truth. They believed themselves a superior people that maintained the highest ideals of civility and civilization. Nazism, in Baumeister's view, was a response to the threatened egotism of the German people. When the Germans were crushed and defeated in World War I, the Allies imposed harsh conditions on Germany at Versailles. The humiliation of being forced to surrender to the demands of "inferior, uncultured nations" was perceived as an insult to German national pride.

Baumeister argues against the belief that cruelty and violence are committed by evil people. He claims that normal people can become evil through circumstances. Few people embark on lives as perpetrators of evil with fully developed abilities to inflict harm and violence. Even normal, otherwise moral individuals can slide down the slippery slope to absolute evil. According to this view, the Nazi genocide shows that under certain conditions even normal people can overcome the natural aversion they feel toward the use of violence and cruelty.

In *Hitler's Willing Executioners: Ordinary Germans and the Holocaust*, Daniel Goldhagen argues against the type of explanations offered by Milgram, Browning, and Baumeister. He argues that the Holocaust was perpetrated willingly, not only by Nazis and the state, but also by many ordinary Germans, who were motivated not by a sense that they were true victims, not by social or psychological pressure, nor by a coercive state. Goldhagen claims that ordinary Germans held "eliminationist" anti-Semitic beliefs about Jews that led them to slaughter millions of defenseless Jewish men, women, and children, systematically and without pity. These "were not ordinary men, but ordinary members of an extraordinary political culture, the culture of Nazi Germany, which was possessed of a hallucinatory, lethal view of the Jews."

What turned these people into brutal and sadistic killers? Goldhagen's study shows that, even before Hitler's rise to power, ordinary Germans believed in a particular type of anti-Semitism, which held that Jewish influence on Germany was seditious; that the Jews were extremely powerful, wicked, demonic, and destructive; and that they were not human and must be eliminated. They further believed that these characteristics were essential racial characteristics that could not be changed or eradicated except through total extermination of the Jews themselves. This collective and hallucinatory fallacy led them to believe that the Jews ought to die. Not only did they believe that German Jews ought to die but that all Jews should be wiped out so that no germ of Jewry remain that could reconstitute itself. Racial anti-Semitism was so deeply embedded in the Germans that the total and comprehensive elimination of the Jews seemed the moral thing to do. The brutal extermination of the Jews—men, women, and children—was carried out deliberately, willingly, mercilessly, and with joy, not with indifference, and with the assent of every significant institution in Germany. Hitler unleashed, harnessed, inflamed, and perfected German racial anti-Semitism, but he did not invent it.

POLITICAL CRUELTY

There is no equivalent in human history to the genocidal destruction of Jewry committed by the German people. But if Goldhagen is correct, and I believe he is, no one is immune from the ability to inflict cruelty on other people. For example, Jews were prominent in the Communist Party of the Soviet Union, one of the more violent movements in this century. Six of the original twenty-one Bolshevik Central Committee members in 1917 were Jewish—including Kamenev, Zinoviev, Trotsky, and Sverdlov—as were twenty percent of the early party delegates. Jewish Bolsheviks contributed to some of the greatest crimes that were committed in the name of Communism. They participated in the brutal atrocities of Bolshevism, including Lenin's forced famine in Ukraine, the Stalinist purges, and the efforts to destroy Judaism and Jewish culture.

These assimilated Jews saw both Judaism and anti-Semitism as obstacles to achieving an atheistic, classless, and prosperous society. Soon after the Revolution, the *Yevsektsiya,* the Jewish section of the Communist Party, launched the effort to destroy the institutions of Jewish life. One notorious show trial took place in Kiev on the eve of *Rosh Hashanah* 1921 in the District Court Building in Bogdan Chmielnicki Square, the same hall in which the blood libel trial of Mendel Beilis was conducted in 1911. Nora Levin, author of *The Jews in the Soviet Union Since 1917,* quotes from the show trial transcript:

The first of the defendants was an old woman who said she sent her children to *cheder* (Jewish school) where, the court said, "their ideas were darkened by the study of religious and other counterrevolutionary subjects." When the judge asked her why she didn't send them to Communist schools where they would be freed from religious superstitions, the woman answered that she was not a "low-class shoemaker or tailor," but had come from a family of rabbis and *mohalim* (circumcisers) and could not poison her own children with Communist teachers. After she was led out of the courtroom, a witness dressed as a rabbi with traditional beard and sidecurls, was then brought in. When asked why he poisoned Jewish youth with religious fairy tales and chauvinistic ideas, he answered: "I'm doing this deliberately to keep the masses of people in ignorance and bondage to the bourgeoisie." When someone in the audience shouted that the witness was "a lying ignoramus," he was immediately arrested. Another witness was called, a stout man bedecked with gold and diamonds. He declared that the Jewish bourgeoisie used religion to keep the Jewish masses in slavery and numbed their desire for freedom from the yoke of capitalism. A local Hebrew teacher, Moshe Rosenblatt, rose to defend Judaism and remind the court that just ten years before, in the very same room, similar attacks on the Jewish religion were made by the anti-semitic Black Hundreds: "Today you, like real anti-semites and haters of Jews, are repeating the same insults." When the audience broke into a storm of applause, Rosenblatt, too, was arrested. The *Yevsektsiya* prosecutor then summarized "the case against the Jewish religion" and asked for a sentence of death on the Jewish religion. The judge brought in the desired verdict.

This trial, and others like it, were followed by a period of synagogue and Jewish school closures and the abolishment of Jewish institutions at the hands of the *Yevsektsiya*. By the late 1930s, to complete the destruction of organized Jewish life in the Soviet Union, many Jewish intellectuals were killed as enemies of the state.

The cruelty of the Bolsheviks, including Jewish Communists, knew no bounds. Baruch Berman, a Jewish teacher whom I met in Moscow in 1987, told me several years later that he carried a deep personal shame for the sins of his grandfather, Matvei Berman. His grandfather, he explained, was the first director of Stalin's Gulag, the Soviet concentration camp system for political prisoners. Stalin's enemies were imprisoned, tortured, and often murdered on fabricated charges in the Gulag. Matvei Berman administered Stalin's Gulag camp system and was responsible, according to Alexander Solzhenitsyn, for the death of several million Soviet citizens in these camps. The Soviet leaders who managed the system saw themselves as idealists who were preserving the Revolution by eliminating the enemies of the people. In reality, they were misplaced idealists who demonstrated that no one is immune from the ability to inflict cruelty. The question still remains to be answered: How can we avoid crossing the line?

ISRAEL: LIKE ALL THE NATIONS?

How do we maintain our moral and spiritual bearings in a world that does not always share our principles? This is precisely the moral challenge the Zionist movement has faced since its beginnings in

1897. Zionism, the aspiration to restore a sovereign Jewish home-land, is part and parcel of Judaism. Beginning with God's covenant with Abraham, Isaac, and Jacob, the people of Israel and the land of Israel have been inseparable. When Moses led the Israelites to the land that God had promised them, they created the first society to be guided by the teachings of Torah. King David made Jerusalem his capital three thousand years ago and, ever since, Jewish hearts have turned in its direction during times of prayer. The sacred prayers and texts of Judaism reinforce that Israel is the symbol of its people's aspirations for peace and equality, justice and civility. How-ever, from the time that the Romans destroyed Jerusalem in 70 A.D. until the State of Israel was founded in 1948, Jews were prevented from fulfilling the dream of returning to Zion. Since then, Israel has had to fight a series of five wars in order to preserve its security and independence.

I remember the first moment of my own awareness of Israel. In 1957, I saw a documentary film about Israel that included a picture of a child's twisted bicycle. The image illustrated the bloody cruelty of the Palestinian terrorists who had attacked an Israeli kibbutz and shot a child riding her bicycle. The horror of senseless violence di-rected at innocent Jewish children little more than a decade after the Holocaust frightened me. Were we not safe anywhere?

As I grew up, my notion of the Jewish state was very idealistic. I was raised to believe that Israel embodied the eternal hope of the Jewish people, that one day we would be free in our own land to build a state based on the Jewish principles of justice, peace, and freedom. Each week, I put money in the *pushke*, the Jewish National Fund "blue box," whose proceeds helped to pay for reclamation of arable land, the purchase of farm equipment, and the building of a new society. I understood Zionism as both a political movement that created a safe haven for persecuted Jews and a spiritual movement for the regeneration of Israel as a model society. I was influenced by the teachings of Achad Ha'am, Aaron David Gordon, Martin Buber, and others who were committed to Arab–Jewish brotherhood. They saw Israel as a "light unto the nations," a nation that would constitute itself as a moral example of modern statehood, especially in relation to the Arabs.

The early Zionists were meticulous in establishing a legal basis for the purchase of land and had no difficulty purchasing land from Arabs. They were attentive to their relations with the Arab inhabitants, many of whom were drawn to the area from outside by the growing prosperity stimulated by the Jewish settlements. They wanted peaceful coexistence with their Arab neighbors, and they dreamed of a land where all its inhabitants shared in a common prosperity. The Zionist movement was deeply devoted to creating a society based on moral principles. When Zionist settlement began in earnest at the beginning of this century, there were fewer than 500,000 Arabs in the region and none considered themselves Palestinians.

The Arab response to the Zionist settlers was uncompromising hostility. The Muslim Arabs saw Palestine as their legacy and believed in the Islamic teaching that the entire Middle East belonged to them. Arab guerilla units attacked the Jewish settlers and opposed any compromise. In 1947, when the United Nations decided to partition Palestine into two states, a Jewish state and a Palestinian state, Israel accepted the compromise. The Arab states invaded Israel and were defeated. Not only did they forfeit the chance to have a Palestinian state, but many Palestinians living within Israel chose to flee, or were pressured to leave, and became refugees.

The tragedy was that Israel's Arab enemies would not allow the young state the luxury of a moral approach to politics. Under the constant pressure of Arab attacks and their fixation on the destruction of the Jewish state, Israel abandoned its moral mission in favor of security and a strong military. What greater tragedy was there than to confront an enemy as implacable and violent as any we have ever known at the very moment when we had the first opportunity in two thousand years to create a moral society and to regenerate the Jewish soul? The Palestinians were our worst nightmare, an enemy sworn to our destruction, a foe steeped in a tradition of political

108

violence, an adversary who would commit any atrocity in their war against the Jews.

After my junior year in college, I left the United States for Israel and enrolled as a freshman at the Hebrew University of Jerusalem. I did not return to the United States for three years. During this period, I immersed myself in Hebrew and the study of Jewish literature and earned a bachelor's degree in Jewish thought. I studied the Torah, the Talmud, the *Midrash*, the Kabbalah, Maimonides, and the modern Jewish thinkers.

During my years in Israel, I came to see another dimension of Judaism. At that time in Israel, the only religious options were to be Orthodox or secular. I traveled in intellectual circles where religious practice did not matter as long as one was engaged in the serious study of Judaism and its sources. There was no real religious conflict in Jerusalem at that time. Jerusalem was a city of writers, professors, and poets, where literature, scholarship, and poetry mattered. The only time we sensed any religious conflict was when we would venture into the ultra-Orthodox neighborhood of Meah Shearim to buy the holy books that we dissected analytically or to explore a synagogue.

We lived with another, more exciting, kind of tension. Our professors at the university were the leading intellectuals of the young country, men and women who were preoccupied with defining Judaism in modern, Zionist terms. The petty denominational differences that exercised American Jews were not their concern. The academics of Jerusalem inhabited a loftier plane, seeking to define the life and destiny of the Jewish people—whether as a nation or as a religion. The fierce debates among these great minds, drawing on all of Jewish history and literature to marshal their arguments, were electrifying.

What was it that created this intellectually charged atmosphere in Jerusalem? I believe it was the sense of common purpose among Jews that, after two thousand years, we were now free, each in our way, to delve into the heart of our own Jewish civilization. The ideas of Jewish history mattered and had real-life implications: We were building a new Judaism on the foundation of the past but with an eye toward the future. We sought to define Judaism for ourselves, indifferent to the constraints imposed by the outside world. We wrestled with many questions: Are we a unique people with a higher moral standard, or are we a nation like any other? Could we afford the luxury of morality in a region where morality could lead to national weakness? Could Judaism thrive in a free society, or is it an anachronism that should best be left behind? Are we Israelis or are we Jews first?

As Jewish intellectuals, we thought we were able to penetrate to the core of world civilization through the records of its oldest living people. We sought to understand why Jews survived and what is the meaning and purpose of our place in the world today. We argued every point of view as if our lives, and the life of the Jewish people, depended on it. All of Jewish history fell on our shoulders; it was both a burden and a blessing. I felt deeply that I had become a part of Israeli society, and Hebrew became my daily language. Although I returned to the United States after graduation, Israel has always been my other home and its challenges my own.

The great challenge facing spiritually oriented Zionists today is how to achieve reconciliation with a bitter enemy without compromising the security of Israel. If we do not resolve the Palestinian issue, how can we preserve the integrity of the Jewish soul while ruling over a conquered people? This moral dilemma troubled me so much that in 1981, I decided to spend several weeks in Israel trying to answer these questions for myself. I arranged to divide my time between meetings with Palestinians, the spokesman for the Israeli military command in the West Bank, and my longtime Israeli friends, most of whom are intellectuals and university professors.

110   I spent most of my time with Palestinian nationalists who opposed the Israeli occupation of the West Bank in various ways. I spent time with Raymonda Tawil, a former political prisoner in Jordan who later

became Yasir Arafat's mother-in-law. She was head of the Palestine Press Service in East Jerusalem and was under Israeli curfew restrictions. She argued that the Israelis had nothing to fear from the Palestinians. In her view, the main problem was "the psychological inability of Israelis to see themselves as anything but victims," when the true victims were, in fact, the Palestinians living under Israeli occupation.

Raymonda Tawil introduced me to Halil abu Ziyyad. Halil had recently been released from an Israeli jail after a ten-year sentence for involvement in a terrorist organization. Since his release, he had opened a modest bookstore in an Arab neighborhood in Jerusalem and was hoping to get a new start in life. He was a genuine and sincere friend, and we spent many evenings talking about his hopes and dreams for his people. He introduced me to his friends, some of whom openly admitted their participation in terrorist activities. One night, Halil invited me to meet him at Bir Zeit University, deep in the hills of the West Bank. He would be speaking to a group of students about the Palestinian view of Zionism and invited me to attend. Despite anxiety about traveling alone into hostile territory, I drove that night along the hilly back roads of the West Bank to the village of Bir Zeit. When I arrived, twenty students were sitting around a campfire in the darkness as he began his talk.

Halil explained that, in his view, Zionism was the tool employed by British colonialism to extend its rule over the Middle East. He argued that the Zionists were foreigners with no connection to the Land of Israel, who purposefully sought to expel the Palestinians from their homeland. He distorted the actual historical record and ignored the long history of Jewish devotion to the land and the efforts on the part of Zionism to reach a genuine peace with the Arabs. I left his lecture crushed and defeated, depressed by the realization that we shared no common ground. Although I continued to meet with Halil, my optimism about reconciliation between Palestinians and Jews on an individual level had evaporated. Several months later,

I read in *The New York Times* that Halil had been expelled from Israel on the charge that he was a military commander of an underground terrorist cell in the West Bank.

Although I hoped to see in the human face of a Palestinian friend the mirror image of the human face of a Jew, all I really found were distortions and illusions. If Halil could not see me and my people in a human and humane light, how could peace ever be achieved? Ever since that chilling experience, I have had little hope that Palestinians and Israelis could ever find common ground. I came to see that the Palestinian vision is based on an illusion about Zionism and that Halil had little interest in seeing the reality of two people linked together by a common destiny. My experience led me to conclude that there may be no real possibility of reconciliation between Palestinians and Israelis in the near future. The only possible solution, I concluded, is that there should be an amicable separation—divorce with an equitable distribution of property.

At the same time, I am equally troubled by what the conflict with the Palestinians has done to the Zionist dream. Most of the Jews who have settled in Israel came there because they sought a safe haven from oppression in their native lands. Most Israelis are refugees or the children of refugees from the Holocaust, Arab lands, Ethiopia, the Soviet Union, and other eastern European countries. They arrived in Israel already knowing that the world can be a dangerous and oppressive place. Unlike the early Zionist idealists, they seek safety and security through strength and see the moral dream of Zionism as a naïve and impractical anachronism. How can they live according to spiritual and moral ideals when their enemies are committed to their destruction and continue to use terror against innocent civilians? Although the Zionist founders sought to create a state that would be a "light unto the nations," a moral state based on justice and equality, Israel has been denied that possibility.

The moral challenge facing Israel today is how to deal with competing and irreconcilable claims between Israelis who believe that they have the right to settle throughout the Land of Israel and Palestinians who believe that all of Palestine is theirs. Since both sides claim equal rights, the only solution is for both sides to accept a territorial compromise. Only in this way can each side preserve their dream as a goal for the future. In the meantime, only compromise coupled with measures that create mutual confidence can provide hope for a future of peace and coexistence.

This aim requires that Israel struggle seriously with the moral dimensions of the conflict. While Israel must hold the Palestinians to account for violations of security agreements, Israel too must abandon its efforts to dominate and coerce the Palestinians. While Israel must combat Palestinian terrorism and Islamic fundamentalism with unconventional means, it must treat innocent Palestinians as persons and respect their human rights and dignity. Although this stance is difficult to maintain in the face of an enemy who does not abide by civilized rules, Israel should differentiate between Arab terrorists and civilians. Israel should also continue to educate its citizens about how to treat non-Jews living under Israeli rule.

Meanwhile, developments within Israel offer little hope that the Jewish homeland will soon become a "light unto the nations." I view this era as another Generation of the Desert, the name given to the forty-year period after the Exodus from Egypt, when the Israelites wandered in the Sinai Desert. As soon as they had received the Torah, they turned immediately to arguing among themselves, sniping at Moses, longing for the familiar security of slavery rather than the insecurity of freedom, and dividing into factions. Our generation, although it has already reached the Promised Land, is no different. The world is a narrow bridge, and the Jewish people, who have crossed too many bridges in too short a span, have suffered much. Israel is still in need of healing from decades of war, terrorism, and constant siege from its neighbors before it can return to pursuing its founding vision.

The people of Israel have not yet recovered from the wounds inflicted on them in the last fifty years. Holocaust survivors bear their wounds stoically. The Jews from Arab lands are still struggling to

113

overcome the disadvantages of centuries of poverty and discrimination. Soviet immigrants will require a generation to recover from the damage inflicted upon them by the Soviet system. Ethiopian Jews are making a rapid and dislocating transition into the twentieth century. The fundamentalist Orthodox Jews have not yet adapted their spiritual orientation to the realities of the modern world. The hostility of Jewish fundamentalists to liberal Judaism shows that Jews can still inflict cruel wounds on each other. It will require time to create harmony among such dissonant voices. Still, I expect that within my lifetime, Israel will achieve the prophetic dream of security within its borders, freedom within the land, civility among its people, justice within its gates, and peace with its neighbors.

THE MORAL BARRIER

What do the Holocaust, Bolshevism, and conflict in the Middle East teach us? What turns people into brutes? What begets cruelty and violence? Evil perpetrated by human beings is a human problem, not God's responsibility. Although none of us is born evil, we may become evil under certain conditions. We do not become evil because God permits us to, nor because of our desire for wealth or power. Nor is threatened egotism, misplaced idealism, innate sadism, or social, psychological, or group pressure sufficient to explain why we cross the moral barrier. We become evil when we deceive ourselves, ignore the truth, and choose to cross the moral barrier to act out our delusions. Germans committed genocide against the Jews because their culture fostered delusional fantasies about Jews and reinforced the belief that extermination of the Jews was the only solution. Jewish Bolsheviks committed their atrocities because their ideology promoted the belief that revolutionary violence was a necessary means toward creating a communist dictatorship. Palestinian use of terrorism continues to flourish because of the Palestinians' religious belief

114

that no moral constraints apply in the holy struggle to spread Islam throughout the Middle East. In each case, good people have been educated and trained wrongly and, as a result, have crossed the moral barrier between good and evil.

When I was a young faculty member teaching at Wesleyan University, I became friendly with Phil Hallie, a philosopher. Phil had just published his now legendary book, *Lest Innocent Blood Be Shed*, the story of the inhabitants of the French village of Le Chambon and their pastor, who had risked their lives to save five thousand Jews from the Nazis. One evening, after welcoming me in his "Shalom Garden," Phil explained that after years of studying human cruelty, his heart literally gave out. He thought that he had saved his own life by turning to the study of human goodness, and he was captivated by the story of Le Chambon. When he died in 1994, he left behind him the finished manuscript of what became *Tales of Good and Evil, Help and Harm*.

Phil Hallie explored the fine line between good and evil and the "lucid mystery" of the moral choice to help another person. He explored this mystery through several stories, including that of his own life and the "ambiguous decency" of a Nazi officer in Le Chambon who had looked the other way when the villagers rescued the Jews. Phil believed that each of our lives is a moral hurricane with a calm eye of goodness in the center. He reminds us that preserving the stories of good and evil is one of the ways we can sustain that ethical center.

The capacity to inflict cruelty and violence on another person has many causes but cannot be unleashed unless a moral barrier against evil is breached. A person becomes evil by choosing to do evil or by failing to make the choice to resist evil. Evil exists not in the eyes of the beholder but in the failed moral choices of the perpetrators. Evil occurs when education fails to erect an impervious barrier against wrongdoing. The moral and spiritual teachings of Judaism are that barrier. The strongest barrier against choosing evil is the conscious, intentional choice to do good.

How do we know what is the right moral choice? We each face daily choices about what we do. The moral compass does not initially come from within. We are not born with a clear sense of right or wrong, the ability to choose between good and evil. An individual's character is a matter of choices—not fate, destiny, or nature. Every person has two impulses—one for good (*yetzer ha-tov*) and one for evil (*yetzer ha-ra*). Judaism does not believe in original sin but does believe that a person is, or becomes, what he or she *does*.

Judaism has a realistic and honest appreciation of human nature. While humans are basically good, it is easier for them to do wrong than to do right. The good impulse, rooted in altruism and selflessness, is weaker than the evil impulse. The good impulse is passive, with little power or influence over human conduct. The evil impulse is a powerful source of human energy. Impelled by egoistic urges, it is the active, dynamic part of the human soul that is responsible for action. It is impossible for a person to act only with the good impulse because it lacks the vitality necessary for action. The evil impulse is the source of vibrancy and life that drives the human being. The ancient rabbis felt this so deeply that the authors of the medieval *Avot de-Rabbi Natan* said: "When a man stirs up his passion and is about to commit an act of lewdness, all parts of his body are ready to obey him. On the other hand, when a man is about to perform an act of piety, all his parts become laggard, because the impulse to evil in his innards is ruler of his entire body, whereas the impulse to good is like a man confined in a prison."

The Talmud recognized the power of human impulses and did not think there was anything unnatural about it. This led the rabbis to write in the *Sayings of the Fathers*: "Who is a hero? One who conquers his own evil impulse." The rabbis did not deny the existence of the evil impulse nor did they hold sentimental illusions about human nature. They recognized that the challenge to maintain one's self on the straight path was a difficult challenge. They believed that it could best be met by an honest understanding of human character and by a discipline that might guide an individual through difficult choices.

Judaism teaches that we cannot ignore our instincts and impulses nor can we surrender to them. The tradition even says we cannot worship God with the good impulse. The highest form of worship is when we harness the energy of the evil impulse and channel it in the right direction. Judaism calls the evil impulse a "blaze" and recognizes the power of this red-hot energy. What counts is to restrain the blaze when it threatens to burn out of control and to let it burn at the right time and place. Passion cannot be easily restrained, but it can be channeled in morally and socially productive ways.

The ultimate barrier between good and evil, and the only reliable moral compass, is the moral law of the Torah. Morality is an acquired sensibility and it is developed through education. Human beings do not inherently possess the ability to choose goodness without being educated to do so. Our understanding of good and evil develops as we are taught what is right and what is wrong. When we disregard the fundamental moral laws of the Jewish tradition, we lose the only reliable moral anchor that we possess. The moral laws of the Torah and the Jewish tradition provide a clear and dependable guide.

THE CODE OF *MENTSHLICHKEYT*

There are not many issues on which we follow the authority of the past for its own sake. Morality, however, is the one area where the accumulated wisdom of the past may be the most compelling guide to us today. The moral law of the Torah teaches us that justice, the passionately impartial and equitable treatment of all people under the law, is absolute. This requires the pursuit of truth and impartiality in all social, legal, and human relations: "Justice, justice, shall you pursue!" (Deuteronomy 16:20). Basic justice may not be compromised, in favor of neither the rich nor the poor: "You shall not render an unfair decision: do not favor the poor or show deference to the rich; judge your neighbor fairly" (Leviticus 19:15).

Special protection must be accorded to the most vulnerable members of society. Compassion for the weak is a matter of empathy for the human condition that we all face. The poor, the homeless, the immigrant, and the indigent have rights equal to the most powerful member of society. We must remember that we too were once strangers in a land not our own: "You shall not oppress a stranger, for you know the feelings of the stranger, having yourselves been strangers in the land of Egypt" (Exodus 23:9). "Remember that you were a slave in the land of Egypt and that the Lord your God redeemed you from there" (Deuteronomy 24:18). The Torah offers a special warning about the treatment of all defenseless individuals: "You shall not ill-treat any widow or orphan. If you do mistreat them, I will heed their outcry as soon as they cry out to Me" (Exodus 22:21–22).

We place great responsibility on an individual's social responsibility. Our tradition tells us that our moral responsibilities do not change with the circumstances. Even if society permits injustice, each one of us has individual responsibility. We must act to correct injustice even if it means going against the grain of society. As the *Mishnah* tells us, "In a situation where there is no humanity, strive to be human." However, our moral responsibility does not mean that we should carry the burden alone to the exclusion of our other responsibilities in life: "It is not your responsibility to complete the task, neither are you free to ignore it."

Compassion is the basis of the Jewish social outlook. We are responsible not only for the immediate members of our family but for our neighbors, regardless of their race, color, religion, or national origin, and for Jews living in the land of Israel and throughout the world: "If, however, there is a needy person among you, one of your kinsmen in any of your settlements in the land that the Lord your God is giving you, do not harden your heart and shut your hand against your needy kinsman. Rather, you must open your hand and lend him sufficient for whatever he needs" (Deuteronomy 15:7–8). Some commentators read this passage as defining a hierarchy of Jewish charitable responsibility. They say that our first responsibility is to help members of our own nuclear and extended family. The second level of social responsibility is for us to support the needy within our communities regardless of whether they are Jewish or not. The third level of responsibility is toward needy Jews in the land of Israel.

Torah teaches us that the greatest moral vice is hatred. It commands us: "You shall not hate your kinsman in your heart . . . You shall not take vengeance or bear a grudge against your kinsfolk. Love your neighbor as yourself" (Leviticus 19:17–18). To "love your neighbor as yourself" is a duty of the heart that commands us to love other persons as we love our own self. Rabbi Akiva commented that this is the fundamental principle of the entire Torah. His belief that love, empathy, and compassion are fundamental duties of the heart stems from the principle that we are each created in the image of God. Hillel stated this also when he said: "Do not do to another what is hateful to you." We can never see ourselves as being inherently superior to another person. For when we do, we open the door to treating the other person as inferior. Inferior treatment of another person is a form of violence and cruelty. We must even treat those whom we hate on the basis of justice and may not act toward them out of impulse.

Although we might want to take advantage of the misfortune of our enemy, we may not. We must be a *mentsh* even with those who do not treat us with *mentshlichkeyt*: "When you encounter your enemy's ox or ass wandering, you must take it back to him. When you see the ass of your enemy lying under its burden and would refrain from raising it, you must nevertheless raise it with him" (Exodus 23: 4–5).

119

These moral laws help us avoid the kind of moral failures that lead to evil, violence, and cruelty. When we see ourselves as victims, it is too easy to see other people as our victimizers and as perpetrators of evil. Judaism teaches us not to see ourselves as victims but to actively counter, resist, and fight all forms of oppression. We must hate the oppression but not the oppressor. Our spiritual resistance to evil remains moral and principled and does not become personal and vindictive. When we think that it is necessary to commit one wrong in order to achieve a noble end, we open a door that we can never close. It is impossible to reach good results with evil means because a corrupt method contaminates the very goal itself. This is evident in the Jewish laws governing the conduct of war. Although "war is hell" from any perspective, an ethic has been established that prevents its conduct from sliding into annihilationist mayhem.

The Geneva Conventions governing the humane treatment of captives of war, the international treaties limiting nuclear weapons, and the agreements governing the use of chemical and biological weapons are all attempts to regulate the moral use of lethal military force. The biblical prohibition against wanton destruction prohibits destroying a specific target without a compelling justification: "When in your war against a city you have to besiege it a long time in order to capture it, you must not destroy its trees, wielding the ax against them. You may eat of them, but you must not cut them down. Are the trees of the field human to withdraw before you into the besieged city?" (Deuteronomy 20:19). The wanton destruction of fruit trees is prohibited because they themselves are not the enemy. In addition, trees are a source of food for noncombatants, and the destruction of trees is an attack upon civilians that will continue to harm them long after the cessation of hostilities. In a larger sense, this case establishes the principle that war may be directed only at the combatants, not against civilians, and should be limited in scope rather than total. The German war against the Jews is the most vicious example in history of wanton destruction directed against a group of human beings. But there are other, lesser examples of unjustifiable devastation in modern history. Moreover, any nuclear warfare is unjustifiable from a moral point of view.

While we each have the capacity to be brutal, the moral teachings of Judaism are an attempt to inhibit this capacity. Cruelty reinforces further cruelty and violence is habit forming. Once a moral threshold is crossed the first time, it is easier to cross it the second. The Talmud says, "When a person commits a sin and repeats it, it becomes a permitted act in his eyes." Judaism emphasizes avoiding the crossing of that threshold in the first place. But when we do cross the line, the Jewish remedy is to begin by thinking about and sincerely regretting the mistake. Regret will actually lead to a willingness to stop the offending behavior. It then becomes important to acknowledge, through public or private confession, what one has done in order to empty the heart of its burden of guilt. Finally, we must make a personal resolution never to repeat the behavior.

To be a *mentsh*, a humane person, living by the code of *mentshlichkeyt* with all the struggles implied in being human, is the goal of Judaism. *Mentshlichkeyt* does not refer only to the specifically mandated moral laws of Judaism but, in a wider sense, to a humane outlook that is both high-minded and appreciative, but only up to a point, of human moral failings. Occasional lapses in personal behavior are expected, but in matters of ultimate integrity, the code of *mentshlichkeyt* has little tolerance for error.

The code of *mentshlichkeyt* recognizes the equality of all people and dismisses all distinctions among people based on extrinsic values such as wealth or other privileges. A sardonic Yiddish proverb pokes fun at human pretensions and at the person who thinks that wealth is a substitute for intelligence, character, and talent: "With money in your pocket, you are wise, handsome, and you sing well, too!" The code of *mentshlichkeyt* holds that wealth only increases one's responsibility to help the less fortunate, rather than one's status. Money saddles a wealthy person with a great burden. As Sigmund Freud said, "There is really no advantage in being a rich man if one is a Jew; other people's miseries make it impossible to enjoy too much one's own happiness." Other Yiddish sayings remind us that a *mentsh* should not envy another person: "You can not chew with someone else's teeth"; that we are mistaken to think that "it's good to learn to shave on someone else's beard"; and that, regrettably, "We always have a good appetite at someone else's feast."

To be human is to struggle throughout our lives with moral challenges and the constantly changing and unpredictable patterns of our lives. Our struggle involves learning how to cope with the difficulties we face as well as learning how to avoid the mistakes that bring suffering to others. We learn how to follow the path through life that brings us higher up the rungs of the ladder. Imagine a world where we are in fact guided by the moral principles of the Torah, where we teach our children the Jewish code of *mentshlichkeyt*, and the moral laws of the Torah. Imagine a world where we live by the principles of compassion, love, and fair treatment. Imagine a world in which genocide, revolutionary violence, and religious hatred would be unthinkable.

To strive for *mentshlichkeyt* is a struggle. There is too much in this world that tempts us to treat others badly. To be a *mentsh* is to struggle with the challenge of goodness, and the passage through life requires courage. As Nachman of Bratslav said: "The world is a very narrow bridge; the key thing is not to be afraid at all." Sometimes we experience periods of straight progress, happiness, and comfort. But at other times, we slip on the rungs of the ladder. Sometimes we suffer because of things that happen without reason. We turn to find healing and renewal by nurturing the divine spark within us. At other times, we are victims of our own choices and the failed moral choices of others. But there is no life without struggle. The best we can ask of ourselves is to have all the courage we need to face the struggle. That is what it means to be human and why *A mentsh heyst a mentsh veyl er mentsht zikh*—"A person is called a *mentsh* because he struggles."

Chapter Four

THE INWARD AND
OUTWARD PATH

Our heart is an altar. In whatever you do, let a spark of the
holy fire burn within you so that you may fan it into a flame.
—*Baal Shem Tov*

REHEARTENING JEWISH LIFE

Judaism is a spiritual discipline that guides us along a particular
path. The Jewish path is the means by which we raise the sparks,
guide ourselves through the struggles of our lives, and move up the
rungs of the spiritual ladder. The rituals of Judaism are the steps on
the path, the embodiment of our spiritual teachings, and the expression of our spiritual aspirations. They are also the shared symbols
that communicate the spiritual meaning of Judaism among Jews
from one generation to another.

The Jewish way of life is the outward expression of an inward
spirituality. But for many of us today, it is enough to feel spiritual
in our hearts. We do not always feel that we need to express our
spirituality through someone else's rituals. Is it not enough for us to
be spiritual in our own way? If we can find our own individual spiritual path, why do we need Jewish rituals at all?

The spiritual heart of Jewish rituals is not always evident in the intricate details of Jewish practice. Jewish rituals are often presented as laws rather than as guidelines to spiritual and moral improvement. What does it matter if we eat beef but not pork, or drive on the Sabbath, if our hearts are good? What is the spiritual element in the Jewish rituals that is hidden from view behind layers of legalism? Many people are troubled by the focus of Jewish practices on outward behavior rather than the inner experience.

Jewish religious practices came from the hearts of those who were struggling up the stages of the ladder. Those who followed the practices understood the heart-knowledge that was conveyed by the ritual without even putting the message into words. When we put our own feelings into words, we speak only for ourselves in that moment. Jewish rituals are the Jewish way of speaking from the heart without saying more than is necessary. For example, the act of saying *kaddish*—the memorial prayer for the dead—has a powerful emotional effect on the mourner and all those who hear it, even though there is no mention of death in the prayer. When we put our feelings into a ritual that expresses what all of us feel, we create a bond between ourselves and others that goes beyond the moment to all people and all time.

The practice of traditional Jewish ritual is called *halachah*, which means "the path." *Halachah*, as the distinct pattern of Jewish practice, has its origins in the Torah. The content of the *halachah* is the *mitzvot*, which are the commandments that prescribe all aspects of Jewish behavior from morning till night, from Sunday to the Sabbath, from birth until death. The *halachah* includes religious behaviors such as the observance of the Sabbath and festivals. It prescribes the normative practices for daily prayer—the proper ways to pray, what to say, and when to pray. It prescribes the moral conduct that we are required to follow in relation to other people. It establishes the laws pertaining to family life and sets the standards for community life, business, political conflict, and war, down to the smallest details. It is the comprehensive system of regulated Jewish behavior and includes every area of individual, familial, communal, and societal behavior.

Most Jews today, except for Orthodox and some Conservative Jews, do not accept the *halachah* as their path. *Halachah* is understood differently by each of the modern denominations of Judaism. For Orthodox Judaism, *halachah* is the system of behavior that Judaism has codified as religious law. Conservative Judaism sees the *halachah* as law but recognizes that the law needs to be modernized, updated, and liberalized by rabbis who themselves follow *halachah*. Reconstructionism views *halachah* as the historical folkways and ethnic practices of the Jewish people that are subject to change by modern, committed Jews. Reform Judaism believes that the *halachah* itself is not obligatory and that the rituals Jews find meaningful today are a matter of personal conscience.

Our ancestors believed that God commanded us at Mount Sinai to follow the *mitzvot*. They believed that all the *mitzvot* that have been added over time were anticipated at Sinai and that there is nothing new under the sun. They understood the *mitzvot* as what God expects from us. They thought that change is possible only if it adds to the *mitzvot*, not if it takes away or eliminates *mitzvot*. Many *mitzvot* are found in the Torah but many others were developed over time by our rabbis. They are all part of one seamless tradition. The Talmud itself seems to admit that many *mitzvot* are no more than what we as humans have concluded that God wants from us. The *mitzvot* are the human interpretation of what the infinite God wants from us. Many of the *mitzvot* are not from God, they are from us, but they are what God would want from us, if He could tell us.

This was also my grandfather's position: "Everything new is prohibited by Torah." There is logic to this point of view, but there are problems with it as well. Significant changes did occur within the *halachah*. For example, this same grandfather, who came to this country from Russia, had never seen a grapefruit until he arrived in Cleveland in 1913. He faced a new situation: When you drink grapefruit juice, what blessing do you say? Do you say the blessing over fruit—*borey pri ha-etz*—or over beverages—*shehakol nehiyeh bide-varo?* He concluded that grapefruit juice is a beverage, not a fruit, and issued a ruling that others followed. Once he decided, it was as if the Torah had already anticipated this new situation. He did not consider himself to be establishing a new law so much as discovering a *mitzvah* that was implicit in Torah, "a law from Moses at Sinai." Like all followers of the *halachah*, he denied that he had established anything new on his own.

Most Jews today cannot accept the notion that *halachah* is God-given through Moses at Sinai. We understand ritual as the way that each culture creates a shared set of symbols, translates its particular beliefs into practices, and embodies the specific shared values of a culture. We do not have the faith that God ordained the *halachah* and anticipated every future situation in which it could be applied. We understand that the *mitzvot* were developed by our ancestors, who believed them to be holy and sanctioned by God. The *mitzvot* came about when Moses and our other ancestors heard the inner voice that guided their path in the world. They followed the inner voice with absolute certainty along a path that became the *halachah*. When we inherited this path, it sometimes came down to us as an inflexible law without the original spiritual dimension that it once had. Our ancestors' dynamic spirituality has become our incomprehensible law.

We can integrate Judaism into our own spirituality and incorporate our own spirituality into Judaism if we think of Judaism as "the inward and outward path" rather than *halachah*. The inward and outward path is not one that views the *mitzvot* as laws to be followed blindly. No *mitzvah* should be part of the Jewish path unless its meaning is understood. Nor should we ever reduce Judaism to the performance of *mitzvot* without the spiritual dimension. We should never imagine that their purpose is just the doing. Their purpose is the inner experience. Too often the *mitzvot* are seen today by traditionalists as ends in themselves: The more you observe, and the more strict you are in observance, the better. Even traditional Judaism rejects the cult of excess in performing *mitzvot*. The Kotzker Rebbe said that the second commandment against making idols includes the prohibition against making idols of the *mitzvot*. We should not let the observance of the *mitzvot* hide the true inner content of Judaism.

Mitzvot are the records of the spiritual experiences of our predecessors, who turned their experiences into the *mitzvot* and bequeathed them to us. Their experiences are footprints they have left for us in order to guide our steps toward finding the divine spark within the world. They point us in the direction of the experience of our predecessors, but we must also find our own way. We must create new paths for ourselves and for those who come after us, just as those who came before did for us. To be Jewish is to be part of a tradition that offers the wisdom and experience of our predecessors even as it invites us to create our own path. Judaism is a tradition about how we can experience the spiritual dimensions of life and strengthen the image of God within ourselves. This means that each person must find which *mitzvot* speak to each of us even as we add to the legacy of Judaism.

Spirituality cannot occur in a vacuum and must be grounded in actions. The *mitzvot* are the outward expression of inward experiences. We often tend to see only the outer side of the *mitzvah* rather than the inner experience that led to it in the first place. The inner purpose of the *mitzvah* is called the *kavanah*, the purpose, the spiritual heart. As the Yehudi of Peshischa said, "The *mitzvah* is the vessel, but the spiritual intention is the content." We must take every step along the path with *kavanah*, forethought, and preparation. As the Kotzker Rebbe said, "God not only desires your deed, but more so, He desires your intense preparation. The effort is what matters most. All is according to the size of the effort, not the greatness of the deed." Although the *kavanah* is more important than the *mitzvah*, there is no *kavanah* unless it leads to action.

There should be no gap between our inner *kavanah* and our outward actions, our *mitzvot*. The greatest compliment in Judaism is to say about a person—*Tocho kevaro*—"He is inside what he is on the outside." That is called being Torah. At the same time, we are connected to others because spirituality, besides being highly individual, is essentially communal in expression. Judaism places great emphasis on group spirituality. When a stranger or someone unfamiliar with Judaism encounters Jewish rituals, they may be baffled by the experience. To an outsider, the spirituality of the rituals may be imperceptible because of their foreign nature. To an insider, however, the unspoken spiritual connectedness may be a powerful shared force that is just not accessible to outsiders. For example, the theme of freedom implicit in the Passover Seder is understood by everyone, even if it is not always discussed directly. The participants share in the connectedness of an unspoken experience even as they speak openly about other things, such as *matzah* and other Seder rituals.

SHABBAT: "A PALACE IN TIME"

How can we incorporate Jewish spirituality into our daily lives? Every action must reflect a spiritual value if it is to have meaning today. Jewish spirituality is expressed in concrete actions that embody underlying spiritual principles. The most fundamental Jewish spiritual practice is the Sabbath (*Shabbat*). The Sabbath embodies the Jewish spiritual principle that each human being contains God within and that our task is to be Godlike. Just as God rested on the seventh day of creation, so too must we rest and retreat from our daily labor on the Sabbath. Moreover, just as the seventh day marks the end of God's creative efforts and the beginning of our responsibility to complete the work of creation, the Sabbath prepares us for understanding and anticipating our responsibilities. Only by stepping back from the routine of life on the Sabbath can we fully appreciate the deeper values of life.

The Sabbath is the indispensable spiritual moment in the weekly life of a Jew. If there is one spiritual practice that has greater stature than all the others, it is the Sabbath, which is often regarded as equal in importance to all the other *mitzvot* in Judaism combined. The Jewish people are even called "the people who sanctify the seventh day" (*am mekkadeshei shevii*). The Sabbath is given credit for the very survival and preservation of the Jewish people itself. Our sages have said that "even more than the people Israel has preserved the Sabbath, the Sabbath has preserved Israel." The Sabbath is itself Jewish renewal.

The Sabbath is also associated with the female "appearance" of God. The Sabbath is feminine divine-time in the sense that it is free of the harsh, judgmental, and competitive elements that dominate the rest of the week. The Sabbath is time influenced by the holy sparks of divine light, completely unfettered by the power of the broken vessels. The appearance of God is that of the "Sabbath bride" and we are the groom. The Sabbath consummates the marriage between the people Israel and God and unites us with the divine sparks within ourselves and within the world. The Sabbath unites the potential with the ideal, the not-yet-holy with the actually holy.

According to Abraham Joshua Heschel, the Sabbath is a "palace in time," a constructed universe in which our ordinary routine is restructured into sacred time: "The seventh day is a mine where spirit's precious metal can be found with which to construct a palace in time, a dimension in which the human is at home with the divine, a dimension in which man aspires to approach the likeness of the divine." The Sabbath is time elevated from the mundane, detached from routine, and transformed into the sublime. It is a retreat from the productive, mechanical, and laborious activities of the week into a time defined by imagination, expansiveness, and transcendence.

The Sabbath is usually described by what we should *not* do: We should not work, we should not shop, and we are not expected to move through time as we normally do. So how do we describe the Sabbath? It is a day devoted entirely to the regeneration of the body and soul. The Sabbath is a day of rest and joy. Sabbath sexuality is considered especially spiritual on Friday night. Legend has it that we each receive a second, special soul on Sabbath eve that restores us spiritually. Some sources say that the second soul is produced by sexual intercourse on Friday night, the most propitious time of the week. The soul that is created descends immediately on us and leads us though the twenty-five hours of Sabbath. But it is also a day for restoring the body through rest and renewal. The Sabbath is a day for slowing down and listening to what our bodies are telling us. Many people take off their watches and do not answer the telephone on the Sabbath.

CREATING A SPIRITUAL SABBATH FOR OURSELVES

How can we create a Sabbath for ourselves and our families? We can draw upon the Jewish traditions to create an inward and outward path. For example, we can prepare the house for the Sabbath through cleaning and cooking in advance so that we do not have to do any actual work when the Sabbath begins. The traditional Sabbath rituals have spiritual significance. The Sabbath begins at twilight, eighteen minutes before sundown, when it is neither day nor night. Jewish calendars, available through synagogues and Jewish bookstores, provide local listings for Sabbath time. The concern for the exact moment when Sabbath time starts reminds us that there is a precise end to the work of creation and an exact beginning to the first Sabbath of creation. What might appear as an unnecessarily literal preoccupation with the precise minute of the dawning of the Sabbath is really meant to convey the idea that transitions matter and weekday time and Sabbath time are not interchangeable.

The festive Sabbath dinner is a banquet for the body and soul. All other activity stops as the members of the family or the group that celebrates the Sabbath gathers. The normal weeknight routine, whatever it is, stops for this one evening. Time is turned on its head in order to break us of habit, routine, and automatic behavior. The woman or other head of the household lights two Sabbath candles and recites the Sabbath candle blessing. The two candles symbolize the harmonizing of the male and female appearances of God and the tempering of the harsh and gentle sides of our own self. Their light reminds us of the holy light shed by the divine sparks that restores the broken vessels temporarily on Sabbath. The woman who lights the candles represents the power of the feminine appearance of God to bring about harmony in the world.

If there are children present, the parents bless them with the priestly blessing to indicate that we are all priestlike. The blessing for a son is based on Jacob's blessing of his sons and grandsons and the priestly blessing:

May God make you like Efraim and Menasheh: The Lord bless you and keep you! The Lord deal kindly and graciously with you! The Lord bestow His favor upon you and grant you peace!

The blessing for a daughter is similar:

May God make you like Sarah, Rebecca, Rachel, and Leah: The Lord bless you and keep you! The Lord deal kindly and graciously with you! The Lord bestow His favor upon you and grant you peace!

As we sit down to the Sabbath meal, we begin with a song written by Chayyim Nachman Bialik, the leading Hebrew poet:

The sun on the treetops no longer is seen;
Come, gather to welcome the Sabbath, our queen!
Behold her descending, the holy, the blessed,
And with her the angels of peace and of rest.
Draw near, O queen, and here abide;

Draw near, draw near, O Sabbath bride.
Peace be unto you, O angels of peace.

We can conduct a brief service with other Sabbath hymns, such as *Yedid Nefesh*, that we sing together in synagogue or even at the dinner table. This sixteenth-century mystical hymn to the father aspect of God describes Him as the Beloved, the object of our soul's yearning. The hymn is meant to be chanted on Friday evening, at the beginning of the Sabbath, to join together the father aspect with the female aspect of God in a weekly harmony.

Soul lover, merciful father,
Draw Your servant to Your desire.
Your servant will run, swift as a deer,
To bow before Your majesty.
For Your love is sweeter than the honeycomb
Or any sweet taste.

Majesty, Beauty, Light of the world—
My soul is love-sick for You!
Please, God, please, heal her
By radiating Your sweet light upon her
So that she will recover and grow strong
And be Your captive forever.

Ancient one! Let Your tender mercy flow
And show favor on Your favored son
For he has yearned, yes, yearned, so long
To see Your dazzling splendor.
Please, my God, my heart's desire,
Hurry, do not hide.

Reveal Yourself,
Envelop me with your canopy of peace.
Illuminate the earth with Your presence.

Let me rejoice and delight in You.
Hurry, my love, the time has arrived,
To love me as before.

We can follow this with another mystic poem invoking the mother aspect of God. Composed in Safed around 1560, "Come, My Beloved" (*Lechah Dodi*) portrays the Sabbath as the propitious moment of harmony between the father and mother appearances of God and a time of cosmic unity. Once again, the Beloved is the Father image who is invited by the community to join his bride, the Sabbath, the mother. Throughout the poem, the father is called by several code words: "Remember," "Name," "God," and even "King." The mother is called "Preserve," "Sabbath," "Crown," "Shrine," "Jerusalem," and even "King David" and "Messiah." The poem was originally a guide to a community of mystics who went out to the fields around Safed, dressed in white, to receive the Sabbath as it "arrived" from the west with the setting sun.

Come, my Beloved
To greet the Bride.
Let us welcome the Sabbath into our midst.

"Preserve" and "Remember" the Sabbath
Were heard at Sinai as one divine word
From God who is the One, whose name is One.
He rises to His name, His splendor, and praise.
Toward the Sabbath, let us now go.
For the source of all blessing is she.
Before time, before creation, she was formed
As God's last creation, but His first intention.

Shrine of the King, Jerusalem, His royal city—
Rise up, like the Sabbath day, from your ruins.
You have dwelled too long in the valley of tears.
So God will now shower you with His healing compassion.

133

Arise—Shake off the dust!
My people—Adorn yourselves in the robes of majesty!
Our help will come from the Messiah, just a man from the House
    of King David.
Come to my soul, already, Beloved—redeem it!

Awake, awake! O Sabbath Bride—
Your light has arrived.
Arise! My light!
Awake, awake, and burst out in song!
God's glory now shines upon you.

O, don't be ashamed, don't be distressed.
Why are you bowed, and why do you yearn?
In you, O Bride, the poor children of my people find comfort.
For you, Jerusalem will be rebuilt.

Those who destroyed you will themselves be destroyed.
Your foes will be routed.
Your Beloved will soon rejoice in you
As a bridegroom with his bride.

Spread your light to the right and the left
And we will then know how to revere God.
With the help of the Messiah
We will rejoice and celebrate.

Come in peace, O crown of your mate.
Come in happiness and radiance
To the faithful of your treasured people—
Come, O Bride. Come, O Bride!

134

We can then sing a hymn to the Sabbath angels, our own inner-
self striving for Sabbath elevation:

Peace unto you, attending angels, sublime angels
Of the King of kings of kings,
The Holy One, Blessed be He.
Come in peace, angels of peace, sublime angels
Of the King of kings of kings,
The Holy One, Blessed be He.
Bless us with peace, angels of peace, sublime angels
Of the King of kings of kings,
The Holy One, Blessed be He.
And then you will leave in peace, angels of peace, sublime angels
Of the King of kings of kings,
The Holy One, Blessed be He.

We then chant the *kiddush*, the blessing for the Sabbath day recited over wine. The *kiddush* commences with the biblical description of the first Sabbath, and the concluding section describes the sanctification on the seventh day of the Sabbath and the Jewish people. The wine helps to concretize the blessing and to stimulate the spiritual imagination.

Everyone continues the priestlike ritual by washing their hands. Each person fills a cup with water held in the right hand, passes the cup to the left hand, and pours water on the right hand, then passes the cup to the right hand and pours water on the left hand. After the washing, each person recites: "Blessed are You, Lord our God, King of the universe, who sanctified us with *mitzvot* and commanded us on the washing of our hands." Returning to the table silently— so as to not interrupt the blessing and its fulfillment—we cover two loaves of braided *challah* bread to symbolize the double portion of manna that rained down before the Sabbath when the Israelites wandered in the Sinai Wilderness. We place one loaf on top of the other to symbolize the lower and higher spiritual stages of our souls, say the blessing over bread, and eat a piece of the lower *challah*. During the meal that follows, it is customary to discuss Torah, sing Sabbath songs, and conclude with the blessing after food (*birkat hamazon*).

The next morning, the Sabbath observance continues as we make our way to synagogue. After synagogue, we return home with friends for a leisurely Sabbath afternoon meal and discussion around the table. Later, some of us drift off for a nap or a late-afternoon walk to the neighborhood park. The sacred day is yours: Make the Sabbath a time to do noncommercial family activities. Make it a day that you devote to your soul. Enjoy a walk in the woods, swimming in a lake, visiting with friends, reading a good book. Enjoy a nap, eat a leisurely Sabbath afternoon meal, have a long conversation with someone you like. Refresh your soul. The Sabbath is a day like no other. We do not go to work, we do not shop, we do not go to the movies. The pace is different, a sort of alternative time, and it creates a cocoonlike effect.

As dark settles over the day, we light the candle for *havdalah* and chant the blessings over the wine, the candle, and the sweet spices as we conclude the Sabbath and begin a new week:

Behold, God is my redemption. I am confident, not afraid. The Lord is my strength, my might, and my redemption. Someday, we will draw water joyfully from the wells of redemption. Redemption is the Lord's. He will bless His people. God is with us. The God of Jacob is our protection. God, the one who trusts in You, is fortunate. Help us, God! Answer us, O King, when we call. Just as the Jews found light, joy, celebration, and honor—so may we! I lift the wine-cup of redemption and call upon the Lord.

(Over a cup of wine:) *Praised are You, Lord our God, King of the universe, who creates the fruit of the vine.*

(Over spices:) *Praised are You, Lord our God, King of the universe, who creates fragrant spices.*

(Over a braided *havdalah* candle:) *Praised are You, Lord our God, King of the universe, who creates the light of fire.*

Praised are You, Lord our God, King of the universe, who distinguishes between the holy and that which is not yet holy, between light and darkness, between the people Israel and other people,

136

between the seventh day and the other days of the week. Praised
are You, Lord our God, King of the universe, who distinguishes
between the holy and that which is not yet holy.

KASHRUT: THE SPIRITUALITY OF FOOD

The Jewish dietary laws (*kashrut*) are spiritual guidelines to eating.
The Jewish dietary laws today hardly seem to have a spiritual dimension because *kashrut* appears to have degenerated into a com-
pulsive concern for the details of food labels, dishes, and other
regulations unconnected to spirituality. Does it really matter whether
I use one kind of dish soap or another for someone to feel comfortable eating in my kitchen? *Kashrut* strikes many people as a restriction on our personal autonomy and a constraint on one of the most
pleasurable of all human social behaviors. Who really enjoys being
the odd person whose dietary restrictions need to be considered
when one dines out, attends public dinners, or orders airplane meals?
Kashrut can also seem to be an archaic set of ethnic behaviors meant
to keep Jews apart from other people. *Kashrut* often appears to be
an obstacle preventing observant Jews from fully integrating into
non-Jewish settings.

Civilization has developed food customs that restrain human appetite and refine human eating based on notions of justice and differentiation of humans from animals. As Leon Kass points out, the
Jewish dietary laws show how the activity of eating "can be not only
ennobled but even sanctified." Judaism favors vegetarianism as an
ideal but accepts the eating of meat as well as vegetables as a compromise. While the Torah specifies that God intended that Adam
and Eve be vegetarians, omnivorous dietary habits became acceptable by the time of Noah.

The biblical dietary code permits eating the flesh of cows,
chicken, turkey, and fish that have fins and scales. The same law

137

prohibits foods including, but not limited to, pork products (ham, bacon), rabbit, insects, reptiles, rodents, seafood (clams, shrimp, lobster, scallops), and predator birds (eagles, vultures, hawks). Animals selected for food must be in good health and have to be slaughtered with a knife at the neck in a particular way that avoids pain to the animal. The blood has to be drained, and the meat has to be soaked and salted to remove the blood. Finally, that meat and milk cannot be cooked together is in fact a moral statement, asserting that no mother animal should ever provide the milk in which her offspring is cooked.

Biblical *kashrut* has developed from a simple dietary code into today's elaborate array of detailed regulations covering the preparation of food, certification of ingredients in prepared foods, consumption separately of meat and dairy products, and regulations for kitchen implements and utensils. Kosher meat must be certified as *kosher* by a *mashgiach* (*kosher* supervisor) to assure that everything is being done according to *halachah*. Meat products and dairy products cannot be eaten at the same meal, and there is a required waiting period between eating meat and dairy food. Separate dishes, cooking and eating utensils, and often separate sinks, are maintained for preparation and consumption of meat and dairy food. Commercially prepared food has to be inspected at every stage of the process by a *mashgiach*. Packaged goods, which often contain many ingredients, are inspected and certified as *kosher* by several local and national Orthodox rabbinic organizations, and many *kosher*-observant Jews will only purchase certified products. Vegetables and fruits are the only exception to the restriction on purchasing certified *kosher* foods. Many Orthodox Jews will only eat out in *kosher* restaurants, while many other *kosher*-observant Jews will eat in regular restaurants but order only dairy, fish, or uncooked items. In addition, there are many other *kosher* practices that go into great detail about Jewish food rituals.

Today's elaborate and detailed dietary regulations have clouded the original intention of bringing spirituality to the daily routine of eating. *Kashrut* is a spiritual discipline that we might reconsider as an important element in a Jewish lifestyle. What can we gain by *kashrut*? Just as we follow disciplines of healthy eating for medical reasons, we might incorporate *kashrut* as a discipline that leads us to spiritual awareness of the various sources of our food. The spirituality of eating is central to Judaism because the holy sparks are found in everything we eat. When we consume any kind of food, we incorporate into ourselves their sparks. Every item we eat has sparks of holiness. Eating then becomes an act of raising the sparks within the food.

I prefer to concentrate less on the elaborate details and more on the fundamental belief that eating is an intentional act, a compromise with our natural state of vegetarianism, and an opportunity to raise the sparks of our most routine behaviors. Food can be either healthy or toxic to our bodies. Food is a source of pleasure because of the sensual enjoyment of eating, but it can also be a source of illness. Eating requires us to separate the pleasure of food from the danger of eating the wrong foods. Similarly, food can have a beneficial or detrimental impact on our souls. The Jewish dietary code reminds us of our spiritual responsibility toward our own bodies, the environment, and animals.

How is carnivorism spiritually acceptable? The sparks of holiness are everywhere within the universe. Since humans are superior in intelligence to animals, one way to raise the sparks is for a higher life form to consume the sparks found in a lower life form. Thus, humans are allowed to eat the flesh of animals but only under very strict limitations. *Kashrut* is also a concession to the human desire for meat. By permitting but restricting the eating of meat, not every carnivorous instinct is permitted. The restrictions remind us that we cannot give in to our every desire.

Kashrut can serve to create a shared spiritual link among a community of Jewish spiritual seekers and can help establish common ground among different communities of Jews. *Kashrut* is not a food compulsion or a taboo but a spiritual ideal to which we might strive.

How can we apply its principles to our own lives? We could begin with the assumption that there is a great variety and range of *kashrut* practices and no one's personal practice is inherently better than any other. Rather than focusing on the differences among people's practices, we might focus on what they have in common. We might adopt at least a minimal form of *kashrut*, already a widely shared Jewish spiritual practice. For example, we might practice *kashrut* within our own homes as a spiritual statement about raising the sparks and as an affirmation of belonging to the Jewish people. However, outside the home we could apply a less restrictive standard, following a form of biblical *kashrut* that permits certain animals and fish, but dispensing with the requirement that food be prepared according to the *kosher* dietary code.

To Jews who practice strict *kashrut*, this sort of practice might appear to be inconsistent, while to nonpractitioners, any form of *kashrut* might appear as an unnecessary restriction on their personal behavior. Certainly, such compromise requires greater acceptance of diverse forms of Jewish practice on the part of the traditionalist but allows the nontraditionalist a way of creating links to the spiritual tradition. The key is to invest our behavior with spiritual content in a nonjudgmental way and to respect the different ways people proceed along their own individual paths. Followed in good faith, spiritual practices allow us to grow individually within a community that shares and supports our values.

ROSH HASHANAH

Many of the highly personal Jewish spiritual practices have their most profound and lasting impact when we experience them within a circle of friends, family, or community. One voice singing on key is lovely, but a harmonious chorus lifts each voice even higher. The seasonal Jewish holidays afford us each the opportunity for an individual spiritual experience. When we celebrate them together with other people, however, our own experience is deepened.

What are the Jewish spiritual practices that make up the seasonal cycle of Jewish life? The seasons of the Jewish year begin with *Rosh Hashanah*, the Jewish New Year. My personal approach to these High Holy Days is to view them as a series of gates. The entry into the new year is symbolized by passage through any one of seven gates. Each gate is accessible and available if we choose to enter it. We each possess a key that unlocks any of these gates, although not every gate is equally suitable for each of us. We do not enter each year through the same gate we entered the previous year. We pause to consider all of the gates before we choose the one through which we enter. We can enter through one or through several. The only choice we should not have is the choice not to enter any gate at all.

The first gate is the gate of history. Upon entering it, we accept membership in a unique community that has celebrated this holiday for twenty-four centuries. This is the gate we must enter before any of the others. It is the gate through which we are led by our parents, who were first led through it by their parents. Someday, each of us must decide to enter this gate alone, to consider its architecture, and to ask who built it and for what reason. It is the gate on whose pillars are engraved the names of all those who passed through before us. *Rosh Hashanah* begins with an affirmation that we stand, shoulder to shoulder, with millions of other Jews each year just as those who came before stood with their contemporaries. *Rosh Hashanah* and *Yom Kippur* are the largest collective gatherings of Jews around the world. While we might not always appear to have much in common with each other, the holiday reminds us that we share a commitment to create a heaven on earth through our individual and collective efforts. This is the marriage contract between God and the Jewish people that we reaffirm on *Rosh Hashanah*.

The second gate is the gate of love and mercy. This is the gate through which we pass alone, at our own pace, as we are able. As we pass through, we are reminded that this is the gate of judgment tempered by mercy. Indeed, *Rosh Hashanah* is called the Day of Judgment. Although legend and liturgy say that this is the day on which God judges us, it is really we who judge ourselves. We enter the New Year receiving love and mercy to the degree to which we give love and mercy. We look upon ourselves and question our own actions of the year that passed. We wonder whether we will live up to our own high expectations in the coming year. We pass before God like sheep before the herder's staff so that we can examine our own hearts, count our deeds, and search our souls. God, however, is a kind and merciful king who is slow to anger and easy to forgive. We always have another chance. This is the meaning of the Day of Judgment.

The third gate is the gate of creation and nature. Through this gate we pass each year in cycles of growth, change, decline, and rebirth. Considered the anniversary of creation, *Rosh Hashanah* is called the Birthday of the World. Creation is also a process of renewal that takes place within the world, within time, and within us. Just as it is important to concentrate on spiritual renewal, it is especially important to celebrate part of the day in nature to reaffirm the renewal of nature. As we pass through this gate each year, we note the start of the cycle that binds us to the world, to time, and to our pasts and futures.

The fourth gate, that of repentance and remembrance, is the most frequently traveled entrance. The *shofar* is sounded to remind us of the great trumpet on Mount Sinai that urged us to find the voice of God within ourselves. On *Rosh Hashanah*, our prayers bring us absolution for all our private failures, but we can only be absolved for our other failures by resolving the difficulties we have with other people directly. There is no wiping the slate clean without making real changes. The gate of repentance is always open and requires no key. In passing through this gate, we remember who we are, where we are from, what we have done, and where we are heading. It is the open gate that is never closed.

The fifth gate, that of kingship and majesty, is hidden from most people. Historically, *Rosh Hashanah* began as a coronation ceremony in which Jews recalled that our king was different from every earthly ruler. A Hasidic parable also helps to explain the nature of God our King. According to the parable, a king had built a glorious palace full of corridors and partitions, but he himself lived in the innermost room. When the palace was completed and his servants came to pay him respect, they found that they could not approach the king because of the circuitous maze. While they stood and wondered, a pious person came and showed them that the partitions were not real walls but only optical illusions and that the king, in truth, was easily accessible. Push forward bravely and you will find no obstacle. Our God is the King of kings of kings. He rules by a steadfast moral law and expects us to live by its code of goodness. This is the dominant image of God on *Rosh Hashanah*. The holiday reminds us that our task is to create the kingdom of God on earth.

The sixth gate, the gate of personal choice, is wider than the others. It has to be, in order to accommodate the different ways in which people pass through it. Some approach it with their eyes closed and only manage to pass through it because of its wide berth. Others go backwards through it, come at it from all angles, approach it at a run, or happen not to notice that it is a gate and merely pass through unwittingly. The gate of choice requires that we learn how to act deliberately. This is the gate for seekers who see Judaism as a lifelong journey rather than a fixed recipe. We are different and grow from one year to the next. Our year is filled with all the choices that make up our separate Jewish journeys. This gate reminds us of our own personal responsibilities and choices and the memories that we bring through it from year to year.

The seventh gate is the gate of trust and prayer. This is the last gate at which we stand on *Rosh Hashanah*, after we have passed through one or more gates. This last gate is one of confidence—in 143 our ability to enter freely all the other gates.

Finally, one of the endearing customs of *Rosh Hashanah* is the *Tashlich* ("casting away") ceremony on the afternoon of the first day.

We fill our pockets with bread crumbs and walk to a nearby body of flowing water. We stand by the edge and think of the personal traits we would want to discard as we begin the new year. Then, as we take each crumb out of our pocket, we deposit a flaw on it and throw it vigorously into the water. As we watch our individual flaws float away, we silently plan how to eliminate them in the coming year.

YOM KIPPUR

Ten days after *Rosh Hashanah*, we observe the holiday of *Yom Kippur*, the Day of Atonement. In the Torah, the tenth day of the Hebrew month of *Tishre* is a time for "the affliction of our souls," a day of penitence, introspection, and fasting. The Talmud lists six classes of routine activities that are prohibited on this day in order to direct us to "afflict our souls." We are commanded not only to refrain from eating and drinking but also to avoid washing our bodies; using perfume, cologne, or cosmetics; wearing sandals or shoes made of leather; and having sexual relations.

These activities are each defined as physical pleasures that may be enjoyed at all other times. Their denial on *Yom Kippur* is not meant to punish or afflict the body but to promote a means of spiritual elevation through transcending physical pleasure. Very specifically, the Torah invokes the affliction of the "soul," not the "body." *Yom Kippur* is a day on which we give the physical machinery of an individual a rest in order to condition and activate the spiritual capacities of human life. Forbidding these activities is not an end in itself but only a means by which we achieve the spiritual conditioning necessary for reaching the objectives of *Yom Kippur*.

Despite the very strong emphasis on repentance in the liturgy, it is not the fundamental objective of *Yom Kippur*. All that we do on *Yom Kippur* is designed to lead us to what the Jewish mystics call *devekut*, or bonding with God. *Yom Kippur* is a carefully structured drama in many acts involving the entire congregation as the cast. The grand finale of this drama is supposed to culminate in a spiritual experience for each individual and for the congregation at large. The elaborate rehearsals, preparations, dialogues, and performances during the twenty-five hours of the holiday all lead to the possibility of such an experience.

Yom Kippur, understood as living theater, is a vivid recreation of the events leading up to the giving of the Torah to the Israelites at Mount Sinai, the most powerful event in the history of Judaism. However, *Yom Kippur* is perhaps more a celebration of mystical revelation than *Shavuot* and is the closest any of us will ever come to understanding some of the awe and mystery that caused our ancestors to accept the Torah. Tradition tells us, in fact, that after God revealed the Ten Commandments at Sinai on *Shavuot*, Moses shattered them when he saw that the nation had built the Golden Calf. The second set of tablets was given and accepted on *Yom Kippur*.

Each of the six categories of activities forbidden on *Yom Kippur* and the arrangement of the services are key elements in the script that enables us to reenact the mystery of Sinai. The drama begins when we prepare ourselves for the holiday, just as Moses prepared himself for his first encounter with God at the burning bush. God called to him, saying, "Moses, Moses." He responded, "*Hineni*—Here I am." God warned him, "Do not come closer. Remove your sandals from your feet, for the place on which you stand is holy ground." The prohibition against wearing leather shoes on *Yom Kippur* was originally a prohibition against wearing sandals made of leather. It was based on the idea that we are all to act today like Moses at the burning bush, standing on holy ground, ready to meet God. We do not wear leather shoes on *Yom Kippur* in order to imitate Moses, the first mystic in Jewish history. We are all Moses on this day. 145

On the morning of *Yom Kippur*, the Torah portion describes the elaborate preparations of the high priest in the Temple for the Day of Atonement sacrifice. The high priest imitates Moses by taking off his shoes before he enters the Holy of Holies, once a year, on *Yom Kippur*. The other priests tie a rope around him in order to be able to pull him out in case he dies in a state of ecstatic rapture in the Holy of Holies. Like Moses, the high priest is warned, "Look before you, you who are about to enter, and know that if you fail to concentrate upon what you are about to do, not only will you fall dead at once, but the atonement of Israel will be lost as well." On *Yom Kippur*, we are all high priests. In fact, the drama of the high priest is carried on throughout the service. The response of the people on the Temple Mount to the high priest's blessing has always been, *"Baruch shem kevod malchuto le-olam va-ed"* (Blessed be the name of his glorious majesty forever). Once a year, on *Yom Kippur*, we are all transformed into participants in the priestly ritual. Therefore, *Yom Kippur* night (*Kol Nidre*) is the one occasion during the year when the same blessing, *"Baruch shem kevod malchuto le-olam va-ed,"* is said out loud in response to the *Shema*, "Hear, O Israel, the Lord our God, the Lord is One."

Centuries later, in the Middle Ages, the prohibitions against wearing shoes were turned into a prohibition against wearing any leather goods. The prohibition against wearing leather was explained as a concession to the pain of animals and as an admission that, under ideal circumstances, animals should not be used for human benefit. The original mystical intention of the drama, symbolized by removing sandals, was transformed into a moral statement, symbolized by not wearing leather. In the process, the original intention has been obscured.

After being called by God at the burning bush and after the Exodus from Egypt, Moses prepared the nation to receive the Torah at Sinai. He warned the people "to remain pure, to be ready, to refrain from sexual contact, to abstain from food and water." These preparations for the mystical revelation at Sinai, of course, include the same instructions we are to follow on *Yom Kippur*. Since tradition has it that the second set of tablets was brought down on *Yom*

Kippur, the holiday is, therefore, a symbolic reenactment of the events of Sinai and realizes atonement for the sin of the Golden Calf, this time with complete acceptance on the part of the Jewish people.

In its conscious recreation of all of the elements of the Sinai experience, *Yom Kippur* is really about the process of completing the revelation at Sinai. The Torah recounts that when the commandments were revealed, "all the nation witnessed the thunder and the lightning, accompanied by the blast of the *shofar*." Likewise, the closing service, the *Neilah*, concludes with the final blast of the *shofar* trumpet. The Torah continues: "the nation beheld God, and they ate and drank." And thus, the mystical ritual is completed by a feast, which ends the fast.

The liturgical poems, *piyyutim*, which have been added over the centuries to the central service of *Yom Kippur*, introduce the themes of atonement, humility, and mortality. The recognition of the limits of human autonomy are recalled for us in phrases such as "like clay in the hands of the potter, to be thickened or thinned as he wishes, so are we in God's hand" and "like a rudder in the hand of the helmsman, to be guided or abandoned as he wishes, so are we in God's hand." We remember the tenuous condition of our lives. How many of us know instances of deep personal suffering among friends or family? How many of us are free from the pain and anguish that cripple so many others around us? On *Yom Kippur*, we exert control over what we can and pray for protection against that which is outside our control. We are reminded of our vulnerability.

The *Yom Kippur* services lead us from an initial sense of vulnerability and weakness to the eventual affirmation of our power and ability. Having begun with a confession that we are like dust and ashes, we retrace the steps of Moses and the high priest. *Yom Kippur* is a majestic and magical day, for it captures all of the feeling of human life within one day. We pray that we will pass from the hunger and affliction of the day to the elation and mystery of Moses and the high priest.

SUKKOT

Sukkot, the festival that begins five days after *Yom Kippur*, is unique in its symbolism. A *sukkah* is a temporary shelter that reminds us of the fugitive circumstances of our ancestors when they left Egypt. The *sukkah* is also a reminder that many of our ancestors were migrant farm workers during the harvest seasons in antiquity. In honor of the original harvest festival on which it is based, the first seven days of *Sukkot* are called simply "The Festival" and "The Feast of Ingathering." During *Sukkot*, we can eat most of our meals in the *Sukkah* or even camp out under the fall sky. In addition, there is a custom of welcoming a new biblical guest on each of the first seven days of the festival. Each guest symbolizes a spiritual trait on which we might concentrate for that day. In daily order, the biblical guests and their respective characteristics are as follows: Abraham—love; Isaac—judgment; Jacob—dignity; Moses—endurance; Aaron—beauty; Joseph—masculinity; and David—femininity.

On *Sukkot*, it is a *mitzvah* for us to have a palm branch (*lulav*), bundled with three myrtle and two willow branches, and a citron (*etrog*). The seven items that make up the bouquet are also symbolic of the seven daily characteristics and traits. The items are carried in synagogue processions during the weekdays of the festival and during the prayer for fall and winter rain in the Land of Israel on *Hoshana Rabba* (The Great Hosanna) on the seventh day of the festival.

The ninth day of *Sukkot* is actually a separate holiday, *Simchat Torah* (The Joy of Torah), which was added later. This holiday brings to culmination the three fall holidays, *Rosh Hashanah*, *Yom Kippur*, and *Sukkot*. It also marks the end of the cycle of weekly Torah readings and the beginning of the new cycle. It is one of the rare times in Jewish life when, in addition to spontaneous singing and dancing, parody, hilarity, and consumption of liquor within the synagogue are encouraged.

PASSOVER

The *Pesach Seder*, the table ritual of Passover, begins: "In every generation, a person must see himself as if he had personally left Egypt."
Each year, we retell a story about the Exodus from Egypt and plumb
new meanings from an ancient event. Earlier generations, who themselves lived under the slavery of anti-Semitism and poverty, would
contrast the optimism of the *Pesach* story with the sorry events of
their own lives. They could only rely on the promise that God would
save them in the future as He had done in the past: "Next year in
Jerusalem!" they would chant. They would find hope in the biblical
promise: "The Lord freed us from Egypt by a mighty hand, by an
outstretched arm and awesome power, and by signs and portents.
He brought us to this place (Israel) and gave us this land, a land
flowing with milk and honey" (Deuteronomy 26:8–9).

We live in an age when most of our hopes and dreams are ful-
filled. We are relatively safe, secure, and prosperous, and the homeland of Israel is not a dream. What do we have to look forward to
that we do not already have? We can interpret *Pesach* as a holiday
not about our own lives but about our responsibility to others. We
have turned *Pesach* into a reminder of our duty to help others gain
freedom and overcome poverty. But *Pesach* is not only about our
obligation to others. We have let *Pesach* become too directed to
helping others and have lost touch with the personal dimension. *Pesach* is about feeling and experiencing the Exodus from our own
personal houses of bondage.

How can we celebrate *Pesach* in a spiritually appealing way? Some
commentators have noted that the consonants in the Hebrew word
for "Egypt"—*mitzrayim*—are the same as the consonants that spell
the Hebrew word for "self-imposed constraints," *meitzarim*. The Exodus from Egypt is the Exodus from our own self-imposed constraints. Therefore, the spiritual path to seeing ourselves as if we had
personally left Egypt is for us to work on removing our own personal
shackles. *Pesach* is the spring holiday that reminds us that we must

continue to care for our souls. In particular, we are challenged to think about how we cause ourselves to get stuck in our own bad habits and qualities and how we have the responsibility to free ourselves from our own little enslavements.

Pesach is not only about history and obligation. It is about personal insight and spiritual growth. What better forum for resolving our own inner slavery than around the table with the very people—our families—with whom those chains weigh heaviest. *Pesach* becomes a time for taking strong action to resolve our inner conflicts and the conflicts in our relationships. We free ourselves from our own Egypt with our own mighty hands, by an outstretched arm and awesome power. Israel, a land flowing with milk and honey, is within each of us.

SHAVUOT

The holiday of *Shavuot* suffers a sorry fate. It is often regarded as the least significant of the three major pilgrimage festivals—*Sukkot*, *Pesach*, and *Shavuot*—and holds little of the tactile pleasures of *Sukkot* or the drama and majesty of *Pesach*. There are no special rituals associated with *Shavuot* as there are for almost every other major holiday. It doesn't carry the power of the High Holy Days or the amusement of *Purim*. It doesn't serve as a concession to major non-Jewish holidays, as does *Chanukkah*, and it doesn't come at a time of the season when we need a break from our routine, as do *Tu B'shvat* or *Lag B'omer*. In fact, as one of the major Jewish holidays, it doesn't seem to serve much purpose at all. It is the one major holiday whose approach people tend not to notice, as if *Pesach* were the end of the Jewish busy season. Few people tend to plan for *Shavuot* as they do for other festivals. Were it not for the imposition of Confirmation ceremonies upon *Shavuot*, a relatively recent innovation, *Shavuot* might be on its way to becoming a vestigial memory of the older generation. Like the Spanish and Portuguese Marranoes who lit Sabbath candles every Friday night without knowing the origin of the custom, we might have otherwise found ourselves eating blintzes and sour cream each June without knowing why. The sorry fate of *Shavuot*, however, is due not to the vicissitudes of the Jewish calendar nor to the timing of its arrival, but to the very troublesome meaning of *Shavuot* and the message concerning Jewish destiny that it conveys.

In the Torah, *Shavuot* is a festival that commemorates the beginning of the spring wheat harvest. It is a time of gathering and thanksgiving that follows the pattern of agricultural life in ancient Israel. In the period of the Talmud, when Jews were more likely to be town dwellers than farmers, the sages of the time took the decisive action of adding an additional layer of meaning to the festival. The primary meaning of *Shavuot* as an agricultural festival was in danger of becoming lost to a Jewish population no longer attuned to the rhythms of the planting and harvest seasons. Therefore, the sages turned to one of the most vital and memorable events of Jewish history, which they promptly identified with the *Shavuot* holiday. That event, of course, was the central event in Jewish history, the giving of the Torah at Mount Sinai.

Thus, when the agricultural meaning failed, Jewish historical meaning took its place and has animated our celebration of the holiday ever since. We now refer to the holiday as *Zeman Mattan Torateinu*, "the season of the giving of Torah," and only infrequently as "the harvest feast." The memory of Sinai has come to dominate our associations of the holiday of *Shavuot*, and the legends associated with it convey the traditional Jewish conception of the Torah as the essential link binding the Jewish people and God. For example, one *Midrash* tells us that God went to all of the nations of the earth offering them the Torah. Each, in turn, asked what it contained. When God told each nation that it contained laws prohibiting murder, idolatry, and theft, they promptly declined the offer. Only when God came to Israel, did this nation accept the Torah without qualification, saying, "We will observe it and, afterwards, we will ask questions." This unconditional acceptance of the Torah by Israel established a unique covenant, a mutual and reciprocal contract, between the Jewish people and God, valid for all times and in all places.

Shavuot, of course, created a set of profoundly significant memories for the Jewish people. First of all, the events at Sinai mark the creation of a new people on the face of the earth. The Israelites who left Egypt were a ragtag mob, a group of slaves, with little to unite them other than a commonly shared misery and desire to be almost anywhere but where they had been. But they were not yet a people until the Torah was given to them on Sinai and they received it. There was nothing until then they shared and that united them as one. *Shavuot*, therefore, signifies as much the birth of a people as it does the reason for the creation of that people. As a holiday, it commemorates the most sacred event in the life of that people. As a memory and an idea of history, it commemorates the most worldly and secular event, the origins of the life of the people. Therefore, *Shavuot* celebrates the connection between Torah, history, and the Jewish people.

Shavuot has become a minor star in the constellation of Jewish holidays because it commemorates an event that no longer animates the hearts and minds of the Jewish people as it once did. The magic of the moment when Moses heard the divine voice that he recorded as Torah is not credible to many Jews today. Just as the Talmudic sages transformed the emphasis of *Shavuot* seventeen hundred years ago from an agricultural festival to a historical recollection, so too in our own lifetime the holiday must undergo a major transformation in order to survive.

The reason for the breakdown in the meaning of *Shavuot* is clear. Two hundred years ago, the Jewish people were struggling to achieve their civil rights throughout Europe. The non-Jewish world was willing to consider admitting the Jews to citizenship only on the condition that Jews assimilate to the ways of the majority culture. In the interest of the cause of emancipation, Jewish leaders sanctioned fundamental changes in Jewish observance in order to facilitate the smooth entrance of Jews into the general culture. While many Jewish leaders recognized that minor and major adjustments in dress, eating habits, and personal behavior were required in the modern world, others took the occasion as an opportunity to examine the very principles upon which Judaism was based: the validity of the Torah as the covenant that binds together the Jewish people and God.

The major challenge to the idea of covenant came from those who believed that Judaism is a universal religion, that is, a religion of respectful worship and moral teachings that does not differ fundamentally from liberal Christianity other than by the day upon which the adherents of each choose to worship. The universalists stripped Judaism of its uniqueness and promoted the idea that Judaism is defined by its universalist teachings not by its distinctive observances. Furthermore, they concluded, the distinctive observances, which are the product of human invention, are dispensable, whereas the universal teachings, the product of divine revelation, are indispensable and should be accessible to all humankind. The notion that Judaism contains nothing within itself that is not acceptable and accessible to all humanity is not restricted to any one branch of Judaism. Most of us accept the idea, in one form or another, that whatever Judaism teaches must be universally true for all people or it should be discarded.

This is exactly what occurred. Whatever did not fit into the universalist conception of Judaism or did not further the cause of Jewish emancipation was no longer considered worthy of preservation. The idea that the Jewish people enjoy a special relationship with God, inaccessible to all except those who belong to the covenant people, has died a slow and labored death. We have trouble with the idea of a special relationship with God because it excludes those people whom we are so strenuously persuading to accept us. In order to avoid the persistent accusations of Jewish superiority, we have not

153

only eased our burden of observance but have denied the very covenant upon which our peoplehood is based.

However, we have managed to find acceptable substitutes for the original article. We have been able to celebrate *Shavuot* in modern times by creating new meanings, temporary meanings, until we can reinvest and reanimate our celebration with true meaning and purpose. For example, we celebrate the holiday with dairy foods, especially cheese. This custom is based on the agricultural origins of the holiday, which stress the kinship between grain and milk products. Another interpretation holds that Mount Sinai, the location of the *Shavuot* events, is called *har gavnunim*. Although *har gavnunim* means a ragged, many-peaked mountain, playful commentators noticed the similarity between the words *gavnunim* and *gevinah*, cheese. Thus, Mount Sinai became "the mountain made of cheese" and the custom of eating dairy products was born.

Another substitute is the Confirmation celebration. Confirmation has emerged as a result of an attempt to reintroduce the notion of covenant between the Jewish people and God by advocating the importance of having religious-school students confirm their commitment to the covenant. But if we have hopes that the old covenant can be confirmed, I think we will be greatly disappointed. The Confirmation ceremony is meaningless in the face of even greater momentum coming from the direction of those who believe that there is nothing of significance that remains to be confirmed.

THE BOOK OF RUTH

It is customary to read the Book of Ruth on *Shavuot*. The Book of Ruth tells of events that happened around the year 1100 B.C.E. Elimelech, a resident of Bethlehem, took his wife, Naomi, and his two sons across the Jordan River into present-day Jordan in order to escape a famine. His sons married local non-Israelite women, as was common. It was not a source of contention in those days. Elimelech and his two sons died in Moab, leaving his widow Naomi with two non-Israelite daughters-in-law. When Naomi decided to return to Bethlehem, one of the daughters-in-law, Ruth, persuaded Naomi to bring her back with her. When Naomi attempted to dissuade Ruth from returning with her to Bethlehem, Ruth declared: "Where you go, I will go, and where you lie down, I will lie down; Your people are my people, and your God is my God." Ruth returns with her and soon marries a relative of Elimelech, Boaz. Ruth and Boaz, the narrative concludes, were the great-grandparents of King David.

The Book of Ruth is read on *Shavuot* for two reasons. First, the story of Ruth centers on agricultural events—the famine that brought Naomi to Moab, where she met Ruth, and the harvest, where Ruth met Boaz, which encounter initiates the chain of events leading up to the birth of King David. The second and principal reason we read the book on *Shavuot* is that it narrates the tale of the betrothal and marriage of Ruth and Boaz. Without their coupling, there never would have been a King David. And without King David, there might never have been an independent Jewish nation, a Temple, and so many other elements of Judaism that have been passed down from generation to generation. Betrothal, marriage, covenant—whatever we might call it—is the abiding theme of *Shavuot*.

The Book of Ruth narrates the most unlikely, but ultimately the most consequential, betrothal in the history of the Jewish people. The book cries its message out to us: what if Boaz and Ruth had never met, what if Ruth hadn't insisted on returning with Naomi to Bethlehem, what if there was no famine, what if, what if, what if? All of these events were unlikely and could just as easily have never occurred. Where would that have left us? No marriage, no King David, no Solomon, no Temple, no Judaism, no Jewish history, no Jews.

The Book of Ruth is linked to the other unlikely betrothal—the giving of the Torah at Sinai. What if another nation had accepted the covenant before us, what if God hadn't brought us out of Egypt, what if, what if, what if? *Dayyenu* is wrong—it wouldn't have been enough if God had brought us out of Egypt but had not given us the Torah. The whole point was for Him to give us the Torah. What would we have missed if there had been no Torah or, worse, if the Torah were given to another people? But, in both cases, at Sinai and with Ruth, an unlikely marriage took place. That is why we are able to celebrate this holiday and that is why we are able to exist as a people. The covenant theme, the fortunate bond between two significant parties that shapes our destiny, is linked together by the reading of the Book of Ruth on *Shavuot*.

All of the events that take place in the Ruth narrative are the result of human decision and actions. Nowhere in the entire book does God thunder down or even whisper to tell Ruth what course of action to follow. God plays no direct role in the events described in the book and never in fact intervenes. All the unlikely and fateful events are the result of human choice. Yet, we learn in the end that God, the invisible hero, subtly acted behind the scenes to direct the inevitable outcome that made possible the eventual birth of King David.

Perhaps we have something to learn from the idea that God plays no direct role in the course of human events. Certainly this idea is more palatable for those of us who are troubled by the notion of God singling out a special people and relating to them to the exclusion of others. Maybe the very idea of a God who affects human history offends our humanism, our belief in our own will, our understanding that people create history, not God. *Shavuot* poses a problem because covenant, its predominant theme, no longer dominates our thinking.

But the solution to this dilemma emerges from the Book of Ruth. Of course, human history is moved along by human actions. The only destiny we reach in our individual and collective lives is the destiny we ourselves choose. For better or for worse, humanity alone determines the course of history. We live in a universe where there are no voices from heaven and no divine guidance. But this does not mean that God does not exist, nor does it mean that there is no covenant. It certainly does mean that our notion of covenant must be reconsidered.

We have already discussed that God is unknowable, unreachable, inconceivable, and ineffable. Some even say that the infinite God is never truly mentioned anywhere in the Torah—so high and exalted is His infinity. All we find in Torah are human conceptions of God based on our need to portray God in terms human beings can comprehend. But if God is not found in the Torah, where is He to be found? The answer is clear: Only in the most unlikely places can traces be found; even in the hidden, dark recesses can we find hints of God.

The covenant we confirm on *Shavuot* celebrates a marriage between two parties, one of whom is hidden. That is precisely the reason why *Shavuot* poses such a great problem for us today. How can we celebrate a covenant when we never really know who it is with whom we have entered into a binding agreement? The Book of Ruth provides us with the answer: God need not be visible or recognizable in order to be considered as part of the partnership. In fact, His presence is all the more powerful the less it is apparent. The seemingly unlikely and fateful events that take place in the Book of Ruth are no less marvelous than the infinite complexity of factors involved in the production of our universe. And yet, behind and above it all, there is a hidden hand steering the course of Jewish destiny.

Perhaps it is possible to recapture the meaning of *Shavuot* through a new understanding of the covenant. Let us dispense with the simplistic notions of a binding legal obligation between two consenting parties in favor of a more spiritual notion of a covenant between the Jewish people and the reality beyond their understanding. In this way, the Torah was not so much given as received, and what we received was the best guidance available for making critical choices about living and being in the world.

157

THE JEWISH CALENDAR

The creation of new rituals is a time-honored Jewish tradition. As we adapt to changing circumstances and find new meanings, we often reexamine our Jewish lives and practices. We invent new rituals that embody our changing understanding of ourselves and the universe in which we live. We also turn to revive ancient Jewish rituals, filling old bottles with new wine.

The celebration of the New Moon (*Rosh Chodesh*) has become a popular custom, especially among women trying to restore Jewish women's spirituality. Judaism uses the lunar calendar of twelve months, which is adjusted by adding a month seven times every nineteen years to conform to the solar calendar year. The New Year for the Hebrew months occurs in the spring. The order of the months is as follows: *Nisan, Iyyar, Sivan, Tammuz, Av, Elul, Tishre, Cheshvan, Kislev, Tevet, Shevat,* and *Adar*. In antiquity, *Rosh Chodesh* was observed by festive meals and by women not working on this day, although it was not a holy day like the festivals. Special prayers and Torah readings are included in the daily services.

Each month takes on a special character. The sign of *Nisan* is the Lamb, the symbol of Passover. *Pesach* begins on the full moon, the fifteenth of *Nisan*. Other holidays, such as *Tu B'shvat, Purim,* and *Sukkot,* also occur on the full moon, the fifteenth of their month. *Iyyar* coincides with the Counting of the *Omer*, the forty-nine-day period between *Pesach* and *Shavuot*. *Iyyar* 5 is *Yom Ha-Atzmaut*, Israel Independence Day. The holiday of *Lag B'omer* falls on *Iyyar* 18, a day that commemorates the rescue of rabbinical students from Roman persecution during the Bar Kochba Revolt in the second century, as well as the death of Rabbi Shimeon bar Yochai, a hero of the Kabbalists. The sign of *Sivan* is Twins, the Written Torah and the Oral Torah, because the holiday *Shavuot* occurs on *Sivan* 6.

Forty days after *Shavuot*, on *Tammuz* 17, Moses descended from Mount Sinai with the Ten Commandments. Because this was the day on which Moses destroyed the tablets, this has come to be a partial fasting day in the Jewish tradition. *Tisha B'Av*, the ninth of *Av*, marks the anniversary of the destruction of the first and second Temples. It is a fasting day on which we read the biblical *Lamentations*. *Elul*, the penitential month, marks the period of self-accounting and preparation leading up to *Rosh Hashanah*. Three major holidays occur in *Tishre*: Rosh Hashanah, Yom Kippur, and *Sukkot*. *Cheshvan*, the only month with no holiday, is called for this reason *Marcheshvan* (Bitter *Cheshvan*). *Chanukkah* occurs on *Kislev* 25. The tenth day of *Tevet* remembers the beginning of the Babylonian siege on Solomon's Temple.

The month of *Shevat* includes *Shabbat Shirah*, the Sabbath on which we read Moses' and Miriam's Songs of the Sea and the story of the judge Deborah (Judges 4:4–5:31). *Tu B'shvat* falls on the full moon of *Shevat* and, with the first blooms, marks the end of winter in Israel and the New Year for Trees. In the seventeenth century, a new ceremony called *Seder Tu B'shvat* was invented by followers of the false Messiah Sabbatai Tzvi. Based on the *Pesach Seder*, it prescribes a table ritual in which four cups of wine are interspersed with eating different fruits, including pomegranates, dates, figs, and grapes. The four cups of wine symbolize the different images of God, first as father, then as mother, followed by a balance between father/mother and mother/father. The different fruits represent the universe and the various ways that God is present within the world. Finally, "when *Adar* arrives, our joy increases," because this is the end of winter, the month before *Pesach*, and the month in which we celebrate *Purim*, the rescue from Haman's plan to exterminate the Jews.

The New Moon reminds us that the cycle of our world begins anew every twenty-eight days. No matter what was gained or lost in the last month, we can start over again in the new month. For women, the monthly cycle is a reminder of the potential for new life and the closing off of that potential each month. Therefore, women perhaps sense the significance of the changing months more acutely than men.

159

The celebration of the New Moon is known as *kiddush levanah* (sanctification of the moon). In Kabbalah, the moon is the symbol of the mother image of God, the *Shechinah*. *Rosh Chodesh* is, therefore, the monthly festival of the *Shechinah* except on the New Moon of *Tishre*, *Rosh Hashanah*, which is the holiday dedicated to the masculine image of God. For those concerned about the over-emphasis on the masculine God, *Rosh Chodesh*, along with the Sabbath, provides an important measure of balance. The Kabbalists even added a festival on the day before each *Rosh Chodesh* that they called *Yom Kippur Katan* (Minor Day of Atonement), a fasting day marked by penitential prayers and contemplation of personal goals that was to signal the beginning of the renewal of the *Shechinah*.

Rosh Chodesh has been celebrated with a variety of rituals, including lighting special candles, hosting festive meals, and discussing significant Jewish events in the coming month. Songs include *Siman tov u-mazel tov*, which literally means "May your astrological sign favor you and all Israel!" In addition, the following prayer is often recited:

> *May the One who performed miracles for our ancestors and redeemed them from slavery to freedom, soon redeem us and gather our dispersed from the four corners of the earth. Let all of Israel be together! And let us say: Amen.*

SPIRITUAL PRACTICES FOR THE HOME

Until recently, Jewish life was celebrated primarily in the home, not the synagogue. Religious activities took place in the home and parents were responsible for the Jewish education of their children. The shift of the focus of Jewish life from the home to the synagogue has led to Judaism becoming more of a spectator than a participatory activity. How can we restore Jewish spirituality to the home? Too many Jewish ceremonies are conducted in the synagogue because too few parents know how to infuse the home with *Yiddishkeyt*. We can use the popular home rituals of *Chanukkah* and the Passover *Seder* as a model for developing other home rituals. We should seek to empower the family and to make Judaism a matter of the home by incorporating Sabbath celebration into our lives. However, as the traditional family structures have changed, we need to adapt these rituals to our own lives by involving friends and relatives. The key to domesticating Jewish spirituality is for each of us to take responsibility to begin the process, to seek out help along the way from knowledgeable people, and to recognize that there is more than one right way.

When a Jewish boy is born, he is circumcised on the eighth day and welcomed into the covenant of Israel through the *brit* (covenant) ceremony. The *brit* symbolizes that he is a member of the Jewish people and that he carries with him throughout his life the responsibility to raise the sparks in the world. He is expected to do this through a lifelong devotion to listening to his inner voice and the divine voice within the Torah, through developing intimate relationships, and through making the world a better place through his actions. That is why we wish him and his parents the following greeting as part of the *brit*: "Just as he entered the covenant, so may he enter Torah, the wedding canopy, and good deeds." A short service at home or synagogue is conducted, during which the circumcision takes place. The surgical aspect of the *brit* ceremony is carried out by a *mohel* who is trained in the medical and religious skills of circumcision. The ritual part of the ceremony can be conducted by the *mohel*, a rabbi, and the parents of the child.

A *zeved habat* (the gift of a daughter) or *brit banot* (covenant of daughters) ceremony has been developed, especially among Sephardic Jews, to welcome a daughter into the covenant. It is essentially the same as the *brit* ceremony but without circumcision. The service can be held at the home or synagogue and various roles can be assigned to family members and friends. The text of the ceremony can be modified so that the parents can speak of the family traditions they wish to transmit to the child and emphasize the connections between the generations.

Our names are our history. Hebrew names link us to the biblical figures who bore these names and to our more recent ancestors who carried them. Our Hebrew names are an integral part of our Jewish identity. The naming of a child as a way of linking the past and the future is an integral part of the *brit* ceremony. In the eastern European Jewish tradition, children are named after deceased relatives whose names have not already been memorialized within the family. The first name chosen is that of the grandparents, followed by those of other close relatives. The practice involves giving the child the exact Hebrew names of the chosen relatives. Many people today choose an English name that may or may not have a connection with a Hebrew name; a similar-sounding name; or the English equivalent of a traditional Hebrew name. I believe, however, that the significant Jewish element is the Hebrew name and that parents should consider giving their children modern Hebrew names that serve as both their English and Hebrew names and that memorialize a relative.

The Hebrew name of a child has three components: the child's name, followed by *ben* (son of) or *bat* (daughter of), the name of his or her father, then the name of his or her mother. This is how we are called to the Torah, how we are addressed in Jewish ritual ceremonies, and how we are remembered after our death. Our name is a valuable form of Jewish identification. The other valuable information we need to know is to which of the three ancient divisions of Jews we belong. Were our ancestors *Cohanim* (members of the priestly class), *Leviim* (levites) who assisted the priests, or *Yisraelim* (ordinary Israelites)? Traditionally, this aspect of our identity is transmitted through the line of the father.

162   The basic elements of the *Bar* or *Bat Mitzvah* are the acceptance of the child into the arena of Jewish responsibility as indicated by an *aliyah*, the call to bless and read from the Torah scroll publicly and chant the *Haftarah*, the weekly reading from the Hebrew Proph-

ets. A boy reaches *Bar Mitzvah* at thirteen, whereas a girl is *Bat Mitzvah* at twelve in recognition of the fact that adolescent development proceeds at a different pace for each. In addition, the child should give a *derush*, a learned explanation of the Torah portion. Among non-Orthodox Ashkenazic Jews, the custom is for the child to begin to wear the *tallit* (prayer shawl) on that day. Orthodox men begin to wear a small *tallit* undergarment from a very early age and the full *tallit* after they are married. Sephardic boys begin to wear the *tallit* from the age of five or six. After the child completes the *Haftarah*, the family and friends shower him or her with candy.

The focus should be on the religious ceremony rather than on the party. In our family, we have a tradition that the centerpieces at each of the tables for the celebration should consist of decorative, nonperishable food items. The next day, the *Bar* or *Bat Mitzvah* child helps deliver the food baskets to elderly adults, new immigrants, and hungry indigents. This practice helps us to share our joy with others while reminding our children that their own good fortune is not always available to others.

The dedication of a new home is celebrated with a *Chanukat habayit*, a ceremony in which a *mezuzah* is fixed to the right frame of every doorpost in the house, except the bathrooms. A *mezuzah* is a small decorative case containing twenty lines from the Torah written on a parchment scroll. The case is attached in a slanting position from left to right two-thirds of the way up the frame. As the *mezuzah* is attached, the family says: "Praised are You, Lord our God, King of the universe, Who has commanded us to attach the *mezuzah*." Symbolically, in this ritual, the home is the Jerusalem Temple, the dining room table is the altar, the meal is a spiritual offering, and those sitting around the table are priests.

MOURNING AND *SHIVAH*

The mourning ritual, "sitting *shivah*," is a skillfully crafted set of practices that helps focus the mourner on moving through the various stages of grief. Traditional Jewish mourning practices require that adult relatives observe a seven-day mourning period for a parent, child, sibling, or spouse. The period of mourning begins as soon as the funeral is complete and is observed in the house of the deceased. The mourners return from the cemetery and have a "meal of condolence" that is prepared for them by their friends and family. The mourner may not study Torah, leave the house, have sex, or bathe, although he or she may wash his or her face with cold water. The mourner should stand or sit on a low bench or stool but not on a comfortable chair. The only exception to these rules is allowed on the Sabbath that occurs during the *shivah* period. The *shivah* period ends after seven days, or earlier if *Rosh Hashanah, Yom Kippur, Sukkot, Pesach,* or *Shavuot* should occur during *shivah*. Friends and relatives are expected to visit the mourner. They should not greet the mourner or initiate conversation but should wait until the mourner approaches them. They should comfort the mourner but should not joke with him or her. They should arrange for food to be delivered to the house of mourning. The mourner should not feed or otherwise provide for his or her guests.

These mourning rituals are a form of etiquette that guides our behavior in an awkward and uncomfortable situation. We are all uncomfortable around death and tend to shrink away from confronting it directly. Rather than permitting us to retreat and hide from death, the *shivah* rituals offer a precise etiquette for confronting death. Neither the mourner nor the community can hide from death; they are brought together in a way that reaffirms life and the connection between people at a time when our natural inclination is to withdraw. The *shivah* rituals are spiritual practices that help restore heart and soul to the most vulnerable and tender moments in our lives.

We can now see how the Jewish spiritual practices can reintroduce heart and soul into Jewish life—"rehearten" our Jewish lives. They can serve as our instructions for lighting the fire. Our task is still to find the clearing in the forest and sing the *niggun*, the melody that is in our hearts and in the hearts of those who came before us. We should see their practices as outward expressions of their inner journey, human aspirations that transcend their time and place. Their hearts can speak to us across the generations, not as commands, but as gentle suggestions from their wise hearts.

Are there indispensable ingredients to the inward and outward path? There is indeed an irreducible minimum set of steps in the lifelong pursuit of Jewish learning, Jewish spiritual practices, and acts of kindness that is the Jewish path. This is, in fact, the basis of rabbinic Judaism, according to its founder, Rabbi Yochanan ben Zakkai, who said: "The world stands on three pillars: Torah, devotion, and deeds of kindness." Although ben Zakkai's followers understood his words in different ways, we can develop our own modern spiritual Judaism and still remain faithful to the basic principles of the ancient faith.

Chapter Five

BECOME AN EAR THAT HEARS WHAT THE UNIVERSE IS SAYING

You must cease to be aware of your own self but become an
ear that hears what the universe of the Word is saying within
you.

—*The Maggid of Mezritch*

Judaism is a culture in which learning and teaching,
cogitation and reflection, intellectual effort and theological
pursuit, are esteemed and elevated to the highest ranks of its
precepts.

—*Norman Lamm*

MAKERS OF MEANING

We are all makers of meaning. We can each see the same
event, hear the same words, read the same story, see the
same movie, or know the same person. Yet, if we were each asked
to describe what we experienced, we would each probably explain
the situation differently. Rarely does our perception of an event,
person, or experience coincide with someone else's. We each bring
our own personality and orientation with all our prejudices, insights, and judgments to what we experience. A folktale from the
Buddhist tradition illustrates how we interpret our experiences.
An elephant stood among a group of blind people. One person
touched the tail and thought the elephant was a stick; another
person found the ear and thought the elephant was a fan; yet another touched the great torso and thought the elephant was a wall.

167

None of them saw the whole elephant but drew conclusions about it based on the limited information they actually had.

I don't mean to say that our perceptions are wrong or that we are like blind people who grope around aimlessly. We perceive most things incompletely because we cannot immerse ourselves in what we are experiencing. We hear words that others speak, we read someone else's writing, we encounter another person, but we never fully know what is in the speaker's thoughts, the author's mind, or the other person's heart. Our perceptions are clouded by all of the interpretive biases and perceptual limitations that we bring to any given moment.

We do not acquire the meaning of things; we create them. This belief opposes that of the fundamentalist, who believes that meaning exists in things and is waiting to be acquired by us. He believes that the meaning is there waiting to be uncovered and that there is only one meaning. The fundamentalist deceives himself because even his "truth" is a construct of his own perception. He deludes himself into believing that his truth is the only truth and that all other versions of the truth are illegitimate.

Judaism does not sanction fundamentalism. That may be hard to believe, since, even today, there exist proponents of Judaism who claim that their way is, has been, and always will be the true way. They are able to fool most of us because they appear to be credible spokesmen for Jewish authenticity and they often have greater knowledge of Judaism than the audience they address. Who are we to doubt them? Yet, fundamentalist claims about Judaism always turn out to be false because they represent only a particular interpretation of Judaism and not even a particularly appealing one at that. Judaism has a far greater spiritual diversity than the Jewish fundamentalists either know or recognize. As Gershom Scholem once said, everybody takes their own slice out of the big cake.

The great divide between spiritual Judaism and fundamentalist Judaism cuts across the Torah. What do the fundamentalists believe? They believe that God dictated the Torah word for word to Moses

168

on top of Mount Sinai. Moses copied down the words faithfully and added nothing of his own. This became known as *Written Torah*. Moreover, God also conveyed to Moses other teachings that Moses did not transcribe. This became known as *Oral Torah*. The Written Torah is the tradition of divine wisdom whose meaning is waiting to be acquired by every generation. Whenever a sage offers a new interpretation, a new law, or a new practice, he is not inventing something of his own. He is merely acquiring something that has been waiting until now to be revealed from within the Oral Torah.

This fundamentalist approach denies that we ourselves bring any personal meaning to Judaism, because all meaning is ready and waiting there for us to discover. Yet, even the most ancient traditions of Judaism do not support such fundamentalism. The *Mishnah* states that anyone who does not believe that "the Torah is from heaven" (*Torah min ha-Shamayyim*) will not be rewarded with life after death. The fundamentalists claim that this belief is actually based on three important truths: First, that God dictated every word of the Torah to Moses at Mount Sinai. Second, that because the Torah is, in its entirety, divine, we may not choose to overlook or change any biblical law or teaching. Third, that all laws stemming from the Oral Torah have the same weight and stature as those inscribed in the Written Torah.

But the fundamentalists are wrong on all three counts: The Torah itself does not claim that God dictated every word of it—only the portions about the events at Sinai. The later commentators were divided between those who believed that the entire Torah as we know it was dictated to Moses and those who, like ancient Rabbi Ishmael, believed that Moses, or others, composed parts of the Torah. Fundamentalism is not even supported by the Torah.

The fundamentalist view also collapses when we try to explain some of the contradictions within the Torah itself. These contradictions serve as internal evidence that the Torah went through a process of human transmission. For example, the Ten Commandments appear twice with very minor variations. If every word is dictated by

God, how can there be two different versions? Even the most traditional authorities say that God spoke one word but people heard the same word differently and so two versions were recorded. Other sages said that men heard one version and women another, so both accounts were written down. That the Torah is not God's spoken version but rather the version that people heard undermines the fundamentalist argument. Even the more than 600,000 Israelites were makers of meaning of the divine voice.

There are many laws in the Torah that the rabbis of our tradition have acknowledged could not or should not be followed. For example, all Jewish authorities agree that the principle of "an eye for an eye" should not be applied as punishment for causing bodily injury to another person. Rather, punishment should be limited to monetary compensation and other forms of noncorporal punishment. The rabbis have few reservations about changing *Torah min ha-Shamayyim* while still claiming the inviolability of the Torah.

If the Written Torah is indeed the way that Moses and others heard the divine voice, the Oral Torah is the way that Jews through history have heard the same divine voice. While this might actually mean that the Written Torah and the Oral Torah stem from the same divine source, it also implies that God's voice is always filtered through the human mind and imagination.

HEARING THE VOICE OF GOD IN THE TEXT

All Jewish sages indeed believe in the divine origins of Torah, but what that means is open to wide interpretation. I do not doubt that Moses heard the voice of God at Sinai and communicated what he understood from his experience to the Israelites. Moses probably could not communicate his awesome encounter in words commensurate with the experience. He did make meaning out of the voice that he heard and communicated it to others, who recorded it for posterity. This process of interpretation is what Jewish tradition calls *Midrash*. *Midrash* literally means to search out implicit meanings by means of a biblical passage. *Midrash* is also an original Jewish literary technique of explaining textual nuances such as puzzling words and phrases, gaps in the text, curious repetitions, contradictions with other verses, and obscure meanings. It is also an imaginative process of uncovering new meanings and interpretations in familiar verses.

Midrash is also a spiritual process of attempting to hear the voice of God in the received text. *Midrash* tries to uncover the original experience behind the recorded text so that we might feel as though we are present at Sinai alongside the 600,000 and more who stood there. It is an attempt to overcome the barriers of time and place that separate us from the immediacy of the experience of standing at Sinai.

Finally, *Midrash* is also how each generation keeps the Torah alive by reading it through its own lens. Every generation reads its own values into the Torah. Rabbi Ben Zion Gold has pointed out that each generation's relationship to Judaism can be measured by their understanding of the weekly Torah reading. The fundamentalists read their own values into the Torah. That is their *Midrash* on the tradition. Every generation claims its own version of Torah to be the original version. Every generation is wrong. Torah is like a moving panorama. As the tradition itself says, "the gates of interpretation are never closed."

Torah is Moses' *Midrash* on his experience at Sinai. It is what Moses communicated about his encounters with God, but it is not the same as the encounters themselves. Every description is a *Midrash*. Every translation is *Midrash*. All there is, is *Midrash*. There is no literal meaning. We each hear the divine voice differently, even Moses.

171

The meaning of Torah exists in the mind of the beholder. There is no right or wrong interpretation, only the layers of meaning that are waiting to be uncovered. Torah prepares us for life, where everything depends on our perception of things. *Midrash* trains us to ask the right questions about the meaning of things when the meaning is never simple. The Kabbalists even say that we can take heart from the 600,000 who stood with Moses at Sinai because each of them heard the echoes of the divine voice individually. Each one of us is supposed to see ourselves as if we personally stood at Sinai. The tradition says that the Torah was heard differently by each of the 600,000 who stood there more than three thousand years ago. So there are at least 600,000 different versions of the truth. That is still true today. We must turn to the Torah to discover the 600,000 different ways of defining truth. Judaism and fundamentalism cannot coexist. The process of creating Torah is continuous and ongoing. We must find our own personal Torah, our own understanding of the spiritual truth today. We must learn the truth of those who came before us. But, we must also see ourselves as if we personally stood at Sinai.

There is a Jewish custom that encourages each one of us to make a Torah during our lifetime. While this suggestion leads some people to support the purchase of a Torah or to pay to have a letter inscribed on a new Torah, I have something else in mind. Each one of us can make the Torah our own by making our own *Midrash*, by coming to our own unique understanding of Torah.

What happened at Sinai? Moses heard the inner voice—he became an ear that heard what the universe was saying to him—and communicated it to others, who then added to it themselves. Torah is the way that Moses and his generation understood and recorded their calling to a higher purpose. We study Torah to understand the way in which the divine voice has been heard by those who came before us, to learn their wisdom, and to penetrate their experience. But we must also experience, on our own, the call to discover the divine presence for ourselves and within ourselves. This is the very meaning of Torah.

Like Moses, we must each become an ear that hears what the universe is saying to us. We can train ourselves to do that by first becoming an ear that hears how those who came before us heard the divine voice in the text. Learning Torah helps us to recapture the experience of our predecessors and prepares us to hear what the universe is saying directly to us.

JACOB'S DREAM

To understand Torah as a means to hear what the universe is saying to us, let's look at an example of how the midrashic process works. The biblical narrative beginning with Genesis 28:10, which is known as "He Went Out" (*Vayetze*), describes Jacob's departure from the home of his parents, Isaac and Rebecca. The narrative follows immediately after the account of how Jacob deceived his blind father by masquerading as his twin brother, Esau. Although he did not resemble Esau in any way, neither physically nor in personality, he was able to deceive his father into giving him the blessing of the firstborn, which was Esau's birthright.

The conflict between Rebecca's two sons, Esau and Jacob, began in the womb. During Rebecca's pregnancy, "the children almost crushed one another inside her." In an oracle, Rebecca heard the voice of God say to her: "Two nations are in your womb, two separate peoples shall issue from your body, one people shall be mightier than the other, and the older shall serve the younger." This prediction about the destiny of her twins would come true. Ever since she heard God's voice, Rebecca conspired to advance Jacob over Esau. Esau, whose name means "hairy" or "rough one," was born first and is described as "ruddy, like a hairy mantle all over." Then Jacob emerged holding on to the heel of Esau as if still trying to win the battle for firstborn status. His name, Jacob, means "heel-holder" or "'follower." The portrait of the twins suggests that the destiny of Esau and his descendants is dependent upon brute force, while the future of Jacob and his descendants, and thus the future of Israel, depends on the divine spirit.

173

The narrative is driven forward by the dynamics of deception and manipulation. By custom and law, the firstborn in ancient Israel succeeds the father and inherits a double share of the father's estate. The father, however, can annul the birthright and transfer it to another son. The intervention by a father into the course of natural right and destiny is a common theme in the Torah: Even before they were born, God predicted that Jacob would usurp Esau's birthright. The stealthy Jacob traded food to the hungry Esau in exchange for the birthright. Later, their mother, Rebecca, conspired with Jacob to deceive Isaac into promising the birthright to the younger son. It should be no surprise, then, that Jacob, when he blessed his sons and grandsons for the last time, himself shifted the birthright of his grandsons, from Menasheh to Efraim. Jacob even denied his own firstborn, Reuben, the birthright because Reuben had slept with Bilhah, Jacob's mistress. The switching of birthright parallels and foreshadows the intervention by God into the destiny of nations: God favors the people Israel, the least of all the nations of the earth. The transfer of the birthright advances the Torah's narrative. Without it, the cascade of events that led from God's call to Abraham to God's favoring of the Jewish people could not have happened.

Esau discovers the final deception of the stolen blessing and decides to kill Jacob in revenge. When their mother hears about this, she tells Jacob to flee to her brother Laban until things cool down. She then turns to Isaac and somewhat disingenuously tells him that she is disgusted with Esau's Hittite wives and does not want Jacob to marry a woman from the Hittite tribe. The Hittites were concentrated in central Anatolia (Syria/Turkey), but some had apparently migrated southward and controlled Hebron, where Rebecca and her sons lived. She persuades Isaac to give Jacob one more instruction: Jacob should go to his Uncle Laban and choose a wife from within the ancestral family. In order to escape Esau and to follow his mother's advice about choosing a wife, Jacob decides to leave Beer-sheva for the ancestral town of Haran, where Uncle Laban lives. Both Isaac and Rebecca were descended from Abraham, who had lived for many years in Haran, about 850 miles northeast of Beersheva in what is today the border region between Turkey and Iraq.

Along the way, Jacob passes through Luz or Beth El, outside of Hebron. Here he has the first of two dreams that are to shape the course of his difficult life. After the first dream, he swears that if he returns from the impending journey safely, he will build an altar at the site. From Beth El, he proceeds to Haran, where he is exploited by his Uncle Laban for twenty years. Laban deceives him by substituting under cover of darkness the less desirable daughter, Leah, for Jacob's own choice of a wife, the more attractive Rachel. As Nahum Sarna points out, in *Understanding Genesis*, "the perpetrator of deception was now the victim."

The second pivotal dream in Jacob's life occurs twenty years later, on his return from Haran, right after he has escaped from Laban and before he is to confront his brother Esau in a final struggle or reconciliation. In that dream, Jacob is renamed Israel, which means "one who has struggled with beings divine and human." Back home, he survives the rape of his only daughter, Dinah, the death of Rachel, and the kidnapping and disappearance of his son Joseph. Jacob's entire life, as if to mirror or repay his earlier stealth and deception, is filled with adversity and struggle. The Bible scholar Michael Fishbane, in *Text and Texture*, sees Jacob's life as a series of routine human struggles and trials in which he proves worthy of being an ancestor of his people: "He is Jacob the 'overcomer,' the 'prevailer' named Israel."

Here is the full text of Jacob's first dream according to the Jewish Publication Society's translation of the original Hebrew text:

Jacob left Beersheva and set out for Haran. He came upon a certain place and stopped there for the night, for the sun had set. Taking one of the stones of that place, he put it under his head and lay down in that place. He had a dream: a stairway was set on the ground and its top reached to the sky, and angels of God were going up and down on it. And the Lord was standing beside

175

him and He said, "I am the Lord, the God of your father Abraham and the God of Isaac: the ground on which you are lying I will give to you and your offspring. Your descendants shall be as the dust of the earth. You shall spread out to the west and to the east, to the north and to the south. All the families of the earth shall bless themselves by you and your descendants. Remember, I am with you: I will protect you wherever you go and will bring you back to this land. I will not leave you until I have done what I have promised you." Jacob awoke from his sleep and said, "Surely, the Lord is present in this place, and I did not know it!" Shaken, he said, "How awesome is this place! This is none other than the abode of God, and that is the gateway to heaven." Early in the morning, Jacob took the stone that he had put under his head and set it up as a pillar and poured oil on top of it. He named that site Beth El, but previously the name of the city had been Luz. (Genesis 28: 10–19)

The first question we might ask is whether the translation itself is a faithful reproduction of the Hebrew. Every translation is also a *Midrash* and makes choices in how it conveys the meaning of the original text. Words have connotations, shades of meaning, and associations that might escape even the most careful reader. For example, the Torah scholar Everett Fox has published a new translation from the Hebrew. Fox translates the Hebrew word *malachim* in the dream encounter as "messengers," whereas the Jewish Publication Society translates *malachim* as "angels." The term "angels" is a far more religiously charged term than "messengers" because of its centuries-old connotations in the Christian tradition. "Messengers" is a better translation because it doesn't offer more meaning than is necessary. The two choices in translation effectively illustrate the concept of *Midrash*.

MAKING NEW *MIDRASH*

What are the obvious questions raised by this episode? *Midrash* begins with asking questions. The questions are at least as important as the answers. Some questions are simply the obvious ones that come from a close reading of the text. For example, What did Jacob experience? Was it a genuine encounter with God, who spoke directly to him, or was it a dream in which he imagined God speaking to him? Did he dream of the encounter or did it actually happen? What is the character of Jacob that we discover here, and how does it fit with our image of him? What caused the dream and what are his feelings about it?

What is the significance of the stairway (or ladder) and the gateway to heaven? It does not appear to have a specific purpose or function in this narrative, at least not in relation to Jacob or God. Jacob does not ascend the ladder to the sky. God does not descend on it. God does not speak to Jacob from the sky but appears beside him when He is ready to speak.

What is the significance of the curious phrase that the angels/messengers were "going up and down" on the ladder/stairway? Why were they not first "going down" and then "going up" as we would expect of such beings? Who are the angels/messengers and what is their role in this episode? The angels ascend and descend on the ladder/stairway, but their movement seems to be strictly ornamental. They appear entirely in the background, neither speaking nor serving any evident purpose.

Other less obvious questions arise from having greater knowledge about other parts of the Torah. For example, what is the role of Beth El itself? Abraham had already built an altar at Beth El (Genesis 12: 8) two generations earlier, yet there is no reference here to Abraham's altar, only to Beth El's earlier name, Luz. If the name Beth El is already more familiar than Luz, why mention Luz here at all? A thousand years later, Beth El became the site of a renegade Israelite sanctuary that was widely condemned for its sinful practices. Why

177

emphasize the location of the holy site as Beth El here if the same name were later to symbolize corrupt worship? Is there something significant in the fact that both his pivotal dreams occur at the site of shrines on the border of the Land of Israel, once in his going there, and the other upon his return?

Are there subtleties of language that we can only grasp in the Hebrew? The word *sulam* for ladder/stairway is a *hapax legomenon*, a word that appears only once in the Torah. Moreover, the passage is characterized by a cacophony of verbs. Is there a verbal pattern in the Hebrew that is not readily apparent in the English? The verbal sequence is thirty-six verbs in nine verses: *left, set out, came upon, stopped, set, took, put, lay down, dreamed, set, reached, going up, going down, stood, said, lie, assign, be, spread, bless, protect, go, bring back, leave, do, promised, awoke, said, know, shaken, said, took, put, set up, poured,* and *named.* What is the function of repetitive single words or brief phrases within the narrative such as "stones"? Are there other significant literary patterns that command our attention? As we find later on, Genesis 32 appears as a parallel episode using some of the same verbs (Jacob "left," "set out," and "came upon") in describing Jacob's return from Haran and the occurrence of his second dream.

The obvious significance of the episode as a critical juncture on his life's journey is apparent. Still, so many questions are left unanswered. Why? To draw us in to explore his experience, to discover meaning in the mysterious gaps and unanswered questions, and to allow us to read ourselves, our heart, and the values of our time into the story.

Let us now turn to answer just one of these questions. Our first responses, which look to the Jewish tradition and represent the diversity of approaches to the Torah, are all examples of *Midrash.* *Midrash* does not mean that any imaginative interpretation is valid. It means a sincere effort to penetrate into the text. It can offer insight into one word, a phrase, a verse, or an entire narrative. It can often mean that a word or phrase can be explained by another verse.

Sometimes, *Midrash* can be an imaginative or invented legend or story that fills in a gap in the biblical narrative.

DREAM INTERPRETATION

What did Jacob experience? The biblical episode itself provides no more information besides the fact that Jacob had a pictorial vision of the ladder/stairway and heard the voice next to him promising him a glorious destiny. While it is obviously a series of powerful images, it is presented almost cinematically and without any dialogue from Jacob until it is over. The text does not tell us his understanding of what occurs while he is inside the dream. The lack of interior explanation gives rise to a variety of midrashic interpretations among our ancient sages, who probed the mysterious passage for greater insight. The interpretations can be classed according to several broad approaches that emerged over time.

Some interpreters wondered about the nature of dreams. Dreams were often understood in the *Midrash* tradition as prophecies. The content of a dream, therefore, required interpretation. Some interpreters believed that the dream could be interpreted in a general sense, while others believed that every element in the dream was a symbol that had to be interpreted. They saw Jacob's dream as a prophecy of the future of the Jewish people. Nehama Leibowitz, in *Studies in Bereshit* (Genesis), called it a dream about "the ladder of history." An early *Midrash*, *Bereshit Rabba*, by fancifully identifying Beth El with Jerusalem, saw this as a dream predicting the future building of the Jerusalem Temple and the institution of sacrifices. The sacrifices would ascend to God, and God would cause His love and protection to descend upon the people Israel. Another early *Midrash* sees the dream as a foreboding of the coming exile of the people of Israel from their land and the rise and fall in their fortunes throughout history. The ladder is the destiny of the Jewish people and the ascending and descending angels are the rise and fall of Jewish destiny. Within the dream, however, God promises to watch over the people for all time. The *Midrash*, therefore, turned this into a dream of comfort and assurance. Yet another *Midrash* saw the ascending angels as the angels that had accompanied Jacob to the border of Israel and the descending angels as those who would accompany him on the journey to Haran. Now that Jacob was about to leave Israel for the next twenty years, one contingent of angels departs (ascends) as another arrives (descends).

Similarly, the *Zohar*, the major Kabbalistic work, sees the vision as a dream in which Jacob is shown the future of his people. The *Zohar* employs a technique called *gematria*, in which each letter of the Hebrew alphabet has a corresponding numerical equivalent based on its order in the alphabet. The *Zohar* notes that the *gematria* of the Hebrew word "ladder" (*sulam*) is equivalent to the Hebrew word for Mount "Sinai" (*sinai*). This suggests an association: The ladder Jacob saw is actually a symbol of Mount Sinai and the angels are the Israelites who would someday receive it.

Avraham Yehoshua Heschel of Apt, known as the "Lover of Israel," saw this passage as a predictive dream in which Jacob saw the future of Israel. The ascending and descending angels were the many exiles that the Jewish people would someday face. But he added another conclusion: The purpose of the exile of the Jewish people among the nations was to raise the sparks of holiness. What did he mean by raising the sparks through exile? He explained that Israel went into exile in order to increase the Jewish population through the addition of converts to Judaism. (This is an example of how bold *Midrash* can be.)

Many other *Midrash* makers saw this episode not as a dream but as a perfect example of solitary prayer. Their approach hinged on the multiple meanings of the Hebrew term "to come upon a certain place." They concluded that "to come upon a certain place" means to have a profound prayer experience. Because their own tradition also taught that one of the names for God is "Place" or "Abode" (*makkom*), they created meaning based on a word association: "He came upon a certain place (*makkom*)" meant that Jacob encountered God. They also noted that this event took place at night. Jacob was the first man to pray at night in the darkness of an intimate moment with God. They concluded, therefore, that this must have been the origin of the evening prayer service *Maariv*. As one *Midrash* says: "The forefathers established the three daily prayer services: Abraham established the morning service, Isaac established the afternoon service, and Jacob established the evening service, as the verse says, 'He came upon a certain place.' " (The *Midrash* assumes that the reader knows that the verse continues, "He stopped there for the night, for the sun had set.") These *Midrash* makers understood this episode in this way because spirituality for them meant the solitary, intense, and interior experience of praying. They took the liberty with the text of overlooking the dream and its content while focusing only on the imaginative word association of "come upon" and "place."

SPIRITUAL AWAKENING

Other *Midrash* makers took this approach further and saw the episode as a mystical encounter between Jacob and God. One rabbi quoted in *Bereshit Rabba* assumes that the word *makkom* was used in two senses—to denote both a physical place and God. He reads "He came upon a certain place" as "He encountered the Abode." The *Midrash* then asks why is "the Abode" a name for God? Its answer is that the universe exists within God! Thus, God is not really *in* the world as much as the world resides *within* the all-encompassing depths of God, who embraces the world: "Why is the Holy One, Blessed be He, called 'the Abode'? Because He is the abode for the world and the world is not His abode." Jacob's encounter was, for them, a mystical experience in which he realized that not only is God within him, but he is truly within God.

This midrashic approach eventually led to further interpretations of Jacob's ladder. The *Zohar* explained the ladder as the stages of human spiritual development. In the dream, says *Zohar*, Jacob realized that when a person is fully developed in all his spiritual capacities, he achieves unity within himself and draws the presence of God into the world. This meant that Jacob himself was the ladder connecting heaven and earth.

Yaakov Yosef of Polnoye wrote that Jacob had a moment of great spiritual awareness when he realized that "a human being is a ladder placed on earth." For him, the angels are ordinary Jews who feel themselves filled with divine purpose in this world. They represent the different stages of human spiritual development, some higher and some lower. He also suggested that spiritual development is never steady but involves constant ups and downs. "The whole world is called a ladder. Even the truly faithful Jews who have reached the highest rung are not able to stand there but go up and down." No one is able to remain on the spiritual heights. He added that "even the learned person is a ladder who is sometimes placed on earth." Ultimately, he maintained, the human task is to live in the mundane world while drawing higher and higher to the ideal. "A human is a ladder who is rooted in this physical, earthly world but whose mind reaches heavenward when he strives to harmonize his behavior with his thoughts."

Avraham Yehoshua Heschel of Apt saw Jacob's dream as a moment of spiritual awakening. A human being is both the ladder and the angels. The dream is a reminder that God depends on our human spiritual quest: "Each person must realize that a human being is a ladder placed on earth amidst the physical and material world. His head, however, reaches heavenward because he cleaves upward to heaven by virtue of his mind and the root of his soul. When a person elevates his heart and mind to worship God, he raises all the angels upward. All the divine forces depend on his action.''

Avivah Zornberg, an erudite and insightful modern commentator, has written a fascinating modern explication, *Genesis: The Beginning of Desire*. She integrates classical *Midrash* and rabbinic commentary with insights drawn from modern literature, including the writings of Milton, William Shakespeare, Franz Kafka, Jean Paul Sartre, Sigmund Freud, modern literary critics, and many others. She reads the Torah as we would literature—a coherent narrative about character, the human condition, and ''all the complexities and contingencies of experience.'' She finds echoes and resonance within the text that lead us back and forth to suggested meanings. The biblical characters come alive as she plumbs the text for a deep understanding of their character and the dilemmas they face. She approaches the Torah as an enigmatic text that challenges us to uncover its multiple layers of meaning. Torah is a mystery about human disenchantment, incoherence of meaning, and the absence of God. It is also a seeking of meaning in the face of mystery and absence.

Zornberg takes her midrashic cue from Wallace Stevens: ''Not to have is the beginning of desire.'' She states the theme of Genesis: ''Out of the human response to God's absence, to the unintelligible and the fragmented, life is generated.'' The process of making meaning, *Midrash*, means ''the process of inquiry, interpretation, re-membering.'' She draws on insights from the classical *Midrash* along with modern literature and psychology. She takes us deep into the character of Jacob. Jacob leaves his family and goes out into the world. His dream marks his passage into a ''dark night of the soul'' that lasts throughout much of his adult life as he struggles with a sense of God's presence and retreat. As he goes out ''into a world of darkness and exile, order and coherence are endangered.'' Even as he sees a ladder to heaven, he lies down on the ground as if shunning the call to ascend. But God stands with him, guaranteeing him protection, assuring him order within the chaos. God is with him even in the darkness.

MAKING MODERN *MIDRASH*

We still know nothing further about how Jacob himself understood his experience or whether any of these midrashic explanations are correct. Jewish sages of each age projected their own values into the episode and filled in the gaps in the text with their own conjectures. *Midrash* is the voice in the text that they heard through the filter of their own experience. Each *Midrash* maker reads the same text, but each hears a different voice. There is no authority in Judaism that determines that any of these interpreters is more correct than any other. The rabbis say: "All of these are the words of a living God." They mean that fundamentalism has no place in the process of making meaning. All meanings, sensibly and thoughtfully drawn, are valid. All we have, then, is the human urge to make meaning out of the voice in the text.

Midrash is the heart of the Oral Torah. Is every meaning, interpretation, and new idea virtually present within the Oral Torah just waiting to be discovered and presented as *Midrash*? Or does each generation make its own *Midrash* and justify its own innovation by hitching it to the authority of an earlier tradition? Do we discover hints and develop Jewish beliefs by reading between the lines, or do we read our preconceived beliefs into the texts? Probably both. While I do not believe that everything is presaged in the Oral Torah, I do believe that by listening to the voice of God in the text we can find our own unique voices.

We have tried to understand how those who came before us understood the voice of God speaking within them. We know that Jacob heard the divine voice within himself promising him and his descendants a noble destiny. We also know the various ways that many of our ancestors understood what Jacob heard. Now, we must try to hear the voice of God speaking within us as we venture out on our own journeys. We have to bring our own meanings to the text.

Midrash is an ongoing process of digging deeper in the latent meaning of our sacred texts. How can we learn to hear the voice of God in a text? The first way is an active intellectual and cognitive effort to make a close reading. This is difficult to do because we have often come to see biblical narratives as children's fairy tales or mor-alizing sermonics. We must begin by reading the text with fresh eyes. The most important challenge we face is to ask the right questions, for the questions endure, whereas the answers come and go. We look for curiosities in the text, as did the ancient *Midrash* makers. We read the various commentators and *Midrashim* to learn the right questions to ask: What are the differences between the various trans-lations? How can the original Hebrew clarify the differences and nuances among the various English translations? Are there subtleties of language that we can only grasp in the Hebrew? What are the obvious questions of meaning, character, motivation, and plot raised by this episode? What is the significance of curious phrases, images, and individual words? Are there any extraneous words that do not appear to be absolutely necessary, and why might they be included? Are there any gaps in the text, missing information, or curious omissions? Are there any internal references or parallels to other biblical episodes, narratives, phrases, or words? Is there a pattern of word repetitions? Are there other significant literary patterns that command our attention? We ask each question without taking any answer for granted. This technique involves intellectual effort and thoughtful reflection. If we have asked the right question, the answer will follow. We begin to make our own *Midrash*.

We can also turn to a teacher or a book to guide us through the *Midrashim* and commentaries that others have discovered. In most every community in North America, there are competent teachers who are able to engage in a close reading of the text with you and others. Be careful to avoid the teacher who says there is only one valid meaning to the text—his or her own! The teacher who gives you the answers rather than the questions, who sees Judaism as an authoritarian system rather than a journey of inquiry and discovery, is not a true Jewish teacher.

The active technique of close reading, questioning, and intellectual effort leads to asking the right question of the biblical text. As we begin to answer our own questions, we create a dialogue with the Torah. In this dialogue, we hear the voice of God in the text. We hear the same voice that Moses heard and that our ancestors heard as they felt themselves standing at Sinai.

SPIRITUAL JEWISH EDUCATION

How can each of us become an ear that hears what the universe is saying? If we can hear the voice of God in the text through the active, intellectual effort at close reading, we can hear the voice of God within the universe by the active, spiritual exercise of close listening. The meditative technique of close listening, of ceasing to listen to our own voice, and hearing what God and the universe are constantly saying to us, is an important step on the Jewish path.

How can we teach this ability to hear the voice of God in our sacred texts and to become an ear that hears what the universe is saying? There is an ancient Jewish custom that was used to introduce a child to the study of Torah. It was common practice until a generation or two ago throughout the Jewish world. A child would begin his formal Jewish education at the age of five with a celebration in the synagogue. His parents would bring him to the teacher and write for him on a slate all the Hebrew letters, from *aleph* to *tav*, in honey. Then, they would tell him, "Lick, sweet child, lick. May the words of Torah be as sweet as honey in your mouth."

No matter where we live today, there are too few children for whom the words of Torah are as sweet as honey. What can we do to change this? What can we do to improve our spiritual condition today? What can we do to encourage the spiritual search, to provide a spiritual home for Jewish seekers within Judaism? What can we do to provide ourselves with a community of shared concerns and connection to others, and give expression to our deepest feelings? How can we help put the spiritual outlook of Judaism into words that speak to us today?

There is no clearer expression of this Jewish outlook than in the poignant testament of a mother to her child when they were trapped in 1940 by the Nazis in the Warsaw Ghetto and faced certain death. Despite the horror of contemplating her own death and that of her infant, the mother wrote a poignant letter of hope to her child just before they were murdered by the Nazis. In this letter, reprinted in Jack Riemer and Nathaniel Stampfer's *Ethical Wills: A Modern Jewish Treasury*, the mother ignores their inevitable end and explains to her child the Jewish mission to repair the world, the very world that is about to destroy them. Rather than urging revenge, the mother writes the following:

> Judaism, my child, is the struggle to bring down God upon earth, a struggle for the sanctification of the human heart. This struggle your people wages not with physical force but with spirit and by constant striving for truth and justice. So do you understand, my child, how we are distinct from others and wherein lies the secret of our existence on earth? This is your mission, your calling, your purpose on earth.

We should remember that education is not a process of filling empty vessels but of helping the soul to regain the wisdom it once had by cultivating the inner voice and the deep inner sense. We need to revise our definition of education to accommodate our spiritual perspective. Avraham Yehoshua Heschel of Apt offered a Jewish definition of education. Education is the process of preparing a holy vessel to absorb the divine sparks. He explains: "The Hebrew word for 'education' (*chinnuch*) comes from the same word as 'sanctification' (*Chanukah*): This means that everything that stands ready to be sanctified, to become filled with divine holiness, must become a ready vessel and receptacle able to receive the holiness. Likewise education is called *chinnuch* because we prepare the child to be able to receive holiness when he grows up.''

The core problem facing Jewish education was defined earlier in this century by Franz Rosenzweig in his famous essay, ''Towards a Renaissance of Jewish Learning.'' He said:

> We have no teachers because we have no teaching profession. We have no teaching profession because we have no scholars. And we have no scholars because we have no learning. Teaching and study have both deteriorated. And they have done so because we lack that which gives animation to learning and education—life itself.

The fundamental problem facing Jewish education is not the failure of congregational schools or the inadequate preparation of teachers. These are symptoms of a much deeper problem—the very meaning of Judaism itself for adults and children today. Who is able to create a school on the basis of Jewish values when those very values, the source of the dilemma, are obscure? It is futile to discuss educational improvement until we bring about the renewal of Jewish life and learning.

IS MY HEART HARDER THAN STONE?

The key to the improvement of Jewish education is adult education. There is an ancient story told about Rabbi Akiva, one of our greatest spiritual teachers. The storyteller wonders: So great a teacher as Rabbi Akiva must have come from a wonderful background. What were his beginnings? When were his remarkable talents revealed? Was he a child prodigy or the son of a scholar? The answer surprises us: Rabbi Akiva was forty years old before he was touched by Jewish learning. Nothing up to this point in his life had really touched his heart. He had not yet encountered anything that fully gripped his heart or gave his life direction.

Soon after he turned forty, Akiva passed by a rock that had been worn away by the force of a constant drip of water. It occurred to him that if water could have such a powerful effect upon a rock, there must be something in his own life that would have the power of the water upon stone. He asked himself, "Is my heart harder than this stone?"

Akiva searched for the force in his life that would act upon his heart like water upon stone. Soon after, for the first time in his life, he heard a teacher explain a passage of the Torah. At that moment, he realized that his life's calling was to learn Torah, to allow his cold heart to be touched and even broken by the powerful effect of Jewish wisdom. The story goes on to explain that Rabbi Akiva went to school with his young son the very next day. He learned alongside his son to write the *aleph*, *bet*, and so on, until he learned the entire Torah.

Since then, our tradition has recognized the importance of lifelong and adult Jewish learning. Maimonides even teaches us that if an adult and a child both need a Jewish education, the education of the adult should take precedence. Just as we are obligated to educate our children, we are obligated to educate ourselves: "Every Jew is obligated to learn Torah, whether we are poor or rich, in good health or ailing, in the vigor of youth or very old and feeble."

How does Akiva's experience apply to us? In Judaism, learning Torah has always meant more than understanding the meaning of the five books of Moses. Learning Torah means acquiring all the wisdom that a human being can acquire, all the knowledge that can be gained about the human condition, all the truths that we can discover in the tenuous path of life. As Jews, we learn the truth from those who came before us. We become an ear that hears what the wisdom of earlier generations is saying to us, even as we listen to our own hearts and think for ourselves. We begin with Torah, the way that our ancestors heard the truth, wisdom, and knowledge of their day. But, we continue to explore the texts and history of those Jews who have lived within every culture, across every century, as they struggled to answer the same questions that we ask today.

Why should any one of us study Torah? Each one of us, at some point in our lives, asks Akiva's question: "Is my heart harder than this stone?" We lead our lives within this world somewhat precariously. Judaism helps us to navigate the world, to fill it with magnificence, and to occasionally reach glimpses of eternity. The study of Torah is an encounter between our soul, our own inner voice, and the voice of God in the text. We find our own deepest self in this dialogue between our soul and the voice of God in the text. Too often we are intimidated by the text itself or have been taught to treat it with amused indifference. But what if we were to have a soul-to-soul dialogue with the Torah? What if we were to see the ancient biblical figures not as cartoon characters but as struggling humans like ourselves?

RECOVERING THE TORAH

We should study Torah to learn about ourselves. How do we begin to study Torah? We can begin by creating a Torah study group among our friends, colleagues, and acquaintances. A Torah study group can become very intimate, so the choice of participants is critical. We then face the question whether to have a teacher or to make this a participant-directed group. Often a teacher can be a helpful resource who can provide us with direction, suggest books to read, and facilitate the group. Because a Torah study group should empower us to develop our own relationship with the text, the teacher should be someone with knowledge who participates equally in the inquiry and respects the integrity of the process and that of the participants. He or she should not be a lecturer who has all the answers.

If you decide to have a self-directed group without a teacher, you might begin by studying the weekly Torah portion. Each member or, even better, two members of the group can prepare a weekly Torah discussion. You can begin with the text and several resource books such as those included in the appendix. Then, you can experiment with different kinds of discussions: How much do you want to rely on the interpretations of others? How personal do you want to take the discussion? What other approaches work for the group? The key is to let learning touch our hearts as water wore away Akiva's stone. There is no one right way. There is only the right way for each one of us.

We can also bring these learning groups into congregations so that we can make our synagogues more spiritual places. The more we take responsibility for our own Jewish learning rather than rely on others to teach us everything, the more we will rehearten Judaism and our synagogues. The more we bring our hearts and souls back into the synagogue through creating communities of learners, the more we will change the culture of the congregations. By bringing Judaism from the outside in, we will breathe new life into our congregations. And when adults become involved in Jewish learning within our congregations, we will help renew and restore life to the congregational schools.

We are witnessing today the beginning of a renaissance of Jewish learning that is occurring largely outside of congregations. The most effective forms of Jewish education today are Jewish camps, day schools, and adult classes. Thus, we are educating more Jewish children and adults, but they may be unable to find a home within congregations. As a result, "customized communities of seekers" have sprung up—*havurot*, study groups, *minyanim*—small groups of connectedness in which people can develop their Jewishness. The challenge is to bring every member of the Jewish community into such a group and every group back into the congregation.

Jewish spiritual education must also cultivate the deep, inner sense of Jewish principles through spiritual techniques such as meditation. Jewish meditation involves stopping ourselves from the active intellectual effort of thinking, reflecting, and pursuing in order to listen quietly, attentively, and undisturbed. Jewish meditation begins in a comfortable location, preferably a private room close to nature and away from the urban sounds of traffic, machines, and people. We begin with a chant—usually a *niggun*, a line of prayer, or a biblical verse that has personal significance. After chanting, we focus on breathing in and out. The inhalation is an act of contraction, of drawing in the power of God, just as God contracted within Himself to create a world. The exhalation is the creative outflow of divine energy. The breathing pattern is an acquired technique that works as long as we are not self-conscious. After a while, we reach a deep state of meditation; our breathing flows naturally, our mind becomes still, and our active thinking process stops. In this meditative state, we listen to the inner voice. We listen to the sounds around us. We hear the deeper sounds of the natural world, of the breeze, of birds, of the universe. Over time, we begin to hear what the universe is saying to us. God speaks in deeds and His vocabulary is the universe.

A SPIRITUAL JEWISH CONGREGATION

We stand today at the crossroads—do we continue Judaism as it is, or do we restore the spiritual heart of Judaism? We have inherited a noble tradition that many of us are just beginning to rediscover. At the same time, change has always been a part of our legacy, particularly when we live in societies that are hospitable to us. This time, however, the change that we seek is not to move away from Judaism but to move from the outside in without returning to the closed world of our ancestors.

What would Jewish life look like if we would imagine a Jewish community guided by spiritual principles? Let us start to explore this vision by imagining what a reheartened synagogue might look like. This guide is meant to help seekers re-create our congregations by bringing about some necessary changes. This tour through the Jewish community is partly factual and partly imaginary. Much of what we will encounter exists, but it does not exist altogether in one community.

On this tour, you and I are walking through a new kind of congregation. We begin at the entrance to the synagogue, a new type of synagogue that is different spiritually and architecturally from the cathedral synagogues that have come to dominate the suburban landscape. As we enter the front doors of our mythical Congregation Beth El, the House of God, on a Sabbath morning, we notice the soffet above the entrance: "The world depends on three principles: Torah, devotion, and deeds of kindness." The congregation selected this quotation of Rabbi Yochanan ben Zakkai because it represents the mission of the synagogue. Everything in the congregation refers back to this mission of lifelong Jewish learning, spiritual devotion, and making the world a better place.

The congregation decided to think about the real needs of the people who use the facility. That led the congregation to ask the members what they sought from the synagogue. Through many planning sessions involving regular members of the congregation, they decided to design the building around a series of rooms that could support groups of adults and children. Each room could be customized for the particular needs of a group. The result was the creation of customized services and study groups called *havurot*. The congregation still gets together as a whole for monthly services, but most people feel that the small-group experiences create a deeper sense of Jewish intimacy and connectedness with Judaism.

As we enter, we are struck by the way the synagogue is designed. The design committee concluded that the sanctuary was never full except for the High Holy Days. They decided that rather than design the sanctuary around the needs of people who attend only three days each year, the synagogue should plan around the real needs of the members. That led to a decision to redesign the cathedral and replace it with a series of more intimate mini-sanctuaries.

There is no longer a cathedral-style sanctuary auditorium where the rabbi and cantor officiate from behind formidable lecterns on a raised *bimah* (stage). In fact, there are several mini-sanctuaries of different sizes within the building. Each mini-sanctuary is designed to hold a series of concentric circles of rows of comfortable seats surrounding a small lectern in the center, level with the seats. The lectern is covered with copies of the Torah and prayer books. In one of these sanctuaries, a member of the congregation is standing at the lectern, leading the assembled congregation of fifty people in a vibrant *niggun* at the start of services. As the service progresses, it is clear that most parts of the service are chanted together in melodies that become more and more robust. The energy in the intimate room is palpable, a distinct contrast to the passivity of the traditional cathedral.

In the adjacent mini-sanctuary, a group of people are participating in a new kind of service, known as the "Seeker's Service," that attracts people who want to become more involved with Judaism. Many congregants had felt frustrated that they did not know the meaning of the prayers they were chanting in Hebrew or had difficulty understanding and accepting the meaning of the traditional prayers. This morning, the group began by reading and discussing the meaning of some of the key prayers. They soon turned to chanting these same prayers in a stirring melody that they repeated over and over. As they finished the round, the melody subsided. One member of the group said afterward that this was the first time she had really felt that the service was for her. She explained that she finally felt that there was a place for her in the synagogue because she was accepted on her own terms. She said that made it easier to approach Judaism on *its* own terms.

In another room, a similar group is involved in a Torah study session. Many of them had felt uncomfortable in a traditional prayer

194

service but felt deeply interested in Jewish learning. Many of them now feel that Torah study has transformed their lives and given them a deeper level of understanding about themselves, their families, and their Judaism. This morning they are discussing the different commentaries and *Midrashim*, some classical and some modern, on the weekly portion of Torah.

Down the hall, there is a smaller room set up with comfortable chairs arranged in a circle. The participants are deeply immersed in a meditation exercise based on the words of a Hebrew prayer. Their guide is a young member of the congregation who is leading them in a Hebrew chant and guiding them through a visualization process. Soon, the leader has them all stand up and form a circle. They begin to chant a Hebrew prayer in a meditative way, swaying as they sing. Soon, they are chanting and dancing in a circle around the room, just as their Hasidic ancestors once did.

As we continue, we stop to talk with one of the members of the congregation. She explains that the synagogue has recently recognized that no one kind of service meets the needs of all the participants. Everyone, she says, is at a different point in their own Jewish journey. The key, she continues, is to help empower Jews with the knowledge necessary to be a fully developed Jew. Too many people find Judaism to be a spectator activity in which the rabbi spoonfeeds Judaism to the congregation. However, as people become more involved in their own Jewish growth, it becomes clear that some people want a more participatory service, some want to learn what the prayers mean, others want to conduct their own services, while still others want to study Torah. As people become more knowledgeable, they feel empowered and want their Judaism to be more accessible and personal.

The same congregation also participates with other congregations in a community-wide Torah study program. Every Thursday night, people come from all over the community to one of the synagogues to study the weekly Torah portion. The session is conducted by a different teacher each week. Each teacher has a somewhat different approach. Some have a traditional religious perspective while others are more liberal. Some use the classical commentaries while others offer historical, literary, psychological, or political interpretations. Sometimes the teachers are congregational rabbis and professors of Jewish studies while, at other times, there are guest speakers or panel discussions. There is always a great deal of insight and, usually, strong debate about which interpretation is correct. People enjoy the exposure to different approaches to Torah and the fact that Jews of all persuasions come together to learn Torah. Most people explain that this helps prepare them for the Sabbath and for the reading of the Torah in synagogue.

We return to the synagogue on a weekday afternoon. We find a variety of groups meeting in the different rooms. In one room there is a class of high school children learning Hebrew. The room is equipped with ten computers, one for each student, and each student is seated at a workstation. Some of the students are on the Internet, participating in Hebrew chat rooms with Israeli teenagers. Another computer is arrayed with desktop videoconferencing that allows the student at that workstation to have a live, fully interactive television communication with several Israeli teenagers at the other end. They are collaborating on a model peace agreement for the Israeli–Palestinian conflict as part of a high school course on conflict mediation.

In another classroom, a group of teenagers is participating in an orientation for a youth group trip to Israel. They have just completed a unit on the Hebrew poetry of a noted Israeli poet. Their trip leader, who is leading the orientation, has explained to them that they will spend a day at the kibbutz residence of the poet. They are preparing for this part of their planned summer trip by reading and analyzing themes in his poetry. This is a first-time trip to Israel for most of the students. There are several trips going from their community this summer, each with a different theme. The theme of their own trip is Israeli culture and they are preparing for it by learning about Israeli artists, theater, literature, dance, and television. Other groups are planning their trip based on themes of nature and wilderness activities or ancient archeology and modern architecture.

A group of younger children is studying in a classroom down the hall. The teacher is presenting case studies of moral dilemmas that people often face. The case studies are drawn from the Talmud and *Midrash*, the ancient collection of narratives and teaching stories in the Jewish tradition. Standing outside the room, we ask the synagogue's educational director what is different about these classes. She explains that, in her view, the educational mission for this congregation is to teach our children that Judaism cares more about character than it does about learned mastery of the Torah. She cites a Hasidic story about Rabbi Leib Saras, who once said: "I did not journey to Rabbi Dov Baer of Mezritch to learn from him interpretations of the Torah, but to note his way of tying his shoelaces and doffing his shoes. For of what worth are the meanings given to the Torah, after all? In his actions, in his speech, in his bearing, and in his relation to the Lord, a person must make manifest the Torah." She explains that the only way to develop character is through the engagement on both the spiritual and intellectual level with the moral teachings of the Torah and the Jewish tradition.

In another room, a group of young couples are attending a childbirth preparation class. They have just finished practicing their natural-childbirth breathing techniques and are sitting on blankets and mats on the floor. The rabbi has joined them, and they have just begun to discuss what changes they anticipate in their home lives with the birth of a child. Tonight's discussion is about choosing a Jewish name for the baby. The rabbi has explained the Jewish custom of naming babies after deceased close relatives and has helped them translate the names they are considering into Hebrew. Then, they begin to discuss Hebrew names and how giving their children Jewish and Hebrew names is a critical first step in shaping the child's Jewish identity. Soon, the evening is over and one couple asks the rabbi if the next session could be devoted to learning how to create a Jewish home life when the baby arrives. Another couple asks if the

197

rabbi could help them prepare a home ceremony for the child's *brit* (circumcision), if it is a boy, or a *zeved habat* (gift of a daughter) ceremony, if they have a daughter. They all agree that there is much to discuss and decide to continue to meet as a new parents' support and learning group even after their children are born.

Elsewhere in the building that evening, a group of twenty people are participating in a study group. Their instructor is a professor of Jewish studies who has recently been hired by the local federation as a community adult educator. She is teaching her students a passage in English translation from a classical Jewish text. The students are arguing over the meaning of the passage and its application to today. After the session, we ask the students about their experience. One young man explains that he had left his synagogue after his *bar mitzvah* because he did not think that he was learning anything of value. As an adult, he attended a graduate professional school and had received a very advanced professional education. He realized, however, that he had only a thirteen-year-old child's view of Judaism. He concluded that while his Jewish education had done him a disservice, he would not be satisfied until he pursued his own Jewish knowledge on an adult level. A friend asked him to join this study group, and he was amazed that it had become the focal point of his week. It was something he did just for himself.

He mentions that other friends of his participate in a home study group. The group meets every other week in the various homes of the participants. They are studying Jewish spiritual biographies based on biblical texts about Abraham, Isaac, Jacob, Joseph, Moses, and David. They also plan to read modern biographies of Franz Kafka, Martin Buber, Abraham Joshua Heschel, and Elie Wiesel. They devote a portion of each session to close readings of the primary sources, followed by a discussion of the personal implication of these biographies for the lives of the participants in the group. His friend finds this group to be both spiritually enlightening and spiritually inspiring.

Within the congregation, several new *havurot*, or fellowship groups, have formed. Although they usually meet in the members' homes, several *havurot* are meeting tonight in the synagogue. One *havurah* for single parents is planning a support network within the group to assist working parents when they face emergencies such as when their child is sick at home, the parent has to be at work, and childcare is not available. They are planning a cooperative system of coverage based on the principle that each member contributes a certain number of hours per month to the cooperative. Another *havurah* has recently been formed for adults whose spouses have died. This *havurah* serves as the congregation's main support group for adults who have experienced grief and loss. The group was formed because the members realized that they could not expect the rabbi to perform every role of service to the congregation. They decided that overreliance on the professional staff of the congregation was not necessary. They could help themselves and each other and could also recruit the necessary resources, such as therapists and counselors, to help the members of the group.

As we continue on the tour, we stop to talk to a group of adults planning a new volunteer effort to help the local hunger center. One member of the group is explaining to another that the spiritual responsibility of the Jewish people is to repair the world. Another states that Judaism places great stress on the unity of all people and on our responsibility to the non-Jewish community. Still another comments that Jews have often been accused of believing in the innate superiority of the Jewish people, but this is a misunderstanding of the notion of our covenant. Our covenant, she explains, is the connectedness of a people devoted to the ethic of self-realization and commitment: "We are a people with a unique mission and calling to see the world not as it is but as it can be. While this may be a Jewish imperative, it is by no means limited to Jews. But Jews bear a responsibility to be 'a light among the nations.'"

All the members of this group agree that one of the virtues of a synagogue is that it is a community of different people who share common values. They have worked for several years to organize groups of congregants to support specific programs. One group gathers each Sunday morning in their workclothes, ready for a day of building new housing for low-income families. Another group has developed among members of the congregation a job bank listing positions available for people entering the job market after having been on welfare. They have created a buddy system that allows each new worker to have a mentor who can help teach him or her skills and work habits.

Another group in the congregation is meeting to develop policy recommendations for *bar mitzvah* celebrations. One member of the group feels that the emphasis on the *bar mitzvah* party is excessive and diminishes the spiritual significance of the event. She has recommended that three percent of the money spent on each party should be set aside for support of *Mazon*, the Jewish organization that supports hunger centers, in order to educate the children about sharing their bounty with less fortunate people. Another member argues that instead of spending the money on another party, the money should be better spent on a congregational or family trip to Israel for the *bar* and *bat mitzvah* children and their families. After all, he argues, the children do not remember one party from the next, but a trip to Israel will have a lifelong impact on their Jewish identity.

The congregational membership coordinator stops us on our way out. She wants to remind us that every member of the congregation is encouraged to participate in one of the *havurot* or to volunteer their talents to the congregation. Some members are able to provide counseling and support to people who have been ill or hospitalized, while others offer to help teach Torah to one of the classes. The membership coordinator sees herself not as a dues recruiter but as a matchmaker connecting the members' needs with the congregation's resources. As we leave the synagogue, we notice a large poster in the corridor. The banner on the top of the poster appears in bold letters: "The Guarantee for Jewish Education: Judaism has been proven to be a rewarding spiritual journey when used as directed as part of a conscientious program of moral discipline and regular educational care.''

Once we are outside, we turn to each other and ask: What did it take to achieve this new spiritual Jewish congregation? We agree that congregations should begin to think of themselves not as membership organizations but as communities dedicated to empowering individuals and groups spiritually and religiously. As one friend summarizes it: "We need to become empowered as Jewish human beings because we cannot leave the perpetuation of Judaism to others. It is our own individual responsibility. If we return Judaism to ordinary Jews, Judaism will be vibrant again. We need to trust in the people to preserve Judaism, we need to trust in the individual human spirit because the universal spirit of God that appeared at Sinai makes everyone equal."

We have to accept the challenge of helping the synagogue become more responsive to people like ourselves. An "ordinary" congregant can often influence the organization by giving voice to the concerns of people looking for a spiritual home. Many rabbis share our frustration with the synagogue and would welcome our ideas. After all, what rabbi would not want a committed seeker as an ally in strengthening Jewish life? Still, it is not always easy to break through the status quo, because many people and institutions resist change. The vested interests of people who like things just the way they are can stand in the way. But we need to persevere and not let disagreement deter us. Do not give up on the congregation. We can bring people who agree with us to committee meetings and encourage others to work with us. Our ideas will be heard as more and more people agree with us about the kind of changes that are needed in the synagogue.

Some people will find that their congregation cannot change fundamentally. They might leave the synagogue and create their own *havurah*. While it will be difficult for them to find a new location and organize everything themselves, they might prefer to create something fresh rather than struggle to change an existing organization from within. Many *havurot* today offer some of the opportunities that the ideal revitalized congregation now offers. Still, many members of *havurot* worry that their own small groups might not last. Some of us prefer to cast our lots with existing institutions because we want to be sure that the congregation will be there a generation from now. Others of us will try to change the organization from within because if congregations do not change, the future of Judaism is in great jeopardy.

A SPIRITUAL JEWISH COMMUNITY

The next day, we continue our tour of the Jewish community. We start off at the Jewish community federation, the central fundraising and planning agency of the organized Jewish community. We sit down for a conversation with the executive director, who points out that one of the greatest challenges she faces is communicating that wealth is not the criterion for leadership in the organization. The wealthiest members of the community often contribute proportionately more to the federation fundraising campaign. They have a great stake in how their capital is invested in Jewish social services and education here and abroad. They have the ability to initiate new efforts that can improve the quality of Jewish life. At the same time, any person who is willing to volunteer his or her time, energy, intelligence, and a fair share of his or her personal resources can shape the direction of the community. In fact, the director points out, one of the federation's greatest priorities is to encourage the spiritual and religious quest among adults, because this is the best way to ensure Jewish continuity in the future.

202

The director explains that many people believe that the organized Jewish community is a plutocracy, a hierarchy governed by wealthy contributors and by the major philanthropists espousing Jewish causes. This is true to a certain extent, and many people see it as an obstacle to true democracy within the Jewish community. Jewish philanthropy, however, is also the engine that has facilitated some of the most important and positive developments in recent Jewish life. In recent years, there has been an infusion of financial resources into Jewish education. While money cannot solve all problems, the support of major philanthropic foundations has begun to have a powerful impact on Jewish renewal through their support of Jewish educational and cultural initiatives. We agree that private philanthropy is a powerful source of support for Jewish renewal that has great potential for improving the quality of Jewish life. We also agree that each one of us has the responsibility to contribute what we can to the community to help Jews and others in need. She then suggests that we start our exploration of community resources at the local branch of the community college of Jewish studies.

We arrive at the local branch of the college of Jewish studies early in the morning. One of the students arriving for morning classes explains to us that she never had a real grasp of Judaism until she began studying with one of the teachers at the college. The student explained that her teacher used to teach at a private university but decided that his talents were needed in the Jewish community. Several years ago he moved to this community, where he serves as a community scholar. Here, the instructor found that he could teach adults who were truly interested in a scholarly, knowledgeable presentation of Judaism that went beyond academic objectivity to explore the implications of the subject matter for the students and the community. The student explained that a college-level education should be available to adults throughout their lives, especially since most Jewish adults have had such poor experiences with Jewish education in their younger years. Her classes were filled with adults of all ages and backgrounds, many of whom were somewhat nervous about returning to the classroom. She explained that the atmosphere of the adult community college, unlike her undergraduate years, was free of competition and pressure, and the teachers were dynamic, personable, and engaging.

203

We meet one of the other teachers in the hall, who explains to us that this college is part of a national network of colleges of Jewish studies in nearly every Jewish community. Some large communities have their own facilities, while others are located in the Jewish community centers. Many of them are linked together through live, interactive videoconferencing, which makes it possible for small communities to offer classes taught by instructors who live somewhere else. The smaller communities, he explains, are no longer isolated or restricted geographically from having access to the same teachers as the larger cities offer. Now, every Jew in North America has access to a high-quality adult Jewish education offered by the best teaching minds in the Jewish world.

Our tour continues at the Jewish home for the aged. As we walk into the spacious and airy entrance, we are reminded of Rabbi Nachman of Bratslav's saying that "the true prosperity of a country is measured by its treatment of the elderly." The same statement could be made about a country's treatment of any vulnerable group of individuals, including children, the poor, and the disabled. Adherence to this principle is especially evident in this facility. The director explains to us that he is deeply involved in planning a new assisted-living facility so that elderly adults can live independently and still have access to adequate medical care, friends and neighbors, and other support services.

Nearby is the Jewish community center, which has a large winterized retreat facility on its sprawling campus surrounded by woods. The center is used every Sabbath by various congregations that run Jewish retreats for adults and children. It is an ideal location for people who wish to experience the Sabbath apart from the usual distractions. People come here with their rabbis, teachers, and friends on Friday afternoons and leave Saturday night. For the duration of the Sabbath, they are insulated from television, shopping, school, work, and entertainment. Their time is devoted entirely to Jewish pursuits of learning, singing, resting, praying, and enjoying the camaraderie of their friends around festive meals. The participants describe this retreat as a means of renewing the body and the soul.

We arrive next at a Jewish day school, a community elementary and middle school that follows traditional Jewish practice and is guided by a liberal educational and religious outlook. We stop to talk with one of the parents on the way in and ask her about the school. She tells us that she has always been deeply committed to public education but wants her children to have the kind of Jewish education she never had. She hopes her children will become creative and critical thinkers, morally grounded in the right values, literate in Jewish subjects, fluent in the Hebrew language, and competent in all the general-studies subjects. She mentions that when she discussed the idea of enrolling her children in a Jewish day school her husband objected, claiming it would not "prepare them for the real world" because it lacked the diversity found in public schools. When the parents investigated the school, they found that it indeed lacked racial diversity, but the students came from all the different Jewish backgrounds—Orthodox, Conservative, Reconstructionist, and Reform—and from diverse cultures—the United States, Mexico, Canada, the former Soviet Union, and Israel. The school was actually as ethnically diverse as any they had visited, and the cultural and religious mixture within the school was greater than any they had encountered. Moreover, they appreciated that the school placed a high value on academic achievement and encouraged the personal growth of the students. Because of these cultural values, the students did not feel the same social pressures about fashions, conformity, competition, and drugs that were prevalent in the public schools. The atmosphere was wholesome, and the parents valued the protection their children would gain from some of the pressures children are often subject to in our culture.

205

EMPOWERING JEWISH SEEKERS

At the end of our tour, we sit down to assess what we have seen. We both agree that it is almost instinctual for Jews to be pessimistic about the future of Judaism even as we make glorious contributions to Jewish civilization. Spiritual Judaism sometimes seems so far from the reality of Judaism today. If we look at what Jewish life is today, we are often frustrated by the fact that many of the inheritors of the Jewish spiritual tradition have become fundamentalists, while liberal Judaism is insufficiently spiritual. For many spiritually inclined Jews, there is no place to call home in the Jewish community. We are searching for a middle ground that avoids the close-mindedness of fundamentalist Judaism and the superficiality of cathedral Judaism. We agree that too little attention is paid to the growing renaissance of Jewish learning and searching that is evident all around us today. The return to Judaism, the interest in spiritual Judaism, the phenomenal growth of adult learning, and the return to tradition are all signs of a Jewish revival.

Too many congregations ask what the members can do for the institution, not what the congregation can do for the members. The members are not interested in congregational politics; they want community and connectedness. Too many people come into congregations episodically and are alienated by the fact that if they are to feel connected, they must conform to the congregation. Spiritual growth is not just personal; it involves the search for connectedness with others.

How do we accomplish this? Congregations should be based on small, intimate groups that are created to meet the needs of the members of that group. The congregation must become a community of customized groups rather than an impersonal, mass-membership organization. Each group must define itself, create its own intimate community, and pursue its Jewish journey and exploration together. The role of the congregation is to facilitate the journey of its members through creating communities of seekers. The congregation should see its mission as empowering Jewish seekers through creating opportunities for personal Jewish growth within a group setting.

Too many congregations are organized on the assumption that Jewish expertise resides among the professional clergy. The goal of a congregation should actually be to raise each of its members up to the level of competence of the clergy through encouraging learning, growth, experimentation, and empowerment among its members. The best way to encourage this is to allow for members to practice what they learn in smaller groups. Not every service has to be led by the rabbi; services can be led by members of the smaller groups by and for themselves. The rabbi's role is not to preserve the authority of the clergy but rather to help the members become competent Jews themselves. At the same time, congregations have to change their expectations of their rabbis. The rabbi cannot be all things to all people, nor should the rabbi be spread so thin that he or she cannot focus on the real priorities. We must allow rabbis to become teachers once again rather than managers.

Ultimately, we realize that spiritual Judaism will nurture new communities of searchers and learners. Congregations will inevitably choose to embrace many of these changes because they are its future. Jewish communities are beginning to facilitate the search for Jewish meaning and promote the spiritual search. Jewish seekers will have a profound impact on the next generation of Jewish life, which will continue to evolve in response to the growing number of Jews who bring their own spiritual energy back into the Jewish fold. Spiritual Judaism requires a great deal of personal effort and learning if we are to bring about this rejuvenation of Jewish life. But you and I are certain that we will.

The message of Torah is how to find the divine sparks within the mundane world. The path of Torah is to recognize the cosmic significance of our individual acts. Every human action—thought, speech, and deed—influences the entire universe. The power of our soul can either purify or contaminate the universe in which we live.

Spiritual Judaism guides us in the struggle to bring God into the world, a struggle for the sanctification of the human heart. When we understand that, we will have found the location of the clearing in the forest and will have learned the instructions for lighting the fire. Now, we turn to learn how to sing the *niggun*, the lost melody of Judaism.

Chapter Six

GOD SINGS WITHIN US

My Lord, Open my lips, and my mouth will sing Your
praise.
—*Amidah prayer*

I sought You out and found You in my thoughts.
—*Isaac ibn Ghiyat*

WHY WE PRAY

Prayer is the voice we hear when we listen to what the universe
is saying to us. This is what Martin Buber calls "God singing
within us." God sings within us when we cease to think of ourselves
and listen to what the universe is saying to us. This is the custom of
one of the great Hasidic rabbis who would often delay reciting his
morning prayers so that he could go out to a nearby pond and listen
to the songs of the frogs. When he could hear their song within his
own soul, he knew that he was ready to pray.

Sometimes we pray when we are looking for an answer. The
prayer is our question. In order to hear the answer, we must stop
praying and listen to the voice within. The technique of listening
also involves opening ourselves up to the prayers of other people:
Shema—"Listen! Take these words to heart." When we hear the
voice that sings within the composer, we can understand what

209

moved the hearts of our ancestors. Everything in the universe longs for higher rungs and deeper layers. That longing is prayer. The heavens pray, nature prays, the heart prays.

Prayer is a heart-to-heart conversation with the divine within. We pray at times of powerful pain and distress, pouring out our broken heart in search of comfort and healing. We empty the broken vessel of our heart before we can refill it with the healing light of God. But we also pray in small, unconscious ways every time we are filled with the pleasure, wonder, and awareness of everything around us that we too often take for granted. Every moment of awareness of the divine within the world is a prayer waiting to be shaped into words.

Prayer is also valuable in helping us to break the routine of our lives and to achieve greater spiritual heights. Prayer can be an inward meditation that reorients us away from the mundane and toward the sublime. Prayer is an effective technique to reorder our usual way of being in the world, which is necessary for spiritual growth. As we sever the bonds that connect us to routine consciousness, our soul can soar to the heights.

Prayer is not the words we recite from the prayer book but an experience of the soul. If the words of the prayer book, someone else's words, are not adequate, we can find our own words. Even if we sit or stand silent in the synagogue while everyone around us is reading, reciting, or chanting, the thing that truly matters is what we experience in our privacy. The only prayer that matters is the one that comes from our heart. If our heart is not touched by the written words of the prayer book, we can turn inward and listen to the inner voice. Then, we can turn that voice into a chant, a movement, a melody until it burns in our hearts.

The prayer book is an anthology of biblical psalms and religious poetry composed mostly in Hebrew throughout the ages. It is built around a common structure of certain core prayers that make up each service and, at certain times, the Torah reading. Many prayers written throughout the ages have been layered upon the core prayers or replaced by new prayers. There is no reason why this process of introducing new prayers and replacing others could not continue today. When we find the prayer book limiting, we can develop our own services, using a mix of traditional and new prayers.

There is a deep sense of connection to our ancestors and to other Jews that we can feel when we make the ancient prayers our own. The common structure of core prayers makes it possible for a Jew from any community around the world to recognize and participate in a Jewish prayer service. Prayer within a group also provides something that solitary prayer does not. Spirituality is not only inward and private but also involves establishing a connection with other people. Judaism stresses congregational prayer, not to discount the importance of personal spirituality, but to emphasize our common humanity and spiritual aspirations. Communal Jewish prayer is understood as the sum of our individual efforts directed toward a common goal. A Hasidic story retold by Arthur Green and Barry Holtz in *Your Word Is Fire* illustrates this principle:

Once in a tropical country, a certain splendid bird, more colorful than any that had ever been seen, was sighted at the top of the tallest tree. The bird's feathers contained all the colors in the world. But the bird was perched so high that no single person could ever hope to reach it. When news of the bird reached the ears of the king, he ordered that a number of men try to bring the bird to him. They were to stand on one another's shoulders until the highest man could reach the bird and bring it to the king. The men assembled near the tree, but while they were standing balanced on one another's shoulders, some of those near the bottom decided to wander off. As soon as the first man moved, the entire chain collapsed, injuring several of the men. The bird was never captured. The men had doubly failed the king. For even greater than his desire to see the bird was his wish to see his people so closely joined to one another.

SPONTANEITY AND THE PRAYER BOOK

We pray to express what is in our hearts. In spiritual Judaism, there is a preference for the spontaneous, heartfelt expression of the soul over the formal liturgy of the prayer book. The Talmud says: "Do not make your prayer fixed." Yet it is precisely the fixed language of the prayer book that is so alienating for many Jewish seekers today. Because many of the prayers are composed in the language of the Torah, they are unfamiliar to the modern ear. Because the prayer book often speaks in the voice of "we," not "I," many people have difficulty with the somewhat impersonal language of the Jewish prayers. Because many of us are unfamiliar with the original Hebrew, we rely on the translations that are often written in archaic English and misrepresent the original language. Because the sentiments found in the prayers are often expressions of thanks to a lofty God, they seem to lack the personal language of the spontaneous human heart.

The problem is compounded when we enter synagogues where we are unfamiliar with the ebb and flow of the service, when we do not feel part of the group, and when we sit as audience members listening passively to the rabbi and cantor. If prayer is God singing within us, the song has become tired through repetition and lifeless translations. Once the prayers became required, fixed, and formalized, they themselves became obstacles to spirituality.

The true goal of Jewish prayer, the one that rarely gets discussed, is the spontaneous prayer that is beyond words. True spirituality arises out of the heart of the individual and goes beyond the prescribed prayer book. The following story is told by Martin Buber in *Tales of the Hasidim*:

212

A villager, who year after year prayed in the Baal Shem Tov's synagogue on the Days of Awe, had a son who was so dull-witted that he could not even grasp the shapes of the Hebrew letters, let alone the meaning of the holy words. On the Days of Awe his father did not take him to town with him, because he did not understand anything. But when he turned thirteen, his father took him along on the Day of Atonement, for fear the boy might eat on the fast day simply because he did not know any better. Now, the boy had a small whistle that he always blew when he sat out in the fields to herd the sheep and the calves. He had taken this with him in the pocket of his coat and his father had not noticed it. Hour after hour, the boy sat in the synagogue and had nothing to say. But when the final service began, he said: "Papa, I have my little whistle with me. I want to sing on it." The father became upset and told him to do no such thing, and the boy restrained himself. But when the service began, he said again, "Papa, let me blow my little whistle." The father became angry and said, "Where did you put it?" And when the boy told him, he laid his hand on his pocket so that the boy could not take it out. But as the final service began, the boy took out the whistle and blew a note as loud as he could. The entire congregation was frightened and confused. But the Baal Shem Tov went on with the prayer, only more easily than usual.

The attitude of the father in this fable is present in our synagogues. It makes it difficult for many seekers to find a spiritual home in synagogues today. Often we are drawn to finding our own song, the spontaneous, often silent song that expresses what we feel in our own hearts. We do not need to follow the words that others have written for us.

OUR ANCESTORS' LEGACY

Shacharit, the traditional morning service, begins with preparatory blessings, biblical verses, and psalms leading up to the *Borchu*, the call to public prayer. The heart of the service is the *Shema* ("Hear, O Israel, the Lord Our God, the Lord is One") framed by preceding

213

and succeeding prayers, followed by the *Amidah*, also known as the *Shemoneh Esreh* (Eighteen Blessings), or the Silent Devotion. On Monday, Thursday, the Sabbath, and festivals, this is followed by public reading of the weekly or holiday Torah portion and, sometimes, readings from the Prophets.

Minchah, the weekday afternoon service, takes place while it is still daylight. It is a brief service with a preliminary section, the *Amidah*, and concluding prayers. On the Sabbath, part of the weekly Torah portion is read. *Maariv*, the weekday evening service, takes place at sundown and consists primarily of the *Shema*, framed by preceding and succeeding prayers, followed by the *Amidah* and concluding prayers. Special psalms and mystical hymns are added to the beginning of the Sabbath evening service.

Traditional prayers are classified as prayers that praise God, prayers that thank God, and prayers that ask God for a variety of requests. These petitions include prayers to restore our souls, guide our daily activities, enable us to pray, protect us and the Jewish people, spread peace throughout the world, and heal the sick and suffering.

Over time, new prayers composed by Hebrew poets throughout the ages have been added throughout the service. In earlier generations, it was taken for granted that some prayers could be replaced by modern contributions as long as the core service was preserved. Innovation and the introduction of new expressions were taken for granted. Many of the new prayers were highly personal spiritual statements. As Raymond Scheindlin has pointed out in *The Gazelle*, the line between poetry composed for use in the synagogue and poetry intended for private religious meditation is not clear. Many prayers that have been included in our prayer books began as private, personal, spiritual expressions. The process of including poems in the prayer book that were originally intended for private use continues. The prayer book is not a final, fixed text but an evolving collection of personal additions around a common core.

SHARPENING THE AXE

Prayer is one of the greatest spiritual exercises in Judaism, but we often find it difficult to pray within the synagogue or temple. If our spiritual journey begins with our search for the clearing in the forest, what are the instructions for lighting the fire? Even before we light the fire, we must chop down the trees and gather the wood. But as the Kotzker Rebbe pointed out, "sharpening the axe is as important as cutting the tree." Therefore, we must sharpen our own axes and start with our individual spiritual preparations for prayer.

Too often we enter the synagogue, rush to our seats, and try to catch up to rest of the congregation. Why would we expect prayer to be meaningful without preparing ourselves? Even when we exercise at the health club, we know the value of warming up. The first step in preparing to pray involves a choice of exercises that make us ready for the experience.

Meditation exercises have traditionally been a part of preparing to pray. The Talmud explains that in ancient times, pious people would sit still in a meditative exercise for one hour before each prayer service. We can reintroduce meditation into our religious services by sitting quietly before we enter the sanctuary or by meditating in the sanctuary after we enter. You might experiment with one of the exercises described by Mark Verman in *The History and Varieties of Jewish Meditation*.

The first meditation, called a *shiviti*, involves a visualization technique of the king or father image of God. It is based on the biblical verse, "I have constantly placed (*shiviti*) God before me; He is at my right hand so that I shall not falter" (Psalm 16:8). In this exercise, you can stand with your eyes closed and visualize a partner—the king or father image of God—holding you up as you stand on one foot. By feeling that you can find your balance with the assistance of an invisible partner, you can remind yourself that you have God as your partner during prayer.

The second meditation, introduced by Eliezer Azikri in the sixteenth century, can be done while sitting comfortably in a chair with your eyes closed. This exercise involves visualizing an arrow shot from the far reaches of outer space, moving quickly through darkest space, countless galaxies, myriad stars, the atmosphere, until it reaches its target—you! God is the archer, the arrow is the divine spark, and the bull's-eye is you. The goal of this exercise is for us to visualize ourselves in relation to the Infinite and to remind us that all of the energy of the universe flows toward us, as long as we are prepared to receive it.

The third exercise, introduced by the Piatsetzna Rebbe, is an outdoor meditation in which we visualize the heavens and our place in the universe. With our eyes open and looking up, we look at the heavenly sky and contemplate an imaginary voyage to the far reaches of the universe. Concentrate your mind and think: "I am standing here. Beyond each heaven is another heaven . . . I bless You, to whom my eyes are raised. Whether I can see You or not, I concentrate my vision and gaze upon You."

Each of these exercises can be modified or adapted to meet your own spiritual inclinations. The important point is that we need to devote time to preparing ourselves for prayer. We cannot jump right into a service and expect to find it spiritually engaging. We must sharpen the axe before cutting down the tree.

THE CLEARING IN THE FOREST

Keeping a personal journal is another useful technique in getting ready to pray. We can write down our deepest spiritual longings in a prayer journal that we turn to for inspiration. Because it is very difficult to sustain our ability to pray, we can trigger an openness to prayer by reading what we have previously written or by writing down new prayers that help us to focus on the moment. For example, the thirteenth-century *Sefer Chasidim* preserves an example of a personal prayer supposedly composed by a Jewish shepherd who could only pray by offering to do for God what he knew how to do best—tending sheep: *"Ribbono shel olam,* Lord of the World, If you had sheep and gave them to me to tend, though I take wages for tending from all others, from You I would take nothing, because I love You.*"* This personal prayer came from the heart.

I recently gave an in-class exercise to the students in my seminar on Jewish spirituality. I asked them to write down their own personal prayers to help them focus on what they wanted out of religious services. Their statements can give you an example of how this kind of writing can help orient you to prayer. Here is a sample of what they wrote:

When I look to You I see myself. However, when I look within it does not always happen. I take it as an obligation and honor to match the two so that I become a more whole and spiritual human being. By doing so, I will be able to feel Your presence more strongly in myself.

My dear God, thank you for all that I am, all that I've been, all that I'm going to be, and all that I have. Help me, dearest God, to heal my mind, body, spirit, and attitudes and allow me to enlighten myself to the highest level that I'm capable of being and doing! I ask for these things in a loving and harmonious way. I give thanks to You today for Your being in my heart.

Ribbono shel olam, *Lord of the World, when all is well and at peace within me, then do I have pureness to offer and receive from You.*

217

God, I see You in the beauty of fall: the vibrant colors of leaves, the landscape surrounding me. I hear Your voice in the wind as

the trees You skillfully planted sway. I am enveloped in Your cre-
ation. I pray that I always see so clearly Your work so that I never
again forget what I hold so dear above all else.

Ribbono shel olam, *Lord of the World, Hear my prayer. Thank*
You for today, for blessing my family and for blessing me. I open
up my heart to You—please hear my prayer.

It is very difficult for me to feel that I am in Your company alone,
without people, without everyday occurrences intruding on my
thoughts. When I do achieve that state, it is a magnificent feeling
and I get carried along without effort and am able to see all the
good in the world.

Ribbono shel olam, *Lord of the World, I know Your luminous*
presence resides within everyone and everything in this world. Al-
low me to feel my connectedness to You and the universe, and help
me to shine as a spark of Your glorious creation.

I hope that my prayers, or my way of praying, or how I feel, what
I hope, will be and is heard by Hashem *("The Name"—A He-*
brew term for God). I hope that I am worthy of Hashem's *atten-*
tion. I hope that I concentrate on and show appreciation of all the
good and positive in my life. I wish to learn to take time to pray
and be more serious about it.

Oh Hashem! *I want so much to feel me with You. I need to*
ritualize my beginning prayer. Like saying "hi" to my very best
friend. So, I think I will just say, "Hi, Hashem, *we have some*
important things to discuss today; please hear me and I will try
my utmost to hear You."

God, You have always been a source of light for me. I thank You and pray that I will always be moved by prayer, song, and meditation—as I have been in the past.

May God forgive me of all my transgressions. Wash me with great mercies that I may become pure as snow. Is it not written, most Holy One: "Who can ascend to the hill of the Lord? He that has clean hands and a pure heart." With humility I bow and worship You. May I find great favor in your most holy eyes to begin my ascent to You. There is one thing that I have desired, Hashem: *That I might dwell within the courts of Your sanctuary and inquire of You to make known Your holy mysteries.*

May my acts today be of benefit to all beings. May I recognize and respect all that I meet, in person and in thought, myself included, as manifestations of the same consciousness and all with the same wish to be happy. May I do no harm. May I be awake with and accepting of each moment, just as it is.

Ribbono shel olam, *Lord of the World—The One who has always been near to me, though I have wandered far and near, struggling to reach You more clearly. May I, too, have patience and openness to lift the sparks of all those around me and, in so doing, lift the spark within myself, and mend the world as one.*

Ribbono shel olam, *Lord of the World, I have quieted the noises in my mind and heart and have tasted Your cleansing breath.*

Oh God, allow my mind to be quiet and to be at peace and open to accepting the opportunity to pray. Let me be able to put aside my mundane, earthly thoughts and concentrate on being receptive to prayer to You.

The purity and beauty in the soul of a child, the goodness, the trustfulness, the truthfulness—is that what it is like to be near You?

Dear God, all that You have created is before me. I revel in its splendor. Nothing eludes me; the sights, sounds, smells, colors are vivid and bold. Your presence is supreme, and I am a part of it.

What I hope for is a personal experience of contact with God. I try to focus on His majesty and visualize His presence and feel a connection between us. I might say in my heart: "Oh, God, I feel Your realness all around me and I know You are aware of this. My heart bows down to You even as I feel Your love for me, Your acceptance of me. I want to be a better Jew. Help me to be aware of Your voice and Your presence all around me, not just on Shabbat morning, to feel connected and aware of Your will and of Your holiness. I need to spiritually bow down to Your holiness."

Ribbono shel olam, *Lord of the World, I hope to be able to find a place in my heart where God always is. So that, in turn, I will treat others with love and understanding. If I feel closer to God, I will feel closer to people.*

Ribbono shel olam, *Lord of the World, Help me to think not of myself but to pray with an open heart. Help me to open my soul to Your goodness so that I may fill my whole being with goodness. Help me to reach beyond myself so that I may grow.*

Ribbono shel olam, *My dear God, please teach me to love my children as You love me.*

LIGHTING THE FIRE

Once we have found the clearing in the forest, we can follow the instructions for lighting the fire. One of the techniques for lighting the fire in preparation for prayer is to wear a *kippah* (head covering) and wrap ourselves in a *tallit*, or prayer shawl. Special clothing, uniforms, and costumes are often used to create a feeling, to note a special moment, or to change our self-perceptions. They help make ordinary moments special and raise our level of awareness from the mundane to the extraordinary. The *kippah* and *tallit* can likewise prepare us for prayer.

Wearing a head covering was practiced in ancient times by the Temple priests, Jewish mourners, and women as a sign of reverence for God. At the time of the destruction of the Second Temple, ordinary Jewish males did not wear a head covering. During the Middle Ages, the custom of wearing one gradually took hold, in some degree as a differentiation from Christians who prayed without. By the seventeenth century, it was customary for Jews to wear a head covering at least during prayer and Torah study. Today, the wearing of a head covering—*kippah* in Hebrew or *yarmulka* in Yiddish—has become one of the ways in which Jews of various degrees of observance identify themselves. Wearing a *kippah* is also a way to focus our attention during prayer and other Jewish rituals.

The ritual of wearing a *tallit* during prayer is based on the Torah passage: "The Lord said to Moses as follows: Speak to the Israelite people and instruct them to make for themselves fringes (*tzitzit*) on the corners of their garments throughout the ages; let them attach a cord of blue to the fringe at each corner" (Numbers 15:37–39). Traditionally, the prayer shawl is worn by men during all morning services, except on the ninth of Av, when it is worn only for afternoon services. It is also worn throughout *Yom Kippur*. In Orthodox congregations, the *tallit* is worn by married men, although all males wear the *tallit katan*, an undergarment with *tallit* fringes. The blue fringe, orginally produced by a dye extracted from a rare sea snail, was discontinued in ancient times and was replaced by black or blue stripes woven into the *tallit* itself.

Many women who recognize the value of prayer rituals have begun to wear a *kippah* and *tallit* during services. Many people put the *tallit* over their head in order to exclude outside stimuli and to focus visually and mentally on the private experience of prayer. The inclusion of *kippah* and *tallit* during services can help elevate the prayer experience. They can also have special meaning if we have not previously worn them: They can serve as a symbol of our own Jewish journey.

SINGING THE *NIGGUN*

Originally, in the time of the Great Temple in Jerusalem, the prayers were accompanied by musical instruments and choral singing. When the Temple was destroyed, the instrumental and choral traditions were abolished as a sign of mourning. Playing of musical instruments in the synagogue on the Sabbath was then regarded throughout the centuries as sacrilegious and a serious violation of Jewish law. Reform Judaism restored instrumental and choral music to the synagogue service in the nineteenth century but incorporated the contemporary style of church music—a choir accompanied by the organ—rather than the original Jewish musical tradition of string instruments and voices.

To turn poems into prayers, we need to add melody, a *niggun*. In the Hasidic tradition, a *niggun* is an inspired melody without words, a melody that sings itself. It comes from deep within the soul and has the power to change our consciousness. According to legend, a certain variety of *niggunim* are as ancient as the universe and each one corresponds to a different spiritual state of the soul. A *niggun* can elevate and heal the soul or communicate a spiritual message nonverbally. A *niggun* is God's song within our soul that we hear and bring out with our voices. We never invent, we only discover, a *niggun*.

How do we sing a *niggun*? Start with a simple syllable such as "lye" or "aye," and repeat it. As we repeat the syllable, let our body sway to each beat. Then, listen for a melody to come out of the syllable and the movement, and let all three—the word, the movement, and the melody—carry it along. Listen to the mood that emerges: Is it joyful, playful, or sad? The melody sings itself, depending on where it comes from within us. A joyful melody can even lift us out of sadness or cure melancholy, while a plaintive melody can become a prayer. The melody is repetitive, circular, and can continue for a long time; it does not have a beginning or an end. A *niggun* sung in a group draws on the unspoken connection between the different voices; when one person might be ready to end the *niggun*, another person might give it new life. It communicates among people.

The next step is more difficult: We can substitute a phrase or a verse for the simple syllable and add words. The great Hasidic *niggunim* were often set to simple prayers, verses, or spiritual phrases and became the basis for a rich tradition of spiritual melodies, passed down from generation to generation. The Belz Hasidim, for example, would chant in Hebrew, "God conceals Himself in the beauty of secrecy; may God's radiance illuminate everything and bring my glad song to You, O God!" The Vishnitzer rabbi, who would often lead his group in a *niggun* that lasted all night long, would chant, "There is no limit to God's years and no end to the length of His days." The Bobover rabbi sang, "My son, do not walk in evil ways, restrain your foot from an evil path." The Modsitzer rabbi would sing a healing chant, "From out of distress I called upon the Lord; He answered me and brought me relief."

The final step is to add dance and movement to the *niggun*. We can ready ourselves for prayer or sit around the Sabbath table, tapping the beat and swaying to the melody while clapping. While singing the *niggun*, we can form a circle dance, moving spontaneously to the melody while linking arms or holding on to the shoulders of the person on either side. The key is to follow the biblical advice: "Praise God with all your limbs!"

We should not limit group prayer to the inside of a synagogue building. In warm weather, why not have the prayer group meet outdoors in a park setting, allowing each of us to experience God within nature? Rabbi Nachman of Bratslav said that when we pray outdoors, among nature, the entire natural world comes to our aid and lends strength to our prayers. Even when we pray indoors, nature is with us, for it is the custom that a synagogue have windows to the outside.

SPIRITUAL LANGUAGE

To better appreciate Hebrew prayers and *niggunim*, we might consider learning Hebrew. Judaism teaches that there are sparks of divinity within the letters of the Hebrew alphabet that have a special resonance with the soul. While an English translation might convey the meaning of a poem, a prayer, or a verse, it lacks two critical elements. First, translation can never convey the nuances, word plays, and lyricism of a translation. Second, a translation cannot touch the soul the way the original Hebrew does. Every language creates a different consciousness, and Hebrew produces a unique consciousness of its own. For example, the Hebrew name of the first man, *Adam*, is related linguistically to the Hebrew word for the image of God, *demut*. This implies that the name Adam means "the one created in God's image," a suggestion not available through the English translation. The first letter of the Hebrew name Adam, *aleph*, is composed of two *yods* separated by a diagonal line. *Yod*, the tenth letter of the Hebrew alphabet, is the letter that forms God's name. Starting Adam's name with an *aleph* suggests that he is the unity of the infinite and worldly manifestations of God. Every Hebrew letter, word, and phrase is a door that opens out to new vistas, connections, associations, and hints. While Hebrew is not an easy language to master, a good teacher can communicate enough of a basic Hebrew understanding to help us understand the spiritual dimensions of Hebrew prayers.

RESTORING HEART AND SOUL

How can we restore heart and soul to prayer? If we want to recapture the personal and spiritual power of spontaneous prayer and yet share a connection with people who feel as we do, we need to start at the beginning again. Every prayer began in the spontaneous expression of one of our ancestors. In order to let God sing within us, we need to understand how our ancestors allowed God to sing within them. This involves a close and deep reading of the prayers that they composed long ago. Their prayers can trigger within us a moment when we had a similar experience but did not put it into words as expressively as they did. It requires that we look at their poetry as an expression of their heart, not as a literary document. It is often difficult to do this because we cannot easily look beyond ourselves to another person's experience. Therefore, we will begin by asking ourselves to listen to the voice within their prayers. All these poems have been composed in Hebrew, but they can be read, recited, and chanted in translation.

In the following section, I present a selection of prayers for different occasions. I have chosen them because you can hear the voice of God within their poetry. Some of the prayer-poems are included in the traditional prayer book, but most are not. They are, however, the same kinds of prayers that have been included in the prayer book. They might be useful to us as substitutions for traditional prayers or as supplements that we can turn to when we are looking for more than the standard prayers can offer. We might even want to experiment by composing our own prayers. The prayers in this next section, however, need not all be read at once. We can read through them at our leisure or come back to some of them later.

THE PSALMS

One of the earliest collections of religious prayers are the Psalms, many of which have been included in the traditional prayer book. They are attributed to King David, "the sweet singer of Israel," who lived three thousand years ago, and were probably preserved as part of a repertoire of hymns by the musical and vocal guilds in ancient Israel. The Eighth Psalm, for example, was probably composed under what Nahum Sarna describes as "a magnificent moonlit sky aglow with sparkling stars." The poem conveys the paradoxical image of the awesome divine presence, God's "splendor" in the world, juxtaposed against our own mortality. It reminds us that we are only a little less than divine:

O Lord, our Lord,
How majestic is Your Name throughout the earth,
You who have covered the heavens with Your splendor!
From the mouths of infants and sucklings
You have founded strength on account of Your foes, to put an end
*   to enemy and avenger.*
When I behold Your heavens, the work of Your fingers, the moon
*   and stars that You set in place—*
What is man that You are mindful of him?
Mortal man that You take note of him?
That You have made him little less than divine,
And adorned him with glory and majesty;
You have made him master over Your handiwork,
Laying the world at his feet, sheep and oxen all of them, and wild
*   beasts, too;*
The birds of heaven, the fish of the sea, whatever travels the paths
*   of the seas.*
Lord, our Lord, how majestic is Your name throughout the earth!

THE CELESTIAL FIRE

We hear the voice of God singing within Eleazar ben Kallir, who wrote mystical hymns to the unknowable God. God cannot be described except as ineffable. Whenever we try to describe God, our images falter, our language becomes inadequate. We can only describe God as a fire that is not consumed:

> You are a fire that devours fire; a fire that burns in dry and damp objects; a fire that glows in snow and ice; a fire that lies in wait like a lion; a fire that appears in many forms; an eternal fire that never dies; a fire that shines and blazes; a fire that rages and consumes; a fire that soars like a storm; a fire that ignites without wood; a fire that starts up again every day; a fire that is not whipped up by another fire . . .

LORD, WHERE SHALL I FIND YOU?

Saadiah Longo, in the sixteenth century, penned a hymn to the mysterious, infinite God. This God can only be described by using an oxymoron, as "concealed yet revealed." Consistent with the common wisdom of the Middle Ages, God is beyond knowledge and only God can know Himself. For if we knew the Infinite, we ourselves would be infinite. Therefore, the limitation of human knowledge is self-understanding:

> The living God is the cause, reason, and sustenance of everything that exists. Hidden yet revealed, I have seen Him with my heart's eye. The creator of opposites and unities, I have called Him one and unique. To one who asks me "How can this be?" I say: "If I knew, I would be Him!"

227

The most important medieval Hebrew poet, Judah Halevi, composed many hymns that have been included in various prayer books. One of his most popular poems expresses the longing of the soul for that which is beyond reach. Even as one yearns for the hidden God, one recognizes that God is present within the soul:

> God, where can I find You? Your place is hidden and sublime. Is there anywhere I do not find You? The whole earth is filled with Your presence. You are found within the deepest recesses, and You set the boundaries of the earth. You are the summit for those who are close, and a bastion for those who are distant . . . Although You sit on an exalted throne above us all, You are nearer to us than our own spirit and flesh . . . I have sought Your closeness, I have called to You with all my heart. And when I went out towards You, I found You coming towards me.

GOD AND THE SOUL

In a similar vein, Solomon ibn Gabirol describes a daily meditation. The poet poses like a beggar, with his face and palms raised upward toward heaven. He marvels at the understanding that although God is so infinite that He cannot be contained, the Infinite is most truly present in the human heart. Since God is present in our hearts, prayer is thus God singing within us. The poet calls out:

> *I pursue You day and night,*
> *I raise my hands and face to You.*
> *My thirsting heart yearns for You*
> *Like a beggar at the door.*
> *The heavens cannot contain You*
> *Though You dwell within me.*
> *Can I conceal Your presence within my heart*

When my longing for You overflows within me?
So, I will go on praising You
As long as the divine soul lives within me.

The soul is often depicted in medieval Hebrew synagogue poetry as a lover, as it is in this poem by Moses ibn Ezra:

My soul longs for You at night! My soul longs for her home, strives to reach her source, and yearns for her holy place day and night. She sees Your splendor in Your creations and wants to approach You. Day and night she speaks Your praises. Night and day.

OUT OF THE DEPTHS

Not all prayers are the song of the soul within us. Some prayers arise out of the pain within our hearts. One prayer by an anonymous poet outlining God's obligations to us is written in the form of the Ten Commandments. It conveys the pain of a soul betrayed by human suffering, which it lays at the feet of God:

Do not hold back from answering us when we call You with all our heart. Do not mock our weakness when we call You out of our desperation. Do not shout back at the meek and frail when we stand before You. Do not turn us away from Your door emptyhanded. Do not grieve or humiliate us when we make mistakes. Do not chastise us angrily when we wander or stray. Do not remind us of our youthful sins that we keep secretly to ourselves. Do not oppress us as strangers when we return to You, just bring us closer.

GOD AS KING

God appears to us in different images, some uplifting, others more challenging. Some prayers see God as the Infinite, while other prayers are soulful expressions of our sense of God as king. The High Holy Day prayer book includes a hymn to the King-God, who is both infinite and present within the world. God is not just a king but a king of kings of kings:

> *Blessed be His name and exalted the mention of the King over kings of kings, the Holy One, Blessed be He.*
> *He is the Lord over all His creatures, ruler over all His deeds, mighty above and below.*
> *There is no God in the heaven above and on the earth below beside Him.*
> *Therefore, it is our duty to thank Him and to bless Him.*

The thirteenth-century mystic, Jacob Hacohen, penned a hymn to the king aspect of God, the hidden, infinite God. The king, just and perfect, radiates His hidden light upon the human heart, pouring out divine wisdom upon it:

> May God send His hidden light to open the gates of relief to His servants and to illumine our hearts, sunk in darkness and gloom. May the great King, just and perfect, consider us and open the gates of wisdom for us, just as He did for our ancestors in days of old.

THE *SHECHINAH*

Rabbi Nachman of Bratslav returns to the idea that divinity, the feminine appearance of God, is infused throughout the world, especially in the human heart. For Nachman, this fullness of the heart is the essence of being a Jew:

> Master of the universe, Lord of all, who rules over all—You contain the world while the world cannot wholly contain You: Give me a heart of truth, a proper and pure heart, to serve and revere You, a true Jewish heart. Let my heart deserve to be a dwelling place for your *Shechinah*, let me draw Your great and holy presence into my heart just as Your *Shechinah* dwells in the heart of each and every one of Your holy people. And wherever I go in this world, with Your permission, may I find Your divinity there, come close to You, and unite with You. Purify my heart to serve You truthfully. Concentrate my heart to revere You. Create in me a pure heart and revive in me a proper spirit.

THE YEARNING SOUL

More recently, Rabbi Abraham Isaac Cook wrote deeply spiritual poetry that expresses the longing of his soul to break out of the confines of the physical world and unite with the source of all existence. The following is a meditation by the soaring soul as it yearns to meet God as He reaches out to us:

> *Expanses, expanses, expanses divine my soul craves.*
> *Confine me not in cages of substance and spirit.*
> *My soul soars the expanses of heaven,*
> *Walls of heart and walls of deed will not contain it.*
> *Morality, logic, custom—My soul soars above these,*
> *Above all that bears a name, above delight,*
> *Above every delight and beauty,*
> *Above all that is exalted and ethereal.*

231

I am love-sick—I thirst, I thirst for God,
As a deer for water brooks.
Alas, who can describe my pain,
Who will be a violin to express the songs of my grief,
Who will voice my bitterness, the pain of seeking utterance?
I thirst for truth, not for a conception of truth,
For I ride on its heights,
I am wholly absorbed by truth,
I am wholly pained by the anguish of expression . . .
Great is my pain and great my anguish,
O, my God, my God, be a help in my trouble,
Find for me the graces of expression,
Grant me language and the gift of utterance,
I shall declare before the multitudes
My fragments of Your truth, O my God.

Some of Rabbi Cook's other poetry expresses a universal longing for oneness:

Radiant is the world soul,
Full of splendor and beauty,
Full of life,
Of souls hidden,
Of treasures of the holy spirit,
Of fountains of strength,
Of greatness and beauty.
Proudly I ascend
Toward the heights of the world soul
That gives life to the universe.
How majestic the vision,
Come, enjoy,
Come, find peace,
Embrace delight,
Taste and see that God is good.

Why spend your substance on what does not nourish
And your labor on what cannot satisfy?
Listen to me, and you will enjoy what is good,
And find delight in what is truly precious.

This is the kind of poetry that, in an earlier era, would have been included in the prayer book. His poetry, however, is more personal than many of the traditional Jewish prayers and may provide an attractive alternative for someone who is approaching Jewish prayer for the first time and through translation.

MOMENTOUS PRAYERS

Many spiritual poems are prayers from the soul. The following poem by Judah Halevi is a morning prayer directed to the poet's own soul. He cautions the soul not to believe that the transient gifts of time last forever nor to view the sensual pleasures of the world as anything but illusions. The only lasting pursuit is to "be before Your Lord," the permanent, unchanging source of all life:

Unique one—seek God at dawn, enter,
Let your song rise like incense before Him.
For if you run after the vanities of time
Mistaking enchantments for truth
Wandering after them night and day
Playing by night and sleeping by day—
Know that you have grasped at nothing
More than a tree whose branches will tomorrow die.
So stand before your God and King
Who protects you under His spirit
And let every one in whom the soul lives
Magnify and sanctify His name.

233

Another morning prayer by Judah Halevi counsels us to look inward and meditate upon the soul, the miraculous presence of God within each human being. When we meditate and look deep within our own hearts, we become the ear that hears what God is saying to us—as if we ourselves stand at Mount Sinai. Our meditation is essentially personal and private, and possibly nocturnal, but it leads us to wake up in the morning ready to praise God for the divine within us:

> *My meditations about You have awakened me*
> *And made me aware of Your love.*
> *They helped me to appreciate the soul that You created*
> *And anchored in me—though I do not understand how.*
> *My heart experienced You as sure as if I were standing at Sinai.*
> *I pursued You in my thoughts.*
> *Your presence passed over me as a cloud.*
> *My dreams awakened me from sleep*
> *To bless Your presence, my God.*

Meshullam da Piera, a thirteenth-century Kabbalist, offered the following morning prayer:

> *Singing together, when the morning stars sing at dawn and light*
> *is all about; when the night ends and gloom disperses and my sun*
> *rises in the east; when my dreams awaken me from sleep and my*
> *being wakes up from night sleep—I praise the dawn with music*
> *and greet the day with my song.*

Special prayers appropriate for each day of the week can be chosen. For example, this mystical meditation for Sunday recalls the first day of Creation:

> *May it be Your will,*
> *My God and God of my fathers,*
> *Artist of Creation—*

Just as You have called the world into being on this day,
Unifying Your universe,
Suspending therein the upper and lower worlds
With Your word—
So with your abundant love
Unify my heart,
And the heart of all Your people, the House of Israel,
To love and revere Your name.
Open our eyes to the light of Your Torah.
For with You is the source of life.
By Your light shall we see the light.

There is also this traditional prayer that can be said before going to sleep:

Blessed are You, O Lord our God, King of the universe, who lowers the shackles of sleep on my eyes and slumber on my eyelids; who brings light to my eye—May it be Your will, O Lord my God and God of my ancestors, to lay me down in peace, and to raise me up again in life and peace. May the good impulse control me, and not the evil impulse; save me from the evil impulse, and from serious illness; may my dreams and bad thoughts never frighten me. May my bed be peaceful before You lest my sleep turn into my death. Blessed are You, O Lord, who illuminates the world with His presence.

A PRAYER AFTER HEALING

The Thirtieth Psalm is a prayer of thanksgiving for a person who has recovered from a terrible illness. The poet shares his own terrifying and painful experience in public with a community that supports and nourishes him through his ordeal. He thinks at first that his suffering is the result of divine anger. He soon realizes that God does

235

"hide His face from us." However, it appears so when we are too proud to recognize that God is always with us. The following is a poem that reminds us that God desires our health and life:

> I lift You up in praise, O Lord, for You have lifted me up and not
>   let my enemies rejoice against me.
> Lord, my God, I cried out to You and You healed me.
> Lord, You brought me up from the dead, preserved me from going
>   down into the pit.
> You faithful of the Lord, sing to Him, and praise His holy name.
> For He is angry but a moment, and when He is pleased there is
>   life.
> One may lie down weeping at nightfall;
> But at dawn there are shouts of joy.
> When I was untroubled, I thought, "I shall never be shaken,"
> For You, O Lord, when You were pleased
> Made me firm as a mighty mountain.
> When You hid Your face I was terrified.
> I called to You, O Lord, to my Lord I made appeal.
> What is to be gained by my death, from my descent into the pit?
> Can dust praise You?
> Can it declare Your faithfulness?
> Hear, O Lord, and have mercy on me,
> O Lord, be my help!
> You turned my lament into dancing,
> You undid my sackcloth and guided me with joy,
> That my whole being might sing hymns to you endlessly.
> O Lord, my God, I will praise You forever.

THE FEAR OF DEATH

The fear of death has prompted many poets to caution us to remember our mortality:

Let man remember all the days of his life that he is being led to death. Stealthily he journeys on, day after day; he thinks he is at rest, like a man who is motionless onboard ship, while the ship is flying on the wings of the wind.

Nachman Syrkin, a modern Hebrew author, composed this prayer as he approached his own death with the certainty of eternal life:

Blessed are You, O Lord our God, Spirit of the universe, who has brought me to the bridge across the river of life. When my own dim light will set, fusing into the light that shines upon the world and blends into eternity—the saga of my light will come to an end. At the twilight of my life, I stand with emotion and full awareness before a new dawn. As a man who is about to die and be born anew, I feel a oneness with and responsibility toward eternal existence. This is what our ancestors realized when they said: "Hear, O Israel, the Lord our God, the Lord is one." Blessed is the God of life and death, of light and love.

SELF-IMPROVEMENT

A prayer from the Talmud, included at the end of the *Amidah* prayer, is a prayer for integrity and moral character, for humility, and for divine protection. It also asks for defense against more mundane difficulties, such as an unsuitable spouse. The version included in the prayer book diplomatically removes the reference to "a wicked spouse."

237

My God, keep my tongue from evil and my lips from speaking deceit. May my soul be quiet before those who malign me. May my soul be as humble to all as the dust. Open my heart to Your teaching so that my soul may seek Your commandments. Deliver me from misfortune, from the evil impulse, from a wicked spouse, and from all the terrible things that happen in the world. And for those who scheme against me—quickly thwart their desire and destroy their plans.

The Ari composed this prayer for overcoming our more base desires:

What is it, my nature, why do you always oppress me and treat me each day as if I were your enemy? Day in, day out, you set traps for no reason until you finally snare me. You have been my oppressor and enemy since childhood. You have gnashed your teeth against me in hatred. My soul has wanted to follow you, as if in your shadow you would protect me from distress.

Other prayers have a confessional quality, such as this one:

I know, my God, that I have done violence to myself, that I have brought destruction upon my Temple. My own crimes have trapped me, my lies have risen up against me.

Avrom Reisen was a Yiddish writer from Russia who emigrated to America. His confession is a plea for inner strength:

Teach me, teach me how
To deal with the world, O Lord!
And how I may transform
Evil into good.
If a wild beast lurks
In our humanity,
Let me turn it toward

238

A mild humility.
I've seen a trainer in
The circus tame a tiger;
See him de-fang a snake.
Lord, let me be wiser.
Bless me with patience, too,
And make me iron hard
That I may show mankind
At least such wonders, Lord.

The modern Hebrew poet Zelda offers us the following:

Every man has a name, given him by God, and given him by his father and mother. Every man has a name given him by his physique and by his way of smiling, and given him by his clothes. Every man has a name given him by the mountains and given him by his own confines. Every man has a name given him by the planets and given him by his neighbors. Every man has a name given him by his sins and given him by his desire. Every man has a name given him by his enemies and given him by those who love him. Every man has a name given him by how he celebrates and given him by his occupation. Every man has a name given him by the seasons of the year and given him by his blindness. Every man has a name given him by the sea and given him by his death.

WOMEN'S PRAYERS

The greatest failing of Judaism has been the lack of attentiveness to the spiritual integrity of women. The traditional prayers that have been included in the prayer book were almost all composed by men for men. This does not mean that Jewish women did not develop their own rich spiritual tradition. The Bible includes women's prayers, in particular, Miriam's Song at the Sea (Exodus 15:20–22), the Song of Deborah (Judges 5), and Hannah's Prayer (I Samuel 1:11). Aside from these special prayers, women composed prayers largely on their own, which were not included in the traditional prayer books.

One of the most important records of Jewish spirituality is found in the collections of women's devotional prayers, known as *techines* (petitions). The *techines* were mostly composed in Yiddish, the everyday language of the Jews of eastern Europe. They were published and distributed widely but with little recognition from men. They became the basis of an accepted women's liturgy that paralleled the required daily, Sabbath, and festival prayers for men. More important, however, the *techines* came from the heart and spoke directly to the human condition. They are often the written version of spontaneous prayers that address God intimately. They are among the best examples of spiritual song in Judaism.

There are *techines* for every significant moment in life from birth to death. There are *techines* for safe childbirth, healing after delivering a child, miscarriage, weaning, a child starting school, success in parenting difficult children, a girl's first menstruation, love, betrothal, engagement, marriage, sickness, and death. The *techines* include prayers for every holiday and even emphasize certain minor holidays, such as *Rosh Chodesh*, as having special significance for women.

Many *techines* are private meditations that women recited before performing certain *mitzvot*. A *techineh* for lighting the Sabbath candles expresses a mother's hopes and dreams for her children:

In honor of God, in honor of our ritual, and in honor of the holy Sabbath that the Lord has given us and commanded us to observe, may I perform this mitzvah *properly and may it be valued as equivalent to all of the 613* mitzvot *of all Israel. Amen, may it be Your will! Your words are a candle at my feet so that all my children may walk in God's path, and may the* mitzvah *of my candle lighting be accepted that my children's eyes may be illu-*

mined by the precious and holy Torah. May their planets shine in the heavens so that they may be able to earn a decent living for the spouse and children. Amen!

There is a prayer for pregnancy:

God is an awesome artist who can shape form within form, flawless and perfect in all its dimensions, able to see and hear, to move back and forth. Thus does He shape the embryo in the womb of its mother.

Another *techineh* for pregnancy expresses the anxiety of a mother and her hopes and dreams for her child:

May I, your servant, who am with child—Your creation—carry full term and give birth to a healthy child who will become a pious Jew and serve You heart and soul; one who will love Torah and revere God according to Your holy will, a beautiful plant in the Jewish vineyard for the majesty of Israel. Amen.

A mother's prayer includes a *techineh* for a sick child:

Lord of the universe, how I suffer with worry and anxiety about my little children who have been afflicted with illness! Lord of the universe, what have the little children done? The poor things have not sinned. Remove from them every unfortunate decree, compassionate and righteous one, so that they will soon enjoy the merit of small children who study your Torah each day with their teacher. Enable them to live with their fathers and mothers so that we may be able to bring them to Torah, to the bridal canopy, and to good deeds. May we live to have many children, and grandchildren, in honor and dignity. Amen.

Another *techineh* can be recited at the time of a child's weaning:

Your wonders and protection over all creatures are so great and numerous they cannot be counted. When a child begins to be weaned, You give him (her) teeth with which to chew food. For the precious gift, for the little pearl I have found in my child's mouth, I thank You and praise Your beloved name. May the remainder of his (her) teeth cut through easily so that he (she) will be able to do Your will, to eat and gather strength with which to go to school and study Your holy Torah. May he (she) become a good and pious person, enabling both You and men to rejoice in him (her). Amen.

Rosh Chodesh became an important holiday for Jewish women. One of the *techines* for the New Moon is a prayer for general well-being:

May it be Your will, O Lord our God and God of our fathers, that You renew for us this month and cause good and blessing to come to us. And may You give us a long life—and life in the world-to-come, a life of goodness, a life of blessing. May God sustain us and grant us a life of ample sustenance, with satisfaction and without sorrow. May we be granted clothes in accordance with our status and a life of bodily vigor. May our bones be strengthened. May we be granted a life of awe of God and may our children believe in God, praised be He. May they walk in God's path, and may they succeed in every step of their way. May we be granted a life without shame or reproach. May we not be humiliated in this world or in the world-to-come before the celestial court. Grant us a life of wealth and honor. May we raise our children to Torah, marriage, and good deeds. Dear God, may You give us a life in which You fulfill the desires of our hearts for good. Amen.

242

Most of the traditional prayers, and many *techines*, invoke the merit of the ancestors Abraham, Isaac, and Jacob as we ask God to remember us. Some *techines*, however, invoke the merits of Sarah, Rebecca, Rachel, and Leah. The following prayer for *Rosh Hashanah* even asks that they intercede with God on our behalf:

We beseech our mother Sarah that she pray for us at this hour of judgment so that we may be judged innocent. Have mercy, our mother, on your children. Make a special plea that our children not be separated from us. Now is the time for you to plead for us that God's attribute of mercy will be raised on our behalf. I also beseech our mother Rebecca to pray for her children and for our father and mother, that they should not—mercy and peace—be separated from us. We also beseech our mother Rachel to pray for us that we may be inscribed and sealed for a good year and that we may never know any sorrow. We also beseech our mother Leah to plead for us. May we be nourished by your beloved holy hand. Amen.

FORMING A PRAYER GROUP

How can we navigate our way to a more spiritual prayer life if we are not comfortable or familiar with the synagogue service? As with the Torah study groups, we can form small prayer groups within a congregation or independently, with the guidance of a leader or without. We can begin by identifying a group of people who share our interests and who are willing to meet together on some regular basis, preferably on a Friday night or Saturday morning. New prayer groups can be set up within existing synagogues. This is not always easily done, since many synagogues only want to sponsor one service under their roof. Synagogues should recognize that different people have different Jewish needs. Standard services are often geared to a certain level of knowledge and commitment, and we often feel left out of services if we do not fit the norm. More important, the spiritual life of congregations will be stronger if they customize the services by offering more than one choice and encourage people to find the service that is right for them.

We can form a group within a congregation that will meet at the same time as the congregation does. We can find a teacher through the local congregations who can help us examine the meaning of individual prayers and learn the accompanying melodies. Perhaps we start with only chanting a few prayers each week and gradually increase our repertoire as our familiarity grows. We could experiment with alternative prayers or compose our own prayers to interpolate among the traditional prayers.

The most important challenge is to start at the beginning again by ourselves or with others who are at the same place. We can pursue learning more about the traditional prayers through exploring the way our predecessors heard God singing within them. Or we can restore heart and soul to our own Jewish lives by listening to the song of God within our souls and bringing that song back to Judaism. Then, we will have relearned the *niggun* of Judaism. All we need to do now is to push forward bravely and we will find no obstacle.

Chapter Seven

ISRAEL SINGS ALL THE
MELODIES OF THE WORLD

Jacob was left alone. And a man wrestled with him until the
break of dawn. When he saw that he had not prevailed
against him, he wrenched Jacob's hip at its socket, so that
the socket of his hip was strained as he wrestled with him.
Then he said, "Let me go, for dawn is breaking." But he
answered, "I will not let you go, unless you bless me." Said
the other, "What is your name?" He replied, "Jacob." Said
he, "Your name shall no longer be Jacob, but Israel, for you
have striven with beings divine and human, and have
prevailed."

—*Genesis 32:25–29*

Now that we have found the clearing, lit the fire, and sung the
niggun, we need to explore the ongoing story of the Jewish
people. We need to understand the dynamics of Jewish history so
that we can better understand how we arrived at today's crossroads.
For if we want to understand why the continuation of Judaism is
important, we need to better understand the place of Judaism within
the world. In this chapter, we will explore the relationship between
Judaism and other world cultures, the breakdown of traditional Judaism in the modern era, and the various denominations that constitute Judaism. We will see that Judaism has a moral mission in the
world that compels us to live within, not apart from, the rest of
society.

Judaism has survived, not by closing itself off from the world, but
by fully living within the world and embracing the best in every
culture. Rabbi Nachman of Bratslav said that everything—every na-

tion, religion, philosophy, and science—has its own *niggun* and that each one has a different spiritual source. The *niggun* of the Jewish people is made up of all the *niggunim* of the world and raises all of the individual *niggunim* to their divine source. That is why some Hasidic *niggunim* are even taken from non-Jewish melodies. More important, it means that there is a spark of holiness waiting to be found in every culture. In this chapter, we will see that the Jewish people embrace the best of the cultures with whom we have lived, while attempting to elevate what we have acquired even higher.

THE JEWISH MISSION

The Jewish people are called by many names. In biblical times, we were called "Israel," the name that God gave Jacob after he struggled with the mysterious stranger on the banks of the Yabbok River. After wrestling all night with Jacob, the stranger could not defeat him and conceded at dawn. Before departing, the stranger blessed Jacob and said: "Your name shall no longer be Jacob, but Israel, for you have striven with beings divine and human, and have prevailed" (Genesis 32:29). The name "Israel" means "Struggler of God" and implies that Jacob struggled successfully with God that night and won. But the passage states that Jacob struggled with God *and* men, not just with God. The man with whom he struggled was himself.

The night-struggle is another example of how the Torah describes events that take place within us as truly real events, as if they occurred on the riverbank itself. But this struggle really took place within Jacob's soul at another pivotal moment in his life. Jacob wrestled within himself that night, as he did earlier at Beth El, with both the divine and human dimensions of his soul. In wrestling with God and man, he struggled with whether he would realize the divine within himself or continue as he had up until this point in his life to struggle with and sneak around his brutish brother, Esau. In strug-

246

gling all night with both God and men, Jacob resolved to live on the higher, spiritual level of seeing the divine within himself and seeking the path of God within the world. This earned him the new name, "Israel, the struggler of God." His fight was not with others but with the constant challenge to realize the divine within himself, within others, and within the world. Jacob's descendants became known as the people Israel, and the land in which this people first struggled with creating God's kingdom on earth was called the Land of Israel, the land of struggling with God and men.

The Jewish people have a unique mission and purpose in the world. Our responsibility as "Israel, the struggler of God" is to conduct a moral effort to bring together the divine aspirations and earthly reality. The sparks of light in our world are there for the gathering. The human task is to harvest these flashes of light that were exiled in the world and complete the task that God began but could not complete.

To be a member of the Jewish people is to be counted among those who wrestle with the conflicting pressures of being human and who struggle to raise the divine sparks and see God face-to-face in the world. The struggle is not only an individual responsibility but a communal one. Every effort of the Jewish people should be directed toward helping individuals rise higher and higher on the ladder placed on earth whose top reaches heaven. Likewise, every effort of the Jewish community should serve the mission of realizing the divine in the world.

We are one people with many voices. We are a people to whom nothing human is alien. We embrace all the cultures of the world to learn the best that the world has to offer. But from these, we blend the best that we have learned into our civilization. At the heart of Jewish civilization is the moral imperative to see the world not as it is, but as it can be, to bring down God upon the earth.

247

We are also the people that resist accepting surface appearances. We are an intense, persistent people pursuing the depth of matters, seeking truth even to its innermost parts. We reject the superficial in favor of the profound. Sometimes we seek relief in the distractions of the world because the truth is often a dreadful burden. The novelist Philip Roth, in *American Pastoral*, calls this quality of Jewishness an "uncompromising dedication to the essential, to the things that matter most." As he described it, we sometimes yearn hopelessly for the escape from the burden of truth. The truth fills us with dread and anything other than the truth is empty entertainment. The Jewish path is to confront the truth of life directly.

WHY HAVE THE JEWS SURVIVED?

Throughout history, Jewish communities have attempted to create social organizations that promote the restoration and repair of the world. During the period of the ancient Israelite monarchy, the laws of the Torah, based on the principle that all people are created in the image of God, governed society and were enforced by the king and judges. The governing principles of ancient Israel were justice and righteousness. Although the full implications of these principles were never fully achieved in their time—women were subservient to men and slaves were subject to their masters—the laws emphasized the sanctity of life by establishing protection for the rights of persons and the sacredness of human life. Murder was punishable by death and physical violence was punished by corporal punishment. The integrity of the judicial system and the strict laws of evidence were established to afford all members of society equal protection under the law. Wealth and privilege earned a plaintiff or defendant no special standing in court. Greater protection was afforded to the vulnerable members of society, including women, the poor, orphans, and resident aliens. Despite tolerance of slavery, masters were obligated to treat their slaves humanely and with justice and compassion. Economic activity had to be conducted on the basis of scrupulous honesty. Compassion was the guiding principle in social relations and

248

was to be expressed in acts of kindness and generosity and in forbidding revenge, hateful speech, and cruelty.

According to the Torah, these universal laws are applicable to every society. They were also the terms of the covenant between God and the people Israel that should be enforced by the Jewish community. Morality is the calling of the Jewish people as a whole and of every individual member. Still, human history, as it is portrayed by the Hebrew Bible, shows how wide the gap is between the ideal and the reality. The moral shortcomings of the biblical figures show realistically that the struggle for goodness is constant and requires unrelenting effort. To be human is to struggle and to fail sometimes, but always to return again to the moral effort. When society appears to drift too far from its moral ideals, the Hebrew prophets bring us back to the core principles.

The prophetic message is that moral behavior is a more fundamental principle than ritual practice. Moral behavior reflects the belief that God created us in the divine image and invested us with the responsibility to raise the sparks and repair the world. Ritual practice is the expression of the moral teaching of Judaism and cannot exist apart from moral behavior. The kingdom must be founded on justice and righteousness, not ritual practices. The Jewish ideal is the moral human being who struggles with goodness, not the privileged royal dynasty or temple priest. The prophet Hosea pleads: "Hear this, O priests; Attend, O House of Israel; And give ear, O royal house: For right conduct is your responsibility" (Hosea 5:1).

The realization of this ideal became more difficult to achieve after the Romans defeated the Jewish struggle for national independence and destroyed the Holy Temple of Jerusalem in 70 C.E. The dispersion of the Jewish people resulted in their subjugation to empires that often barely tolerated their presence. Jews living in the Roman empire were members of a vanquished people that refused to disappear and still preferred to render unto God rather than unto Caesar. Under medieval Christian rule, Judaism was a hated and despised religion that should, according to church doctrine, disappear. By their presence, the Jews continued to serve as a reminder of the treachery of their ancestors, who supposedly crucified Jesus. The Church tolerated the "witness people" in its midst and attempted to reduce the quality of their life to as miserable a level as possible.

COMMUNITIES OF RIGHTEOUSNESS

During the late Middle Ages, the Jewish communities in Poland established a new form of community self-governance, the *Kehillah* (community). The *Kehillah* was an internal communal framework sanctioned by the government and based on Jewish values, religious law, and local custom. Membership in the *Kehillah* included all local, tax-paying Jewish residents. The *Kehillah* treasury supported many charitable institutions and voluntary self-help organizations within each Jewish community. The community treasury funded the *cheder*, a schoolroom for the education for poor children, and the regional *yeshivah*, a high school and higher-education institution where select boys studied Torah and religious literature. Every community supported a variety of charities, including a *hekdesh*, an infirmary for indigent Jews, and a *beis yesomim*, or orphanage. Special funds were designated for the *chalukah*, the fund for Jews living in Israel; *hachnasas kallah*, funds for indigent brides; and *pidyon shvuyyim*, the reserve used to ransom Jewish prisoners from illegal detention in gentile jails.

In addition to the funded organizations, every community maintained voluntary organizations, either called *hevrah* (society) or *kehillah kedoshah* (holy community). Every community had its own *hevras bikkur cholim* ("Visiting the Sick Society"); a voluntary medical self-help association; the *hevra kadisha* ("Holiness Society"), the Jewish burial society; and *hevras Shas* ("Talmud Society"), an adult lifelong learning organization.

Each of these community associations exemplified the Jewish

value system of justice and righteousness based on Torah and the accumulated wisdom of the Jewish tradition. All of them personified the Jewish struggle to repair the world through voluntary acts of kindness and compassion.

Many of these institutions have survived in the modern era in new forms. The medieval *kehillah* organization is the basis of the modern Jewish community federations. The *hekdesh* and *bikkur cholim* societies have become the Jewish hospitals throughout the United States. The *beis yesomim, hachnasas kallah*, and *pidyon shvu-yyim* societies have adapted to the modern social-assistance needs in the United States and now provide services, for example, tailored to the Jewish family. The *chalukah* has evolved into the United Israel Appeal.

The mission of the Jewish people today is the same as it always has been—to repair the world. The struggle to raise the sparks and repair the world is an individual and communal responsibility. The struggle is conducted not with force but with moral power and the physical and financial resources that we each can contribute to that struggle. The faithful application of the spiritual tenets of Judaism has preserved the Jews since antiquity. Jews have perceived the world through the lens of these principles—realizing justice, righteousness, and divinity in the everyday. Historically, from the time a Jew woke up in the morning until the time he went to sleep, his day was structured by the practice of Judaism. Through the course of the calendar year, the weekly cycle of Sabbath and the annual cycle of holidays defined the spiritual universe in which he lived.

RAISED ALTARS IN ALIEN PLACES

251

Throughout our history, we Jews have lived in non-Jewish societies. We often saw these societies as alien places, as stations in the course of our long exile, and as temporary shelters on our long, arduous path back to the Land of Israel. We saw our lives there as a challenge because it was impossible to live a full Jewish life under the rule of gentile nations. The weekly Torah readings reinforced the awareness that God had promised the Land of Israel as an inheritance to the sons of Jacob. The poet Judah Halevi lived in Spain, the extreme western edge of the Muslim world, and longed for Jerusalem, in the East: "My heart is in the East, and I am in the remotest corner of the West." The consciousness of exile pervaded the Jewish mind throughout the centuries.

The Jewish sense that our own sins had brought about our exile was expressed in the festival prayers: "Because of our sins, we were exiled from our homeland." They developed the mentality of the victim who blamed himself for his circumstances. They did not only blame the world powers that had plundered the Land of Israel, desolated Jerusalem, and dispersed the Jews throughout the Persian and Roman Empires. They credited God's withdrawal of his protection from the Holy Temple to their own failure to live up to the prophetic challenge of justice and righteousness. They believed that God allowed the Holy Temple to be destroyed because of the gratuitous hatred that became pervasive in first-century Jerusalem. The Temple was destroyed, they thought, because of the lack of civility within society. The Talmud cited, as an example, the account of an otherwise reasonable person and community leader who had humiliated and disgraced his enemy in a public social gathering. Because of this violation of the principle of respect for the dignity of another person, the Temple was destroyed.

The exiles and their descendants never lost hope in the eventual restoration of the Jewish people to their proper place in the world arena. They believed that despite the poverty of their current circumstances, God had not abandoned them. They taught that "everywhere that Israel went into exile, the presence of God went with them." They developed a religious outlook that deferred human gratification to the afterlife because pleasure in this world was elusive. In the afterlife, they dreamed, there would be no sexuality, no commerce, no hatred or envy, and no rivalry. Their souls would enjoy perpetual closeness to God and the illumination of God's radiant presence. They imagined a future age when the vicissitudes of their daily lives would be erased. They imagined a future age when they would be restored to their ancestral homeland, the Holy Temple would be rebuilt, a descendant of King David would reign over the House of Israel, the nations that oppressed them would beg their forgiveness, and they would be free of foreign domination. Some went further in their dreams and fantasies and believed that, in this future age, the restrictions of Jewish law would be lifted, women would have no pain in childbirth, food would sprout everywhere, and human beings would be 160 feet tall.

Despite the sense of alienation and reliance on the unlikely kindness of strangers, we raised our altars in alien places. One of the earliest of these Diaspora centers was the Greco-Roman Empire. The expansion of the Greco-Roman Empire throughout the Mediterranean saw the conquest of Israel, which the Romans named "Palestina" after the ancient Philistines, by Alexander the Great in 333 B.C.E. Many Jews resisted the influences of Hellenistic Greco-Roman culture and religion. In 167 B.C.E., the Maccabees, who opposed the influence of Hellenistic culture on their fellow Jews, launched a revolt against the Jewish assimilationists. They fought against the growing acceptance of pagan worship in Palestine and against the Greco-Roman values that threatened to replace Jewish culture and disrupt the traditional patterns of Jewish life.

In the next century, the thriving Jewish community in Alexandria fully adopted the prevailing Hellenistic lifestyle. They translated the Hebrew Bible into Greek (the *Septuagint*) and embraced the teachings of Plato and Aristotle, which introduced the notion of an impersonal, unreachable, unknowable God. Still, Greco-Roman society deeply believed in and worshiped a pantheon of pagan gods that were anathema to the Jews. Many non-Jewish Greeks and Romans were attracted by the Jewish belief in God and the spiritual and moral teachings of Judaism. A small but significant number of Greco-

Romans converted to Judaism, and a larger number, known as *se-bomenoi* ("God-fearing men"), embraced Jewish belief but did not fully convert to Judaism.

Greco-Roman civilization had little lasting effect on the Jewish culture of this period. In fact, Judaism developed in the first five centuries of the Common Era in clear opposition and open hostility to the pagan and idolatrous culture of the dominant Greco-Roman Empire. The Judaism of this era came to be known as Talmudic Judaism, out of respect for the major written body of Jewish law and lore from this period, and as rabbinic Judaism, in deference to the authors of this corpus. The Talmud and related writings present a comprehensive guide to how Jewish values are embodied in the daily practice and behaviors of the Jewish people. Talmudic Judaism created an architecture of the human spirit that was guided by the principle that the presence of God could be realized in the way that we conduct our daily affairs.

A Talmudic Jew believed that the primary human responsibility is to imitate the moral attributes of God: "Just as He is gracious and compassionate, so you should be gracious and compassionate. Just as He clothes the naked, so you should also clothe the naked." But the Talmud also introduced changes to Judaism and modified elements of biblical Judaism. Religious responsibility, including the requirement of learning Torah and observing detailed ritual commandments, shifted from the priests who officiated in the Holy Temple to the rabbis and every adult male member of the community. Despite the patriarchal nature of Talmudic society, it shifted the burden of being holy from the Holy Temple to the home. Every adult male had the responsibility to be as holy as a priest. Every home was potentially as sacred as the Holy Temple. Every family meal where blessings were recited and Torah was discussed around the dinner table was as pleasing to God as the sacrifices offered by the priests in the Holy Temple. Judaism became the legacy of every member of the community. The Talmudic rabbis introduced other teachings that had not been part of biblical Judaism, including belief in the afterlife, the expectation of a Messiah, and the idea that a convert to Judaism can voluntarily become a full member of the Jewish people.

THE PEOPLE OF THE BOOK

The Arab Islamic expansion in the seventh century defeated and destroyed the Christian Byzantine Empire in the eastern Mediterranean and the Persian Sassanian Empire in western Asia. In the process, Islam took control of areas that had long nurtured highly developed religious cultures. The Islamic strategy of rapid military conquest by small military expeditions enabled the Muslims to extend their control over greater areas than they could govern themselves. The Islamic conquerors often turned to the local population, particularly to the minorities who had been oppressed by the previous regime, to administer the conquered areas. Frequently, the administration of the newly conquered territories was turned over to dissident Christians, Jews, and other non-Arabs who were beholden to the Muslims for having relieved them from the oppression of the previous regime and improved their own status. Thus, the Arab Muslims relied on Jews and Christians in the period of conquest and expansion that began in the seventh century and continued through the Muslim conquest of Spain in 711.

The Islamic conquerors, who came to rely on their Christian and Jewish subjects, developed great respect for the culture of the conquered peoples. Jews living under Islamic rule were treated as a protected minority with religious and property rights. The Muslims, who respected their ethical and monotheistic traditions, called us "the people of the Book," a name that we later began to call ourselves. However, Jews did not have the same rights as Muslims and were required to accept a socially inferior status in relation to them. The Jews willingly accepted their status because it offered a greater degree of legal protection than they had had under Christian rule.

From the Jews, Muslims received teachings about what constituted the moral and spiritual ideal of a human being and incorporated them into Islam. Many of these teachings became the basis of Sufism, the Islamic spiritual and mystical tradition. From the dissident Christian sects of the defeated Byzantine Empire, the Muslims learned about the ancient writings of the Greek philosophers and scientists such as Plato, Aristotle, Plotinus, Galen, Hippocrates, and Dioscorides. Many of these writings had been viewed as heretical by the Byzantine Church, which sought to expunge them. The Muslims, however, viewed them as revelations of ancient wisdom and embraced them as valuable discoveries. Christians were commissioned to translate the ancient libraries into Arabic, and the new manuscripts were soon distributed throughout the Muslim world and studied avidly. The spread of this ancient wisdom contributed to a renaissance of philosophic, scientific, mathematic, and astronomic knowledge from the eighth to the twelfth centuries. As Islam came under great pressure from the Crusades and the effort to reconquer "Christian" lands from the Muslim "infidels," the Islamic renaissance declined and Islam assumed a more conservative, militant, and fundamentalist character, which it has retained until today.

Jews, most notably those living in Muslim Spain, translated many of these great classics of ancient wisdom from Arabic into Hebrew and then into Latin. The Jews developed a highly secular and literate culture of learning based on the writings of Plato, Aristotle, and others, while refining their own ancient heritage of the Torah and the more recent Talmud. The Jews in Muslim Spain produced a rich tapestry of culture that wove together elements of their inherited religious legacy with the imported secular culture of their day. Jewish translators were also directly responsible for transmitting the classical wisdom of ancient Greece and Rome to Christian Europe several centuries before the Italian Renaissance.

Jews living in the Islamic Empire, especially in Spain, contributed new religious concepts and teachings to the Judaism they had inherited. From the classical Greek philosophic tradition they learned that the biblical portrayal of God as a transcendent being with human characteristics, such as emotions, passions, and desires, was inconsistent with reason and required reinterpretation. If God is transcendent, how could He have human emotions, passions, and desires? They concluded that "Torah speaks in the language of the sons of man" through metaphors and allegories that should not be taken literally. They refined their view of God and introduced a new Jewish belief that God's transcendence is so absolute that He is impersonal, unknowable, and unreachable. They came to believe in Aristotle's God—the Unmoved Mover, the First Cause—instead of the God of Abraham, Isaac, and Jacob. They came to the conclusion that intellectual knowledge is a force for unity among people of different religions and is more fundamental a human principle than the divisions among adherents of different religions. They found new modes of interpreting the Torah that validated their new understanding that God is the impersonal, transcendent source of the universal, moral law.

THE UNFINISHED SYMPHONY

Despite the religious sense of living in exile, Jews actually developed a deep sense of belonging to those alien places in which they resided. Jews developed a portable civilization that could be taken with them from one place to another as circumstances required. The circumstances of anti-Semitism frequently required Jews' sudden and rapid departure from lands they had long called home. The Jews were expelled from Rome in 50, England in 1290, France in 1306 and 1394, Spain in 1492, Portugal in 1497, parts of Germany in 1348, Lithuania in 1495, and Prague in 1744.

As we moved from one country to the next, we brought our civilization with us. We brought our own spiritual outlook with us and developed a rich Jewish life within our homes, schools, and synagogues. We also learned from the environment about the dominant non-Jewish culture and balanced the best of it with the best of ours. Out of this synthesis came new expressions of Jewish culture. As we moved from one civilization to another, we brought the cumulative traditions of all the cultures we had absorbed along with us.

Rabbi Nachman of Bratslav once said that every nation, every religion, has its own *niggun* (melody) that comes from the one, original *niggun* of Judaism. If we understand music as a metaphor for culture, we can say that Judaism is both a unique melody and a world music. We have sung our own song and taught this special song to the world. When we entered the Diaspora, we began to learn the songs of other choruses and the music of other orchestras. We learned to play harmony as we added other melodies to our own song line. We also sang the songs that we had learned along the way as we joined the chorus of each new civilization that we entered. In each land, we learned to harmonize the songs of the past with the new melodies that we learned. We taught the songs of other choruses with which we were familiar to the new audiences that we encountered in our travels. Out of this synthesis came new Jewish melodies that were often different from those that had been sung before. But we always returned to the melody. As a popular Hebrew folk song says: "Time advances, the year passes, but the melody lives on forever."

The Jewish people are like an orchestra trained in the best music schools in the world. We have played in the great symphonies of Greece and Rome, the Byzantine Empire, the Golden Age of Islam, medieval and modern Europe, and now the United States and Israel. Our orchestra has not always been welcome and sometimes we have been forced to leave the concert hall prematurely, but we have always absorbed the best theory and practice and applied them to our own score. As we moved from one civilization to another, not usu-

258

ally by choice, we brought the cumulative traditions of all the cultures we had absorbed along with us. We brought the best of what we had learned along the way to each new civilization that we entered. We cross-pollinated different cultures and created a strong and durable Judaism.

Long ago, we taught the world a new melody of faith and morality. Since then, we have acquired all the goodness of the world in our travels through each civilization. Although most of the cultures through which we have passed are now gone, we have preserved the best of what they had to offer and have transmitted it to their successors. We liberated the sparks of holiness in each civilization, often paying the terrible price of suffering in the process. As the Hasidic leader Rabbi Elimelech of Lizansk said, "It is Israel's particular task to work hard at freeing the trapped holy sparks."

For this reason, we believe that the Jewish people is like an orchestra that is writing its own unfinished symphony. We also believe that our mission is to make a symphony out of all the songs of the different peoples of the world based on our history as a dispersed people. And what is that symphony? It is called "Seeing the World Not as It Is but as It Can Be." That is the real theme of the Jewish people. But the symphony has been interrupted and the melody is hard to recapture.

THE CRISIS OF MODERNITY

The breakdown of Jewish life from within began two hundred years ago in western Europe. How did it occur? After centuries of isolation and persecution, the Jews began to seek emancipation and acceptance within the emerging modern societies of Europe. The European Enlightenment philosophers taught that all men are created equal and endowed with certain inalienable rights, including life, liberty, property, and the pursuit of happiness. They argued that there

259

is a universal religion of reason for all people that subscribe to the principle of monotheism and the self-evident importance of ethics. Eventually, the Jews witnessed the French Revolution, which extended the rights of liberty, equality, and fraternity to Protestants in Catholic France, but not to them. The Jews wondered why these rights were denied them.

Jewish Enlightenment figures and the early advocates of Jewish emancipation wanted to prove that Judaism is compatible with citizenship in modern society. They sought to demonstrate that Judaism is a religion of reason based on ethical monotheism. The leading Jewish figure of the time, Moses Mendelssohn, the grandfather of the composer Felix Mendelssohn, explained that the core of Judaism is the belief in one God who watches over humankind and who demands from us a moral life. The ritual laws, he explained, which set the Jews apart from others, are not essential to our religion. There are, he argued, no essential differences between Jews and Christians, only differences in how we express the religion of reason.

The opportunity of acceptance in non-Jewish society led many Jews to think of Jewish rituals as obstacles to their emancipation. They began to dispose of what they saw as an archaic ritual system that reinforced the social isolation of the Jews. The founders of early Reform Judaism in Germany adopted this point of view and argued that ethical monotheism is the essence of Judaism. The rituals, they claimed, were added by human beings over time to isolate the Jews from others and were, therefore, dispensable anachronisms that stood in the way of Jewish emancipation. They subscribed to the concept of the "Judeo-Christian tradition" to indicate that both Judaism and Christianity shared certain fundamental religious truths that had been obscured over time by nonessential differences.

The campaign for Jewish civil rights presented Judaism as a set of abstract principles of ethical monotheism that should be respected and tolerated by non-Jews. In exchange, Jews offered to reform Judaism, to highlight the essential principles, and to discard the anachronistic ritual practices. They defined Judaism as those rational, private beliefs that do not impact on public behavior except in minor ways. Jews and Christians, they said, worship the same God, each in their own way. While Christians worship in church on Sundays, Jews do so in temples. Some early Reform Jewish congregations even shifted their main worship service to Sundays to stress this point. Jews began to look, think, dress, and behave like non-Jews. We confined Judaism to our homes and temples. The slogan that guided assimilated Jews was, "Be a Jew in the home but a man on the street."

The new call to be a Jew inside but a man outside meant that there was a split between our Jewishness and our humanity. While we might be Jewish in the privacy of our own homes or around the dinner table, any public expression of Jewishness was intolerable. Judaism was a private matter, a vestige of the past that made us less than a full human being. This led to the "inside–outside" syndrome, the sense that certain behaviors that might be acceptable among other Jews would be repugnant or dangerous within polite society.

Sigmund Freud used to describe this syndrome as one of the foibles of modern Jews. He related a self-deprecating anecdote about a poor, slovenly dressed Jew who boarded a train, sat down in an empty compartment, made himself comfortable, loosened his collar, and put his dirty feet on the seat across from him. Just then, a well-dressed man, whom he assumed to be a Christian, entered the compartment and sat down in a gentlemanly manner. The poor Jew straightened himself up and sat as a gentleman should. Then the stranger took out a date book, thumbed through the pages, and turned to the Jew. "Excuse me," he asked in heavily accented Yiddish, "when is *Yom Kippur*?" "Aha!" said the Jew, who put his dirty feet back up on the seat before answering. Jews tended to act properly with gentiles, but more comfortably with their own kind.

Recent immigrants from the former Soviet Union often report that this syndrome still prevails there. Within their Russian homes, they knew that they were Jews and they held on to whatever tiny traces of Jewish life were possible. But once they left the apartment,

261

they knew that any public expression of Jewish identity would jeopardize their education, careers, and social acceptance. They lived with an ambivalent pride and shame at having the words "Nationality: Hebrew" stamped on their internal passport. They learned what it meant to be a Jew in the home but a Soviet citizen in the street.

The Jewish mystical teachings had been the predominant theology among European Jewry until the Enlightenment. In rejecting the old ways, we also rejected some of the most powerful spiritual dimensions of Judaism. It was a case of throwing out the baby with the bath water. The rationalist bias of the enlightened Jews in the early nineteenth century left no room for the spiritual dimensions of Judaism. They saw the Jewish spiritual tradition as a roadblock to Jewish social progress and as a black stain on the rational character of Judaism. The casualty of their prejudice was the Jewish mystical tradition. They censured and censored the study of the Jewish mystical tradition as an embarrassing archaism and an obstacle to the modernization of Judaism even though it was that tradition that had offered the most penetrating guide to the ancient Jewish spiritual teachings. The modern reformers saw mysticism as irrationalism, the enemy of rationalism, and so excluded mysticism and spirituality from Judaism.

The other treasure that we nearly surrendered was our nationality. Wherever Jews sought acceptance, they were accused of having conflicting loyalties. How could Jews be trusted when they were seemingly loyal both to their native country and to the Jewish people around the world? Many Jews answered this charge by arguing that Judaism is a religion, not a nationality. There is no Jewish people—only followers of the Jewish religion. Although non-Jews never had any doubt that Jews are a people and a religious group, none denied their peoplehood more than the enlightened Jews. This led to the narrow definition of Judaism as a religion rather than a civilization and the elimination of those beliefs and practices that stressed our uniqueness, such as the peoplehood of Israel and the hope of a return to Zion. We were essentially the same as our Christian neighbors.

This stance led to an absurd situation in 1806, when Napoleon sought to establish whether Jews can be loyal Frenchmen or whether we were a "nation within a nation." He posed a series of questions to an Assembly of Jewish Notables, including the leading rabbis of the day. The notables pointed with pride to the willingness of patriotic Jews to serve in the French army and to fight against Jews in the opposing armies as evidence that Judaism is a religion, not a nationality. The question whether intermarriage between a Jew and a non-Jew was permitted was also instructive. These rabbis and leaders announced that intermarriage was not forbidden by Jewish law, although a rabbi could not perform one. Their disingenuous answer meant that while religiously sanctioned intermarriages were prohibited, civil intermarriages were not forbidden by Judaism.

If Jews and Christians were not different, why not let Judaism disappear altogether? This became the goal, in fact, of some of its most respected figures. Moritz Steinschneider, the founder of modern academic Judaic studies, defined his task as a scholar as "giving Judaism a decent burial." No less a legendary figure than Theodor Herzl, the founder of Zionism, actually proposed the baptism of the entire Jewish people as a solution to the problem of anti-Semitism in Europe three years before he proposed the creation of a national homeland for the Jewish people. The attempts to "bury" Judaism took place even as the body was still breathing.

REFORM AND ORTHODOX JUDAISM IN EUROPE

Judaism today has been defined according to the denominations of Orthodox, Conservative, Reconstructionist, and Reform Judaism.

The division of Jews into these denominations is not a part of traditional Judaism and each of them is a modern phenomenon. Until the eighteenth century, Judaism was defined by a common set of religious practices that were followed by Jews living in different parts of the world despite some regional variations among them. Although Jewish observance was standardized, there were often fierce and partisan debates about the values, teachings, and meaning of Judaism, its beliefs, and even its practices. Jews who followed the same pattern of religious practice would frequently dispute and, sometimes, condemn the opinions and practices of Jews with whom they disagreed. But they studied the same holy texts, prayed the same prayers, and observed many of the same customs.

Although Jews throughout the world had much in common in their outward behavior, they have never wholly agreed on the meaning of Jewishness. The great debates about the nature of God, human destiny, good and evil, the mission of the Jewish people, the meaning of Torah, the purpose of prayer, and the vision of the future have never been resolved among us, nor should they be. The debates are the sign of a dynamic culture struggling with the great questions in a search for the ultimate, yet elusive, answers. As we moved into modern societies, we began to modify and even abandon the standard practices of Judaism. In response to these changes, different factions emerged among the traditionalists and the modernists.

All the Jewish denominations, even Orthodox Judaism, are uniquely modern constructs. Orthodoxy was itself a new denomination in the nineteenth century and has continued to evolve ever since. The traditionalists began to call themselves Orthodox and soon began to divide into different factions. Thus, far from monolithic, Orthodoxy is itself a deeply divided house. Today there are two branches of Orthodoxy, each claiming to be the authentic voice of tradition. Each of its factions differs about whether it is possible to be faithful to Judaism while living within the non-Jewish world or whether separatism and isolation are preferable. Although Orthodox

Judaism is a continuation of traditional Judaism in some ways, it is also a new development in modern Judaism.

In the wake of the Enlightenment, Reform Judaism was founded in Germany around 1815. It appealed equally to traditional Jews in western Europe seeking to enter modern, secular society as it did to Jews who were already estranged and sought to make their way back to Judaism. The Reform movement, which accepted the idea that the Jews are a religious community and not a people, removed the national elements from Judaism. They eliminated all references to the people Israel, Zion, and the Messiah from their prayer books. Some sought to remove Hebrew entirely, the language of Torah and prayer, as a remnant from antiquity. They argued that Judaism is only a religion, not a national culture, so prayers can be said in any language. As one of the founders of Reform argued, "Anyone who imagines Judaism to be walking on the crutches of the Hebrew language, deeply offends it." Early Reformists kept their temples closed throughout the week except for the one hour of weekly prayer on Saturday or Sunday. They introduced the raised, frontal pulpit, in imitation of Protestant churches. The formal, decorous service was presided over by a rabbi, now called the "minister," who wore ministerial robes and who conducted the service with minimal audience participation. The focal point of the service became the sermon, an instructive lecture whose theme was often the civic betterment of the Jews.

The Jewish communities of eastern Europe before the Holocaust were more traditional and yet more spiritual than those in western Europe. The Jews of eastern Europe in the nineteenth century were divided between two opposing orthodox religious movements—the Hasidim and their opponents, the Mitnagdim. Hasidism is the most powerful Jewish spiritual movement in modern Judaism. The Hasidim were mostly Galizianers, Jewish residents of northwestern Ukraine and southeastern Poland, which formed a distinct cultural and geographical region known as Galizia-Podolia. The Mitnagdim

265

were also known as Litvaks, inhabitants of the area that Jews called "Lita" (Lithuania), which included the modern Baltic states and Belorus (White Russia). Lithuania and Vilna (Vilnius), its capital, were famous for their Talmudic scholars and their great academies of learning, called *yeshivahs*.

Galizianer Hasidim and the Litvak Mitnagdim held each other in contempt. Litvaks saw the Galizianers as poor, simple, pious yet unlearned Jews, and generally dismissed them as "horse thieves." The Galizianers saw the Litvaks as learned but dry, punctilious in observance but lacking in genuine piety, clever but spiritually vacuous, and referred to them as *"tselem kop,"* or "corpse-for-brains." The Yiddish writer Sholem Aleichem, a Galizianer, sarcastically described a Litvak as so clever that first he repents, and then he sins.

The conflict between them was the result of differences in religious, spiritual, cultural, and social values. The Hasidim believed in the presence of God within every animate and inanimate object. Their slogan was "No place is empty of God." They taught that the highest purpose of life, and the goal of Judaism, is to discover the divinity within. Hasidism taught a revolutionary doctrine of spiritual individualism. They held that each individual must strive for consciousness of God, which they called *devekut*, or "bonding." The Hasidim believed it was more important to attain the proper spiritual frame of mind, even if it meant delaying performance of the required ritual practices of Judaism. Although Hasidim followed the same basic religious law as the Mitnagdim, they were more concerned with inwardness and personal religious experience than with observance for the sake of observance.

The Mitnagdim saw Hasidism as a profound violation of the value system of Talmudic Judaism. The leader of this movement was the venerable Gaon of Vilna (1720–1797), a Kabbalist, who viewed the Hasidic movement not as a successor to Kabbalah but as a threat to the integrity of Judaism. His leading disciple, Rabbi Chayyim of Volozhin (1749–1821), who founded the famous Volozhin *yeshivah* in 1803, continued to lead the opposition to Hasidism and to articulate the Lithuanian Orthodox ideology. He taught that human beings were created "for the sake of Torah," which meant that devotion to a life of learning Torah is the vehicle for fulfilling God's will. His leading Hasidic rival, Rabbi Shneur Zalman of Liady, the first Lubavitcher Rebbe (1745–1813), argued that while learning Torah was vital, human beings were created above all for the sake of performing God's commandments.

The Mitnagdim believed that the core value of Judaism is the transcendence and hiddenness of God, who communicates to us not through the world but through the Torah alone. God's presence can be found only in Torah, not in the world or in human beings. They treated the Hasidic teaching of the immanence of God as heresy. They criticized the Hasidim for placing *devekut* above Torah and above the punctilious observance of the ritual commandments. They believed that study of Torah was even more fundamental than performance of the commandments. They taught that God had ordained the ritual law in every detail, including specific time requirements for performance of the commandments. They condemned the Hasidic concept that spiritual readiness is more important than the timely observance of the commandments.

The conflict between Hasidism and Mitnagdism led to charges, polemics, sanctions, and mutual recriminations. In the nineteenth century, Hasidism began to abandon its belief in spiritual individualism and accepted the Mitnagdic principle of punctilious observance. This was most evident with the rise of the Chabad-Lubavitch branch of Hasidism. This denomination took hold in the Lithuanian heartland as a synthesis between Hasidic spirituality and Lithuanian Talmudism. As the influence of the liberal Enlightenment began to penetrate eastern Europe, the Hasidim and Mitnagdim settled many of their differences in order to present a united front against the common enemy— modernization, secularization, and reform. The struggle ended early 267 in the twentieth century as the Hasidim and Mitnagdim banded together as the Agudat Yisrael organization in order to fight the growth of liberalism and secularism.

The two basic denominations into which Orthodoxy today is divided are the ultra-Orthodox Charedim ("God-fearers") and the modern Orthodox. In America, the Charedim include Agudat Yisrael, the Hasidim, and the Mitnagdim, who have become largely indistinguishable from each other. The Charedim, who are often distinguished from modern Orthodox Jews by their peculiar style of dress, include Hasidic groups such as Chabad-Lubavitch, Satmar, and followers of the fundamentalist Mitnagdim. They have established their own separatist communities and maintain a network of *yeshivahs* in New York, New Jersey, Baltimore, Cleveland, and Chicago. The most powerful Charedi sect in America is made up of the Chabad-Lubavitch Hasidim, who are characterized by their missionary zeal, messianism, extensive outreach efforts, self-segregation, and rejection of secular learning.

Modern Orthodoxy traces its roots to the Lithuanian Rabbi Chayyim of Volozhin. His son-in-law, Joseph Soloveichik, was one of the founders of the Brisker dynasty of Talmudic scholars, whose more recent descendants included Rabbi Joseph Dov Soloveichik (1903–1995), the leading light of American Orthodoxy. Modern Orthodox Judaism was also shaped by the teachings of the German Rabbi Samson Raphael Hirsch (1808–1888), who taught that one could live within modern society according to the teachings, values, and practices of traditional Judaism. Modern Orthodox Jews believe that there is nothing more important than Torah learning and ritual observance. Still, they believe that Torah learning is strengthened by confrontation with modern secular learning. This outlook finds its institutional expression in Yeshiva University in New York, which includes a modern Orthodox rabbinical seminary, an Orthodox undergraduate college, and several graduate schools, and in the Young Israel synagogue movement.

268 Mitnagdism also produced the Mussar, or "Morals" movement, founded by Rabbi Israel Salanter, a disciple of Rabbi Chayyim of Volozhin, in the mid-eighteenth century. This movement accepted

the Mitnagdic commitment to Talmud study but argued that it must be tempered by attention to character development, which depended on the cultivation of the personal traits of kindness, compassion, and scrupulous honesty and on immersion in Jewish ethical literature. Lithuanian Mussar *yeshivahs*, including those in Slobodka, Telshe, and Mir, were established to promote a dual focus on Lithuanian-style Talmud study and moral character. The curriculum stressed *middos*, personal character traits such as kindness, humility, submission, and steadfast faith. Students were expected to go out of their way to practice kindness toward fellow Jews and remain humble lest their moral accomplishments go to their heads.

Another kind of Mussar *yeshivah* was established in Novogorod (Novorodok). The founders believed that the path to moral character must be achieved through personal tests and trials. Novorodokers were distinguished by their unconventional behavior, which included going out in public penniless or in tattered clothes to afford students the opportunity to learn humility and to allow those who saw them to give them charity, even if they did not actually need help.

Recognized divisions of Orthodoxy today include Hasidim, Mitnagdim, Charedim, and the modern Orthodox. Orthodoxy, which represents about ten percent of American Jewry, has largely become Mitnagdic. While Orthodoxy is the most authentic continuation of traditional Jewish practice, it represents the victory of Mitnagdism and is somewhat of a departure from the spiritual outlook of the past. Orthodoxy has accepted the Mitnagdic value of the supremacy of *halachah* over spiritual individualism. Even Hasidism has embraced the Mitnagdic ideology and views many of the spiritual teachings of its own tradition, such as divine immanence, as heresy. Modern Orthodoxy is under continuous pressure from the Charedi camp to adhere to the stricter traditions of Lithuanian Mitnagdism and to oppose non-Orthodox Jewish denominations vigorously. In the process, Orthodoxy has become less accepting of the Jewish spiritual tradition, including beliefs that are part of its own heritage.

TEMPTING FREEDOMS

A different process of accommodation has characterized the majority of non-Orthodox North American Jews. For the most part, American Jewry has emphasized the needs of the Jewish people at the expense of the spiritual needs of the individual. In 1839, a small band of Jews left the town of Unsleben, Bavaria, for America. The Unsleben immigrants were among the first Jews to settle in Cleveland, Ohio. While the new world was attractive to many, others saw danger in its tempting freedom. Lazarus Kohn, a Hebrew teacher in Unsleben, warned the departing group that the freedom of America could destroy the integrity of Judaism. This is what he said:

> Friends! You are traveling to a land of freedom where you will be able to live without compulsory religious education. Resist and withstand this tempting freedom and do not turn away from the religion of our fathers. Do not throw away your holy religion for quickly-lost earthly pleasures. Your religion brings you consolation and quiet in this life and will bring you happiness for certain in the next life.

The Hebrew teacher's warning was prophetic. Many Jewish immigrants to the United States left their traditions behind in Europe—but not their memories. The first generation of immigrants quickly abandoned the oppressive legacy of poverty and persecution and, with it, their Orthodoxy. They quickly surrendered centuries of belief and practice and embraced the new world with full devotion. Many had already abandoned their Orthodoxy in Europe and became Socialists, Bundists (ethnic Yiddish socialists), or Maskilim (secular Jews). America offered them unprecedented freedom and opportunity but expected, in turn, that they surrender many of the traditions that once gave their lives direction. Still, the immigrants romanticized the world of their fathers—the idealized *shtetl*, the Jewish town, the golden tradition, the fiddler on the roof. The *shtetl* may have been a miserable place but, in comparison to the new world, at least it was familiar.

As Irving Howe explains in *The World of Our Fathers*, the organized Jewish community in America helped ease the immigrants into society and the *shtetl* out of the immigrants. In its early days, the Educational Alliance, the forerunner of the Jewish community centers, sought to Americanize and assimilate the eastern European immigrants. Their earliest members were traditional, Orthodox Jews and secular, Yiddish socialists who were deeply devoted to their eastern European traditions. The immigrants resisted, resenting the efforts of the Alliance social workers to *oysgrinen zikh*, "to take the greenhorn out of the immigrant." According to Howe, the German Jews who ran the Educational Alliance announced that the new immigrants, "slovenly in dress, loud in manners, and vulgar in speech, must be Americanized in spite of themselves."

The Alliance offered physical training for the immigrants because of their "lack of physical courage and repugnance to physical work." Their "medieval orthodoxy" and socialist anarchism were described as a moral menace by the leaders of the Alliance. To correct this, they taught the immigrants patriotic songs, offered them music lessons, and held birthday celebrations for great historical figures ranging from Aristotle to Longfellow. As Howe recounted one participant saying: "We were Americanized at the Educational Alliance about as gently as horses are broken in. In the whole crude process, we sensed a disrespect for the alien traditions in our homes and came to resent and despise those traditions because they seemed insurmountable barriers between ourselves and our adopted land." By World War I, the Educational Alliance realized that the patronizing and humiliating approach could not, and should not, ignore the traditions that Jewish immigrants brought to these shores.

Many of our communal institutions were founded with deep roots in the Jewish tradition. The Jewish homes for the aged, family services associations, and other agencies were established to assist the new immigrants. But, as they grew in the early years of this century,

271

they saw their mission as preserving Jews but not Judaism. For many years, Jewish agencies serving the Jewish community saw their mission in secular, often antireligious terms, rather than as fulfilling specifically Jewish responsibilities. Jewish organizations sought to preserve Jews without Judaism and, in the process, forgot why preserving Jews was important to begin with.

The immigrant dilemma has continued to shape the character of American Jewry. Can we take advantage of the "tempting freedoms" of the new country without "resenting and despising the traditions" that once guided our way in the world? When Isaac Bashevis Singer accepted the Nobel Prize for Literature in 1978, he too made the case for finding a balance between modernity and Jewish spirituality. He said, "I still cling to some truths which I think all of us might accept someday. There must be a way for a person to attain all possible pleasures, all the powers and knowledge that nature can grant him, and still serve God." This is the challenge that we still face today.

DENOMINATIONAL JUDAISM

In 1885, the leaders of Reform Judaism met in Pittsburgh and drafted a statement of their religious principles. They declared that the biblical and Talmudic kosher dietary laws and other regulations "originated in ages and under the influence of ideas altogether foreign to our present mental and spiritual state." Following the precedent of their European counterparts, they liberalized the practice of Judaism. They declared that "we no longer consider ourselves a nation, but a religious community." From then until the years after the Six-Day War of 1967, American Reform Jews were generally committed to a program of religious minimalism and social liberalism. They eagerly adapted to the unprecedented affluence, accep-

272

tance, and freedom that were available to them, while maintaining a social consciousness of responsibility toward those in need.

According to Edward Shapiro in *A Time for Healing*, only twenty percent of American Jewish families belonged to a synagogue in 1930. The great change in American Judaism occurred after World War II. Jews were part of the great middle-class move to the suburbs, where religious affiliation was considered one of the civic virtues. Like their Christian neighbors, Jews began to establish and join synagogues. By 1960, sixty percent of American Jews were affiliated with one. The synagogue emerged as the most important institution in American Jewish life. Synagogues soon offered a wide range of membership services, including Hebrew or religious school, youth groups, adult social clubs, and *bar* and *bat mitzvah* celebrations. Although most Jews were not traditionally observant, they identified and affiliated with the synagogue. This was especially true of Conservative and Reform congregations.

Many of the small, poorer congregations of the pre–World War II era merged with one another and were consolidated into larger ones as they moved to the suburbs. Many members of the more traditional Orthodox synagogues joined younger and more prosperous Conservative and Reform congregations. Synagogues relocating to the new suburbs often built magnificent buildings to reflect their new sense of prosperity and to affirm their parity with Christians and their churches. The religious services conducted in the synagogues became less participatory as the level of congregational knowledge of the Hebrew prayer book declined. Where conducting services was once a lay member's privilege, the synagogues now hired rabbis who were valued for their oratorical skills and cantors for their musical abilities. The professional clergy led the congregation and conducted services. The new dynamic of the synagogue emphasized the elevated stage, more English and less Hebrew, a greater formality that separated the officiating clergy from the congregation, dignity and grandeur over intimacy and spontaneity, and less active participation and more responsive reading on the part of the congregants. Children were not always welcome in the service, increasingly a well-choreographed musical and oratorical performance. Cathedral synagogues came to resemble the mainstream Protestant churches. Judaism became an observer spectacle rather than a participant activity.

CIVIL JUDAISM

American Jewry flourished as anti-Semitism waned and opportunities for Jews to enter new professions grew. Jews assumed many of the characteristics of other suburbanites while maintaining their liberal social commitments. It was often said by sociologists of the period that this generation "had the socioeconomic status of Episcopalians but voted like Puerto Ricans," meaning that they were affluent liberals. They began to assimilate the lifestyle patterns of their non-Jewish neighbors and became indistinguishable from most other Americans. They sent their children to public schools and encouraged them to take part in extracurricular activities after school. On Sundays, and several afternoons each week, they sent their children to the syna-gogue school in order to prepare for the *bar* and *bat mitzvah* ceremo-nies. Because the parents often regarded Judaism itself as an "alien tradition," Jewish education was not taken too seriously. Synagogue schools did not generally instruct the children properly in their ancient heritage or challenge the complacent mediocrity of Jewish life.

Following the Six-Day War, a new, secular form of American Jewish identity developed into what Jonathan Woocher called "Civil Judaism," a form of Jewish identity that is rooted in tradition but modified to reflect the new ways in which Jews see themselves. Woocher identified the elements that constituted the shared beliefs and practices of those who saw Judaism as a communal rather than a private matter. These beliefs and practices found their place as the shared value system of the organized Jewish community.

274

The tenets of Civil Judaism may be summarized as follows: The greatest Jewish value is the preservation and survival of the Jewish people itself. The Jewish people, not the Jewish religion, is the unique source of Jewish survival and continuity throughout history. Every individual Jew is responsible for the security and welfare of every other Jew in his community and throughout the world. Because Israel is the historic homeland of the Jewish people, a safe haven for oppressed Jews throughout the world, and the repository of Jewish hopes and aspirations, the security and welfare of its citizens are of paramount concern. Because the Jewish people in America are threatened by assimilation, the survival of the Jewish people is linked to the survival of the Jewish tradition, its customs, ceremonies, and celebrations. Jews do not necessarily have a personal obligation to follow Jewish law but are expected to view the Jewish tradition with respect. Traditional norms of belief and practice are considered relatively insignificant, and a diversity of Jewish expressions is accepted. The most important Jewish activity is *tsedakah*, or philanthropic support of Jewish causes, especially through the local Jewish community federation fund drive. As American Jews, however, we also have an equal responsibility to pursue social justice within society for all.

Many of these values are not new, in that they promote the traditional values of support for Israel, the Jewish people, and other people in need. What is new, perhaps, is their detachment from the traditional belief in God, Torah, and the commandments. Many opponents of this form of American Judaism criticize it as "survivalism," a reduction to the most secular and banal formulation of survival for survival's sake. They note that this outlook ignores those same religious beliefs that justify the value of Jewish survival in the first place and tolerates a vague formulation of Judaism with little real content or commitment. Many others note that the emphasis on peoplehood, community, and fundraising has alienated many young Jews, who see this as excessive preoccupation with material concerns. They disparage the concern for the group at the expense of the spiritual needs of the individual and deride philanthropy as the measurement of who is a good Jew. Civil Judaism, however, has been the consensus belief of many American Jews for much of the recent past.

CONSERVATIVE AND REFORM JUDAISM

Conservative Judaism remained committed to the principles of traditional Jewish law, especially observance of the Sabbath, the dietary laws (*kashrut*), and Hebrew as the language of prayer services. However, the movement adopted an evolutionary ideology of "tradition and change" that allowed the adaptation of traditional Judaism by learned rabbis to better serve current needs. Conservative Judaism accepted the need for change but preferred to give greater credence to the traditions that were "sanctified by millennia" of practice than did Reform. At the same time, the movement permitted modernization in Jewish belief and practice. For example, Conservative congregations added the late Friday night service as a convenience to its less traditional members, who would normally work, shop, or golf on Saturday mornings. They permitted driving to synagogue, adopted mixed seating of men and women, and included more English in the services. The gap between the religious practice of Conservative rabbis and their congregants has become characteristic of Conservative Judaism. Increasingly, the membership of Conservative congregations became indistinguishable from that of the liberal Reform congregations. Few Conservative Jews observed the Sabbath, kept the dietary laws, attended prayer services regularly, or identified with the ideology of the denomination.

276   Whereas Conservative Judaism teaches the primacy of Jewish law, *halachah* holds no authority for Reform Judaism. In most other ways, Reform Judaism today bears little resemblance to its European origins. Reform congregations today are recommitted to Jewish peo-

plehood, ethnicity, and Zionism. They have reintroduced Hebrew in prayer services and encourage ritual celebrations such as building festival booths on *Sukkot*. Sabbath morning services and more traditional practices have been included in the life of the congregations. Some congregations now encourage wearing *kippah* and *tallit* in synagogue. Not feeling bound to tradition, Reform Judaism has been free to experiment with new kinds of religious services. Many congregations have stressed the exploration of Jewish spirituality through music, healing services, and ritual experimentation. In contrast to their ultra-rationalist legacy, many Reform congregations today stress the experiential and participatory character of Judaism. The level of observance of Jewish practice among Reform rabbis and their congregants is often the same, indicating a certain internal coherence to Reform Judaism. The movement stresses the importance of human autonomous thinking as the criterion for deciding which Jewish rituals have meaning today. The enduring Jewish values of helping the less fortunate members of society and preserving Jewish life through *tsedakah*, or "charity," and *tikkun olam*, or "social action," are held in high esteem.

JEWISH RENEWAL

The 1960s were a period of profound changes in American Jewry that continues to influence the course of the Jewish community today. Jewish studies courses were just beginning to be included in the curriculum in some institutions of higher learning. Being Jewish was now in vogue and the demand for courses about Judaism was part of a general opening of the curriculum. Jewish ideas about spirituality and the imperative of activism spoke to many of us on a deeply personal level. In the Kabbalah, Heschel, and Buber, many of us found confirmation for our own spiritual beliefs and learned that these spiritual teachings came from the very core of Judaism.

Heschel and Buber were also the intellectual and spiritual inspiration for the Jewish renewal movement that began in the late sixties. The Havurah (fellowship) movement—which was founded by Arthur Green, a student of Heschel, and others—began in Boston and, shortly afterward, in New York. It sought to create an alternative to cathedral synagogues. The Havurah was usually a nonresidential location, a modest home or apartment, with a living room that could accommodate fifty people for prayer services and a kitchen that could support home-cooked celebratory meals. The founders of the first Havurah wanted to create an intimate community that shared ritual exploration and experimentation, intense praying, learning, meditation, and celebration. They were inspired by the spiritual individualism of the Jewish mystical tradition—especially Hasidism, Heschel, and Buber—and by the anti–Vietnam War movement. The movement attracted many young Jewish studies scholars and others who have gone on to influential careers in academia and organized Jewish life.

The latest reincarnation of the Jewish renewal movement is rooted in the religious and political ferment of the sixties. In 1986, *Tikkun* magazine appeared as a manifesto of a revitalized left with a Jewish cultural agenda. The first issue declared: "The universalistic dream of a transformation and healing of the world, the belief that peace and justice are not meant for heaven but are this-worldly necessities that must be fought for, *is* the particularistic cultural and religious tradition of the Jews." *Tikkun* is seen by some as the vanguard of a Jewish renewal movement and several *havurot*, identified as "Jewish Renewal," have appeared.

The problem with some of the recent renewal efforts is that they exist outside the structure of the organized Jewish community and, therefore, may not have a lasting impact. Many Jewish renewal efforts have written off the organized Jewish community and avoid involvement with institutions such as synagogues and federations. As a result, many of the new groups do not last beyond several years and fail to bring about broad-based changes in Jewish life. However, many other veterans of the earlier Jewish renewal movement have moved into the mainstream. They see the challenge not as critiquing the organized Jewish community from the outside but as working to revitalize Jewish life from within. In our lifetime, Jewish life revolves around denominations, congregations, and federations. If a spiritual transformation of Jewish life is to occur, it will be within these structures and not in spite of them. Institutions change, and Jewish progress occurs through incremental change within the existing structure.

One example of the ability of the Jewish community to embrace change is found in the "Jewish continuity movement." Since the dramatic and provocative time of the sixties, the organized Jewish community has become the prime mover in support of Jewish education and culture. Jewish community federations and private philanthropic foundations have become the leading force in rebuilding Jewish education. Since 1988, local Jewish communities have begun to invest millions of dollars in "Jewish continuity," the term used to define the efforts of the organized Jewish community to ensure the Jewish future. These efforts involve greater support for teacher training, family education, retreats, and other innovative educational programs. Still, the Jewish future depends on articulating a clear and compelling explanation of Judaism as a spiritual guide to life as much as on funding educational improvement.

Although the early Havurah movement was distinctly counter-cultural, its communitarian values were preserved in several ways. Many small, voluntary groups were formed around the country in the spirit of the Havurah as alternatives to mainstream synagogues. In particular, the Jewish Reconstructionist denomination has embraced the Havurah concept as the model for their congregations. Many large synagogues, recognizing that it is difficult to achieve intimacy within a cathedral congregation, have attempted to create smaller subgroups. These are often called "havurot," but they are often social or educational in their focus.

SIGNS OF RETURN

Because many Jews today are committed to a serious Jewish journey, the widespread fear that Jewish life is on the decline may be overstated. Many of us worry that assimilation will lead the Jewish people in America to the brink of extinction. The 1990 National Jewish Population Study showed a current fifty-two percent rate of exogamy, that is, marriage between Jews and non-Jews without conversion, and other evidence of declining Jewish rates of affiliation. While we will indeed continue to lose many Jews through assimilation, many other assimilated Jews will return to Judaism. Assimilation is not a life sentence, nor is it an incurable condition. It is a stage in the development of a modern Jew waiting to be reborn. The phenomenon of the return of assimilated Jews to Judaism is an important, and underappreciated, feature of Jewish life. Life is a journey with many interesting twists and turns. We are not now what we once were nor what we will be in the future. Many assimilated Jews are only waiting for a guide to lead them on their Jewish journey.

I believe that assimilated Jews who return to Judaism bring with them fresh ideas and approaches and help bring about a revitalization of Jewish life. There are many striking cases of alienated Jews whose Jewishness reawakens at some point in their lives. For example, Theodor Herzl, founder of political Zionism, the most significant movement of Jewish rebirth in this century, was a thoroughly assimilated Jew who eventually returned to his roots. The yearning for wholeness, for completeness, for integrity in Jewish life comes frequently from those individuals who had once been cut off from the living sources of Judaism. There is a human striving for authenticity, for cultivating the essential dimensions of our experience, that challenges assimilation. Many assimilated Jews, who become aware of their own fragmented form of Jewish identity, turn back to their roots in a search for human authenticity.

One of the most powerful statements of the Jewish spiritual return comes from the unlikely figure of Franz Kafka, one of the fore-

280

most novelists of our century. In his famous letter to his father, he writes, "And what sort of Judaism was it that I got from you?" After chronicling his family's superficial Judaism, he continues: "I could not understand how, with the insignificant scrap of Judaism you yourself possessed, you could reproach me for not making an effort to cling to a similar insignificant scrap. It was, indeed, as far as I could see, a mere scrap, a joke, not even a joke. How could I do anything better with this material than get rid of it as fast as possible? Getting rid of it seemed to me the most effective act of piety one could perform." Franz Kafka never performed this act of piety. Instead, he immersed himself in Zionism, the Yiddish theater, Hasidic teachings, and Hebrew in his search for authenticity.

Although Sigmund Freud rejected Judaism, as he did all religion, he did not abandon his Jewishness. Religion, according to Freud, is a system of wishful illusion that grows out of the human desire for reassurance in the face of mortal helplessness. Religion projects the illusion of reassurance onto an invented god. For Freud, however, Jewishness is an inescapable fact of one's being a Jew, an inviolable part of one's existence, and a source of psychic energy. In writing to a friend who was considering baptism, Freud warned: "If you do not let your son grow up as a Jew, you will deprive him of those sources of energy which cannot be replaced by anything else. He will have to struggle as a Jew, and you ought to help him develop all the energy he will need for that struggle. Do not deprive him of that advantage." Although Freud's Jewishness lacked any religious content, he introduced the notion that Jewishness is an essential part of one's identity that cannot be rejected without endangering the whole. The current concern for Jewish identity actually goes back to Freud, an assimilated Jew who recognized the inescapable quality of one's own Jewishness.

Through assimilation, we bring Judaism to the brink of extinction. Inevitably, however, a countermovement appears among those most remote from traditional Judaism, and leads us back to the center. Assimilation has led to alienation from Judaism, but it has also pro-

duced committed Jews whose thinking is emancipated from traditional categories of Jewish belief. Assimilation has made it possible
for us to bring modern sensibilities back to the very heart of Judaism
and to revitalize Jewish life from within. We have not preserved
Jewish life throughout history through closing ourselves off in our
houses of study while the outside world passes us by. We have continued, persisted, and survived because we have opened our tradition
to absorb the influences from the outside. The Jewish future lies not
in choosing between extremes of seclusion or assimilation, but in
incorporating the spiritual influences of the world around us into our
midst and in applying these insights and inspirations to our own lives.

SIGNS OF RENEWAL

What are the positive indications that offer the hope of Jewish renewal today? Many of the countercultural trends of the sixties that
began outside the organized Jewish community have moved into the
mainstream. The growth of academic Jewish studies has had a profound impact on Jewish renewal. Most major colleges and universities in North America have one or more faculty members who are
recognized Judaic scholars, certified by having earned a doctorate
degree in their field. The academic field of Jewish studies has allowed
Jewish undergraduates to continue their Jewish education during
their undergraduate years. For many Jewish students, such studies
are their first exposure to intellectually challenging, competently
taught, and personally inspiring Jewish learning. Many Jewish studies
faculty members have become valuable resources to their local Jewish communities. They represent a high standard of Jewish learning
that is different from traditional Talmud study as well as from congregational Jewish education. But, because Jewish studies have developed within universities rather than within Jewish communities,
they have been oriented toward producing objective academic re-

search rather than toward educating Jews and solving the problems of Jewish education.

Many of these same Jewish studies professors are teachers within the growing national movement of adult learning, which includes continued participation in adult Jewish learning programs, the reading of Jewish books, and the exploration of new religious observances. The reasons for the growth of this movement are complex and varied. The return to Jewish learning during adulthood is often an expression of one's search for spiritual roots or a personal belief system within organized religion and usually also reflects a desire to fill in a serious gap in one's Jewish knowledge due to disappointing experiences in earlier Jewish education. Significantly, the lives of many men and women have been transformed by their involvement in Jewish studies.

CONFLICTING VISIONS

Still, there are conflicting visions about what it means to be a Jew today. The only one that is illegitimate is that which delegitimizes other Jews. Judaism has always been a vital conversation and engaged debate about what it means to be a Jew. The opportunity for different Jewish visions to compete in the arena of Jewish community life is a healthy phenomenon. The only ground rule should be respect and tolerance for the legitimacy of every interpretation that is grounded in a serious understanding of Judaism. The Talmud calls these great debates over the direction and vision of Judaism "controversies for the sake of heaven," because the underlying purpose is sacred. These controversies involve how best to define the spiritual goals of human life and the means to achieve them. The Talmud also says that a controversy for the sake of heaven is destined to continue indefinitely because there can never be any complete and final resolution of the fundamental questions. The only controversies

283

that come to an end are those that are "not for the sake of heaven," that is, debates that do not contribute to the vital conversation of Judaism because they are based on personal interests and power motives. The conflicting visions of Judaism are part of the ongoing process of defining the meaning of Judaism for ourselves. Debates concerning their validity should be conducted fervently, thoughtfully, and with respect for the vision of others.

The criticism by some ultra-Orthodox Jews of other Jews is not a controversy for the sake of heaven. The truly pious person does not accentuate the divisions among Jews. Long a tenet of Judaism is love for *all* Jews. As one Hasidic rabbi said, "Nothing is more precious in God's sight than the unity of His people." Therefore, the ultra-Orthodox attacks upon other Jews is itself a violation of the very spiritual principles of Judaism. Judaism recognizes that each person lives on a different level on his or her own ladder and deserves respect as an individual no matter what form of Judaism he or she practices.

If Israel truly sings all the melodies of the world, we must continue to be open to absorb the best of the spiritual traditions of the world around us. In fact, that is what Judaism has always done. The real challenge is to weave what we absorb from others and what we ourselves compose into the melody of Judaism. Then we can turn our *niggun* into a symphony that all men and women can perform together.

HEAVEN ON EARTH

THE CHILDREN OF OUR ANCESTORS

The journey on which we have embarked is a sacred search for Jewish renewal. It is the same journey that our ancestors took as they set out into the uncharted waters of their day. Every Jewish seeker from Abraham until today set out on a daunting and daring path to discover the right way to live in the world. Our ancestors stood at Sinai, witnessed the destruction of the Temple, created golden ages and a renaissance, dreamed of liberating humanity from slavery and suffering, developed some of the most profound spiritual teachings and practices in the history of human civilization, spawned other wisdom traditions, survived a Holocaust, and built a new nation. Imagine what it felt like to stand in their shoes. Imagine what sort of challenge many of our grandparents faced when they found themselves uprooted from Europe and displaced in America. We are the children of very accomplished ancestors, who have prepared us

285

well for the challenges that we face today. We take courage from them because, as Theodor Herzl said, "If you will it, it is no dream."

At the same time, we also face an unprecedented challenge in creating a modern, spiritual Judaism that is authentic and faithful to its roots. We walk on a steep ridge with a deep abyss on each side. We have to balance our own precious individuality, freedom, and all the wonders that the modern world has given us with the respect for tradition, the commanding voice of God at Sinai, and the fidelity of one hundred generations to Judaism. Can we afford to slip and let the Jewish tradition of hope, righteousness, and moral purpose fall into the abyss? Can we allow the tradition to become so narrow that we worship the past blindly and allow Judaism to become frozen in the past?

We cannot turn Judaism into idolatry by worshiping the past and denigrating the present. Every present eventually becomes a past. If we were to eliminate today's creativity, innovation, and experimentation, Judaism would soon become a petrified relic of history rather than a dynamic force for the future. For example, when we study Torah today, we can learn from the classical *Midrash*. Their teachings were meant to promote critical thinking and open up new questions. When fundamentalists turn the midrashic teachings into dogma and what Jews *should* believe, they distort the very character of the tradition. The past is useful, but Judaism must continue to change and evolve.

Judaism is a journey, not a recipe. We explore, grow, and change as we move up and down on the ladder. We are exposed to new ways of understanding Judaism through our own experiences and through contact with teachers, books, and ideas. Judaism is the means by which we temper the dreams of the past with new visions for the future and plot the course ahead. Judaism is the vehicle for realizing the noblest of human dreams in the real world, within society, with the help of friends, family, and community.

We each have dreams. My dream for Jewish renewal is based on a belief in pluralism and diversity in Jewish life. There is no exclu-

286

sively right path in Jewish life today and no single recipe for Judaism that is appropriate for everybody. I admire the joy of Jewish living, the steadfast loyalty to the difficult path of observance, and the devotion to Jewish literacy among Orthodox Jews. I find myself at home with the serious and purposeful path of Conservative Judaism, which combines tradition with grand experiments in modernizing the faith. I value the experimentation and creativity of Reconstructionist Judaism and its bold efforts to create new rituals. And I cherish the freshness, openness, and acceptance of Reform Judaism. I am comfortable in synagogues of different persuasions, and my own ideal synagogue would contain elements of each.

Judaism does not value conformity. Our ancestors often lived in diverse Jewish communities in which Jews of differing persuasions coexisted. Pharisees, Sadducees, Ashkenazim, Sephardim, Maimonideans, Kabbalists, Karaites, Hasidim, Mitnagdim, and many other movements made Judaism a rich tapestry of differences. These differences often brought disagreement, but the conflicting Jewish visions helped to refine the Jewish journey. One generation's heresy soon became the next generation's orthodoxy. We should keep in mind that the many layers of Judaism were not added without serious divisions about Jewish values. Nor should we forget that contentiousness is the sign of a vibrant, vital culture struggling to define itself in relation to its past and future.

It no longer makes sense to think in rigid, fixed denominational terms that define each of us as a certain type of Jew. Increasingly, the labels and boxes that we use to categorize Jews as religious or secular, Orthodox, Conservative, Reconstructionist, and Reform, make little sense. People often move from one to another during the course of a lifetime. In fact, we should encourage Jewish journeys rather than promote static denominational loyalties.

Most of us seek Judaism in different ways throughout the course of our lives. We ought to break down the narrow barriers that pigeonhole and stereotype us and see ourselves as "just Jewish." As the philosopher Franz Rosenzweig said, all it takes is the simple af-

287

firmation that "nothing Jewish is alien to me." This principle allows us to explore every aspect of our Jewish lives without ending our journey prematurely. Rather than use definitions that exclude and limit, we should deemphasize the Jewish labels and view all members of the Jewish people as sharing a common heritage, a common destiny, and common concerns.

THE JEWISH JOURNEY

What is my dream for the Jewish journey today? I hope that we will someday see that Judaism is devoted to helping the individual realize his or her own innate divinity within communities of righteousness that promote the equality of all people. We will realize that Judaism is the vehicle that promotes human growth and freedom just as much as it is a source of truth about ultimate human values. We will experience living a Jewish life as a source of joy that binds people together in celebration and community rather than as a law that restricts and constrains us. We will encourage Jews to explore their own journeys without attempts to restrict, constrain, or censor new Jewish explorations. We will discover the ancient texts of our people as a source of inspiration and guidance even as we find our own voices and create new texts for those who come after us. Judaism will bring out the best in people, will offer us encouragement to pursue our own dreams, and will guide us to make fateful choices and increase peace in the world.

My dream is that my children will grow up in a world where being Jewish continues to represent being heir to the world's most noble tradition. Their Jewishness will not be reduced to ethnicity but will remain a calling. They will learn as much from their Jewish education as from any other experience in life. They will pursue wisdom through Jewish learning and through every other source available to them. They will preserve their own tradition and make

288

conscious choices about their spouses, families, and friends. They will accept Jews by choice and encourage the lifelong Jewish journeys of both native-born and naturalized Jews. They will feel comfortable living in two mutually reinforcing and challenging cultures—American and Jewish—so that neither one becomes stagnant.

I hope that they will live in a world where it is safe to live as a Jew and where they do not need to be taught about anti-Semitism as a living concern. Israel will be at peace and a source of moral inspiration to the world. They will feel at home in Israel as much as they do here, they will speak Hebrew as fluently as English, and living periodically in Israel will become a part of their lives. They will realize that everyone's destiny is intertwined with everyone else's, and that the good of one promotes the good of all.

I also wish that the Jewish people will respect the different Jewish journeys of its members while encouraging everyone to reach higher and higher. That it will devote the resources necessary to help seekers pursue their own journeys. That it will continue to practice the sacred values of human life by promoting justice for Jews and all people. That it will continue to renew our people by challenging our own institutions, creating new ones, and ensuring that our organizations work constructively to perpetuate Jews and Judaism. That it will respect the differences that make each of us and our many communities distinct. Our congregations will once again become places that promote the spiritual growth of their members by creating communities of learners and seekers within their walls. Each synagogue will become a congregation in which people feel connected by a common sense of purpose.

At the end of this voyage, what is it that I wish for you? I hope that you have found in this book answers to some of your questions, comfort and reassurance about some of your doubts and concerns, and inspiration to explore further and deeper. The *Mishnah* tells us that we should "turn round and round within the Torah," for it contains enough for each of us. I hope that you discover your own place within its deep reservoirs.

RESOURCES

In this section, I have assembled a list of resources for further exploration of the Jewish journey. These resources include organizations, institutions, and suggestions for further reading.

ADULT JEWISH LEARNING RESOURCES

Increasingly, Jewish adults are involved in various forms of Jewish study provided by a range of different sources, including denominational movements and their academic institutions; national organizations; and regional institutions of higher learning. In many cases, you should be able to locate appropriate adult Jewish learning resources in your community by contacting a local synagogue, Jewish federation, community center, central agency for Jewish education, or professor of Jewish studies at a college or university in your area. 291

In this section, I have identified major resources that sponsor programs throughout North America or that can direct you to a local adult Jewish learning resource.

National Denominational Institutions

Yeshiva University is the institution of higher Jewish learning for the
  Orthodox movement.
Yeshiva University
500 West 185th Street
New York, NY 10033
212-960-5400
web site: www.yu.edu

The Jewish Theological Seminary is the central institution of higher
  Jewish learning for the Conservative movement and offers courses
  online.
Jewish Theological Seminary of America
3080 Broadway
New York, NY 10027
212-678-8000
web site: www.jtsa.edu

The United Synagogue of Conservative Judaism is the synagogue arm
  of the Conservative movement and sponsors a range of adult education programs.
The United Synagogue of Conservative Judaism
155 Fifth Avenue
New York, NY 10010
212-533-7800
web site: www.uscj.org

The University of Judaism is the West Coast institution of higher Jewish learning for the Conservative movement and has a large adult education division.
University of Judaism
15600 Mulholland Drive
Los Angeles, CA 90077
310-476-9777
web site: www.uj.edu

The Reconstructionist Rabbinical College is the institution of higher Jewish learning for the Reconstructionist movement.
Reconstructionist Rabbinical College
Church Road and Greenwood Road
Wyncote, PA 19095
215-576-0800

The Jewish Reconstructionist Federation is the national organization of the Reconstructionist movement.
The Jewish Reconstructionist Federation
Church Road and Greenwood Road
Wyncote, PA 19095
215-887-1988
e-mail: jrfnatl@aol.com

The Hebrew Union College–Jewish Institute of Religion is the institution of higher Jewish learning for the Reform movement.
HUC-JIR
1 West Fourth Street
New York, NY 10012
212-674-5300
web site: www.huc.edu

The UAHC Department of Adult Jewish Growth is the adult education arm of the Reform movement.
UAHC Department of Adult Jewish Growth
Union of American Hebrew Congregations
838 Fifth Avenue
New York, NY 10021
212-650-4087
e-mail: ajgrowth@uahc.org

National Nondenominational Organizations

CLAL—The National Jewish Center for Learning and Leadership—offers serious Jewish learning programs from a modern, pluralistic perspective across North America.
CLAL—The National Jewish Center for Learning and Leadership
440 Park Avenue South
Fourth Floor
New York, NY 10016
212-779-3300
web site: www.clal.org

The Jewish Education Service of North America (JESNA) is the national umbrella organization of the central agencies for Jewish education. They can direct you to the appropriate organization for adult education in your community.
The Jewish Education Service of North America (JESNA)
730 Broadway
New York, NY 10003
212-529-2000
web site: www.jesna.org

The Florence Melton Adult Mini School offers a two-year program
of Jewish knowledge in many communities in North America.
The Florence Melton Adult Mini School
255 Revere Drive
Suite 112
Northbrook, IL 60062
847-714-9843
e-mail: bracha@ix.netcom.com

Regional Nondenominational Institutions

The regional colleges of Jewish studies offer Jewish adult continuing
education. Some offer distance-learning programs in Jewish communities throughout North America.

Boston's Hebrew College offers a variety of Internet courses.
Hebrew College
43 Hawes Street
Brookline, MA 02146
617-232-8710
800-866-4814
web site: www.hebrewcollege.edu

The Cleveland College of Jewish Studies offers a range of courses in
Jewish learning delivered by live, interactive videoconferencing
through its National Jewish Videoconferencing Network.
Cleveland College of Jewish Studies
26500 Shaker Boulevard
Beachwood, OH 44122
216-464-4050
888-336-2257
web site: www.ccjs.edu

Baltimore Hebrew University
5800 Park Heights Avenue
Baltimore, MD 21215
410-578-6900
web site: www.bhu.edu

Gratz College (Philadelphia)
Old York and Melrose Avenue
Melrose Park, PA 19027
215-635-7300
800-475-4635
web site: www.gratzcollege.edu

Spertus Institute of Jewish Studies (Chicago)
618 South Michigan Avenue
Chicago, IL 60605
312-922-9012
web site: www.spertus.edu

National Jewish Renewal Organizations

ALEPH is a national umbrella organization for the Jewish Renewal
    Movement. They provide information on Jewish renewal com-
    munities across North America.
ALEPH
7318 Germantown Avenue
Philadelphia, PA 19119
215-247-9700
e-mail: alephajr@aol.com
web site: www.aleph.org

The National Havurah Committee is the coordinating body for independent *havurot* in North America.
National Havurah Committee
7135 Germantown Avenue
Second Floor
Philadelphia, PA 19119
215-248-1335
e-mail: 73073.601@compuserve.com

Elat Chayyim is a spiritual retreat center associated with the Jewish Renewal Movement.
Elat Chayyim
A Center for Healing and Renewal
99 Mill Hook Road
Accord, NY 12404
800-398-2630
e-mail: elatchayyi@aol.com

Jewish Internet sites have become valuable sources for online exploration of Judaism. Two of the most comprehensive sites provide access to many learning resources. These include:
Shamash—The Jewish Internet Consortium web site:
www.shamash.org
Virtual Jerusalem web site: www.virtual.co.il

TORAH STUDY

For a reader who has "not yet" learned Hebrew, there are several important and reliable translations of the Torah. The Jewish Publication Society has produced a complete translation of the *Tanakh*, including *Torah*, *Prophets*, and *Writings* in three separate volumes. The Jewish Publication Society translation also serves as the basis for the Union of American Hebrew Congregations' edition, *Torah: A Modern Commentary*. This is an accurate translation based on exceptional scholarship. Everett Fox has published *The Five Books of Moses*, a translation and brief commentary that is meant to be read aloud. Other useful translations include Robert Alter's *Genesis: Translation and Commentary*, which attempts to preserve the semantic nuances and literary effects of the Hebrew in literary English.

The translation of the *Midrash* on the Torah can be found in two collections. The first, *The Soncino Midrash*, is a faithful English translation of the earliest *Midrash* on the Torah, but much is still lost in translation. The second, *Mimekor Yisrael*, translates many later *Midrashim* and folk traditions. A superb anthology of classical *Midrashim*, arranged topically in translation, can be found in *The Book of Legends (Sefer Ha-Aggadah)*, edited by Chayyim Nachman Bialik and Yehoshua Hana Ravnitsky. The classical Torah commentator, Rashi, is accessible to modern readers, thanks to Chaim Pearl's *Rashi: Commentary on the Pentateuch*. Nehama Leibowitz has published a series of self-guided studies for each of the five books of Torah, beginning with *Studies in Bereshit (Genesis)*. She helps the student ask the right questions and introduces us to the classical *Midrashim* and Torah commentaries.

Robert Alter's *The Art of Biblical Narrative*, a masterful literary guide to the Hebrew Bible, is the right place to start the study of modern approaches to Torah. Burton Visotsky's *Reading the Book: Making the Bible a Timeless Text* is a good, readable introduction to the midrashic approach to Torah. It is paired well with his more controversial close reading of Genesis, *The Genesis of Ethics*, which he presents as a chronicle of a "dysfunctional first family" that is also a profound story about moral development. Nahum Sarna's *Understanding Genesis* and *Exploring Exodus* are classics of modern biblical scholarship that often clarify the biblical text by reference to archeology and ancient Near East religion. Meir Sternberg's *The Poetics of Biblical Narrative* offers a unique and sophisticated approach to the Bible.

Avivah Zornberg's *Genesis: The Beginning of Desire* stands head and shoulder above most other commentaries because of its fidelity and attention to the original voice in the text. That is not to deny the value of many other modern *Midrashim*. It does, however, highlight the difference between a *Midrash* that tries to understand what the voice of God was saying and one that reads our own values and understanding into the ancient text.

Another important guide is Michael Fishbane's *Text and Texture: Close Readings of Selected Biblical Texts*. Fishbane begins with the notion that the biblical text is "rescued speech" about the encounters between man and God, a recorded version of events that remain obscured beneath the reportage. He attempts to uncover the multiple layers of meaning in the rescued speech. But since "meaning unfolds in the process of reading," the reader becomes the interpreter and midwife of meaning. Fishbane is particularly attentive to word repetitions and to stylistic and literary arrangements of the text.

For a modern Kabbalistic and Hasidic approach to Torah, I recommend David Blumenthal's *God at the Center: Meditations on Jewish Spirituality*. He offers a wonderful introduction to the Kabbalistic understanding of Torah along with rich insights on Jewish spirituality. For a contemporary spiritual *Midrash* on Jacob's dream rooted in Hasidism, Lawrence Kushner's *God Was in This Place and I, I Did Not Know It* is deeply moving.

Many of the most recent interpretations of Torah follow the text in a general sense. They do not focus on a close reading or on reading between the gaps in the text as much as on fashioning a personal connection to the narrative. But they do represent a powerful phenomenon of people who have returned to look for the voice in the text. They are what David Jacobson calls "an interpretive retelling" of the original story. I recommend Peter Pitzele's *Our Fathers' Wells: A Personal Encounter With the Myths of Genesis*. Pitzele, who was raised in a Jewish family devoid of any Jewish content, has spent much of his adult life exploring Buddhist, Native American, and New Age spirituality, only to find himself drawn back to his Judaism, of which he knew nothing. As he turned back to studying Genesis, he found himself beginning to draw from his ancestors' wells. His book is the result of his own spiritual seeking and wrestling with the patriarchal imagination of Genesis.

Naomi Rosenblatt and Joshua Horwitz, authors of *Wrestling With Angels*, view Genesis as a survival story narrating humanity's tenuous triumph over its self-destructive nature. In their psychological approach to Torah, they offer practical insights into our own life's struggles, based on the ancient text. David Rosenberg's *Genesis: Contemporary Writers on Our First Stories* is a quirky, eclectic collection of essays by contemporary writers, poets, and dramatists, including Arthur Miller, David Mamet, and others. It is well worth reading as an outsider's approach to these powerful stories. It is paired well with Rosenberg's *Congregation: Contemporary Writers Read the Jewish Bible*.

An important new area of feminist interpretations of Torah has been opened up recently. Ilana Pardes's *Countertraditions in the Bible: A Feminist Approach* introduces a new and compelling approach. She finds undercurrents of matriarchal or antipatriarchal religion in the "counter female voices which attempt to put forth other truths." These "countertraditions" antithetical to biblical patriarchalism call into question "the monotheistic repression of femininity." This book offers many challenging insights that suggest new ways of viewing the hushed voices of women in the Bible.

Ellen Frankel's *The Five Books of Miriam: A Woman's Commentary on the Torah* offers a new feminist *Midrash* on the Torah. She reintroduces the legend that God created a curative spring of water, "Miriam's Well," that surfaced at pivotal moments in Jewish history but disappeared at the death of Miriam, Moses' older sister. Frankel takes the image of "Miriam's Well" as her focal point to indicate that women's voices, prominent in the Torah, have continued as a living tradition visible below the surface of official Judaism. Although this is an imaginative retelling of the Torah, it is compelling as *Midrash*. "Miriam's Well" is a metaphor for the voices of Jewish women, and her commentary takes the form of a dialogue among various women's voices. The voices range from the women of the Bible to our own Jewish grandmothers.

Judith Antonelli's *In the Image of God: A Feminist Commentary on the Torah* examines the portrayal of women and women's issues. Because her commentary is a curious mixture of radical feminism and traditional Orthodoxy, it offers a unique perspective. She argues that rather than seeing the Torah as the basis of patriarchal sexism, we should recognize that the Torah advanced the status of women in its time. She defends the Torah as a feminist document and argues that sexism is not a product of Judaism. Because she does not distinguish between the original meaning of the Torah text and later *Midrashim* and commentaries, she can often read more into the text than is there. Still, this book is a useful reference work.

PRAYER

This book includes only a brief sample of spiritual prayers from the Jewish tradition. If you wish to explore the literature further, I recommend the following: Nahum Glatzer edited an outstanding collection of traditional and nontraditional prayers in *The Language of Faith*. Nahum Sarna's study of Psalms, *Songs of the Heart: An Introduction to the Book of Psalms*, offers rich insights into the earliest biblical prayers. T. Carmi edited *The Penguin Book of Hebrew Verse*, a collection of Hebrew poetry that contains many prayers. Similarly, Raymond Scheindlin analyzes many medieval Hebrew prayer-poems in *The Gazelle: Medieval Hebrew Poems on God, Israel, and the Soul*. The poet Marcia Falk reworks many traditional prayers by removing most references to the transcendent God in *The Book of Blessings*. Barry Holtz and Arthur Green have collected many important Hasidic prayers and statements about prayer in *Your Word Is Fire: The Hasidic Masters on Contemplative Prayer*.

301

For a deeper spiritual orientation to the traditional Jewish prayer service, I recommend Reuven Hammer's *Entering Jewish Prayer: A Guide to Personal Devotion and the Worship Service*. Yitzchok Kirzner offers a traditional and insightful explanation of the *Amidah*, the central prayer in Judaism, in *The Art of Jewish Prayer*. I also recommend looking at different prayer books that are commonly used today. These include traditional Orthodox prayer books such as Philip Birnbaum's *Daily Prayer Book, The Complete Art Scroll Siddur*, and *The Complete Metsudah Siddur*. Conservative prayer books include *The Sabbath and Festival Prayer Book* and *Sim Shalom*. Reconstructionist prayer books include *Kol Haneshamah*. The modern Reform prayer book is *Gates of Prayer. Or Chadash: New Paths for Shabbat Morning* is a Jewish renewal prayer book produced by ALEPH.

The *techines* cited in this book are mostly from collections such as Tracy Guren Klirs's *The Merit of Our Mothers: A Bilingual Anthology of Jewish Women's Prayers*; Nina Beth Cardin's *Out of the Depths I Call to You: A Book of Prayers for the Married Jewish Woman*; Norman Tarnor's *A Book of Jewish Women's Prayers*; and *Techinas: A Voice From the Heart*.

SPIRITUAL JUDAISM

The basic works on Jewish spirituality include Martin Buber's *Hasidism and Modern Man* and *Tales of the Hasidim* and Abraham Joshua Heschel's *God in Search of Man* and *The Sabbath*. The best anthology on the Kabbalah is Daniel Matt's *The Essential Kabbalah*. Other important works include several books by Arthur Green, including *Tormented Master: A Life of Rabbi Nahman of Bratslav; Seek My Face, Speak My Name: A Contemporary Jewish Theology*; and *Jewish Spirituality*. I also recommend Aryeh Kaplan's *Jewish Meditation*. The reader might also read my own books: *The Mystic Quest: An Intro-*

duction to Jewish Mysticism and *What Do Jews Believe? The Spiritual Foundations of Judaism.*

A growing number of books on spiritual Judaism have appeared in recent years. Michael Lerner's *Jewish Renewal: A Path to Healing and Transformation* initiated the recent Jewish renewal movement. Other books of similar persuasion include Arthur Waskow's *These Holy Sparks: The Rebirth of the Jewish People,* and Zalman Schachter-Shalomi's *Paradigm Shift: From the Jewish Renewal Teachings of Reb Zalman Schachter-Shalomi.* David Aaron's *Endless Light: The Ancient Path of the Kabbalah to Love, Spiritual Growth, and Personal Power* is a readable and enjoyable book that can be digested in small bites as one considers the real-life implications of each section. David Cooper's *God Is a Verb: Kabbalah and the Practice of Mystical Judaism* includes wonderful stories about sages such as Rabbi Shlomo Carlebach and holy dreamers as well as specific suggestions for meditative techniques and spiritual practices. Also recommended are David Gordis's *God Was Not in the Fire,* Wayne Dosick's *Dancing With God: Everyday Steps to Jewish Spiritual Renewal,* and Rodger Kamenetz's *The Jew in the Lotus* and *Stalking Elijah: Adventures With Today's Jewish Mystical Masters.*

GLOSSARY

Adam Shalem A spiritually complete person.

Ashkenazim Jews of central and eastern European origin, descended from Jews who migrated from Germany to Poland during the Middle Ages.

B.C. The standard Christian abbreviation for "Before Christ."

B.C.E. The standard Jewish abbreviation for "Before the Common Era," used instead of B.C.

C.E. The standard Jewish abbreviation for the "Common Era," used instead of A.D. (Anno Domini, "In the Year of the Lord").

Charedi The ultra-Orthodox, Jewish fundamentalist alliance of Hasidim and Mitnagdim, opposed to modernization of Judaism.

Chesed Goodness.

Cheshbon Nefesh Self-accounting.

Chovot Halevavot Spiritual responsibilities.

Devekut Bonding, the internal coherence within a human or spiritual connectedness to devotional prayer.

Emancipation The nineteenth-century European movement that sought Jewish political and civil rights.

Galizia The region that today includes southeastern Poland and the northwestern portion of Ukraine, where Hasidism originated.

Halachah The codified body of Jewish law.

Hasidism The Jewish spiritual movement founded in 1750 in eastern Europe by the Baal Shem Tov.

Havurah A customized community of seekers.

Hebrew Bible The holy Hebrew texts that are commonly called TaNaKh (Torah, Neviim, Ketuvim), known in English as Pentateuch, Prophets, and Writings. Christians refer to this as the Old Testament, a pejorative term for Jews.

Hitbodedut Spiritual isolation or retreat.

Kabbalah The medieval Jewish mystical movement, founded around 1200 in Spain, that was the dominant Jewish religious movement in the late Middle Ages.

Kaddish The memorial prayer for the dead.

Kashrut The Jewish dietary practices.

Kavanah Spiritual intention and forethought.

Kehillah A Jewish community.

Kiddush Levanah New Moon celebration.

Lashon Hara Immoral language.

Litvak Lithuanian Jews who were characterized by strict commitment to the observance of the *mitzvot*, widespread literacy in Talmudic learning, and admiration for Torah scholarship.

Mentsh The Yiddish word for a moral human being.

Mentshlichkeyt The Jewish notion of morality and human goodness.

Midrash The imaginative, literary process of seeking the voices and meanings hidden within the text of the Torah.

Mishnah The earliest postbiblical codification of Jewish law from around 200 C.E.

Mitnagdim The Hebrew term for "opponent" of Hasidism.

Mitzvah The Hebrew term for a commandment, ritual, or spiritual practice.

Neviim The prophetic writings including Joshua, Judges, Samuel, Kings, Isaiah, Jeremiah, Ezekiel, Hosea, Amos, Jonah, Micah, and others.

Niggun A Hebrew melody without words.

Rabbinic Refers to the formative, postbiblical period when Judaism was defined by sages known as rabbis; the period in which *Mishnah*, the Talmud, and *Midrash* were composed. This period covers roughly the first six centuries of the common era.

Sephardim Jews of Spanish origin; descended from Jews who migrated from Spain to Europe, North Africa, and the Mediterranean region after the expulsion of 1492.

Shechinah The feminine archetype of God.

Shiflut Humility.

Shtetl An eastern European Jewish town.

Shul Yiddish for "synagogue."

Talmud The Gemara is the elaboration and expansion of the *Mishnah*; together they are known as the Talmud, the great compendium of Jewish law and thought completed around 500 C.E.

Tanakh The Hebrew Bible

Techineh Prayers composed for women.

Temple The First Temple, Solomon's Temple, was destroyed by the Babylonians in 586 B.C.E. The Second Temple was destroyed by the Romans in 70 C.E.

Tikkun Olam The spiritual concept of uplifting the sparks and repairing the broken vessels of the universe.

Torah The five books of Moses: Genesis, Exodus, Leviticus, Numbers, Deuteronomy.

Tzaddik A holy person.

Tzedakah Justice.

Yetzer Hara The wicked impulse.

Yetzer Hatov The good instinct.

BIBLIOGRAPHY

Aaron, David, *Endless Light: The Ancient Path of the Kabbalah to Love, Spiritual Growth, and Personal Power*. Simon & Schuster: New York, 1997.

Aaron ben Jacob of Karlin, *Mishnat Chachamim*. Brooklyn, 1991.

Abraham Joshua Heschel of Apta, *Ohev Yisrael*. Jerusalem, 1964.

Adelman, Penina V., *Miriam's Well: Rituals for Jewish Women Around the Year*. Biblio Press: New York, 1986.

Alter, Robert, *Genesis: Translation and Commentary*. W.W. Norton: New York, 1996.

————, *The Art of Biblical Narrative*. Basic: New York, 1981.

Altmann, Alexander, "The Delphic Maxim in Medieval Islam and Judaism," in *Biblical and Other Studies*, ed. A. Altmann. Harvard University Press: Cambridge, 1963, pp. 196–232.

Amery, Jean, *At the Mind's Limits: Contemplations by a Survivor on Auschwitz and Its Realities*, trans. Sidney Rosenfeld and Stella P. Rosenfeld. Indiana University Press: Bloomington, 1980.

Antonelli, Judith, *In the Image of God: A Feminist Commentary on the Torah*. Jason Aronson: Northvale, 1995.

Ariel, David, *What Do Jews Believe? The Spiritual Foundations of Judaism*. Schocken: New York, 1995.

————, *The Mystic Quest: An Introduction to Jewish Mysticism*. Schocken: New York, 1992.

Avot de-Rabbi Natan, ed. S. Schechter. Vienna, 1887.

Baal Shem Tov, *Kodesh ha-Kodashim*. Mossad Harav Kook: Tel Aviv, 1951.

Baumeister, Roy F., *Evil: Inside Human Cruelty and Violence*. W.H. Freeman: New York, 1996.

Berrin, Susan, *Celebrating the New Moon: A Rosh Chodesh Anthology*. Jason Aronson: Northvale, 1996.

Blumenthal, David R., *God at the Center: Meditations on Jewish Spirituality*. Harper & Row: San Francisco, 1988.

Brener, Anne, *Mourning and Mitzvah: A Guided Journal for Walking the Mourner's Path Through Grief to Healing*. Jewish Lights: Woodstock, 1993.

Brown, Moshe, *Jewish Holy Days: Their Spiritual Significance*. Jason Aronson: Northvale, 1996.

Browning, Christopher, *Ordinary Men: Police Reserve Battalion 101 and the Final Solution in Poland*. Harper Collins: New York, 1992.

Buber, Martin, *Hasidism and Modern Man*, trans. Maurice Friedman. Horizon: New York, 1958.

————, *Tales of the Hasidim*, trans. Elga Marx. Schocken: New York, 1948.

————, *Ten Rungs: Hasidic Sayings*. Schocken: New York, 1947.

Cardin, Nina Beth, *Out of the Depths I Call to You: A Book of Prayers for the Married Jewish Woman*. Jason Aronson: Northvale, 1991.

Carmi, T., *The Penguin Book of Hebrew Verse*. Penguin Books: New York, 1981.

Chayyim of Volozhin, *Sefer Nefesh ha-Chayyim*. Vilna, 1824.

Cohen, Arthur, and Mendes-Flohr, Paul, eds., *Contemporary Jewish Religious Thought: Original Essays on Critical Concepts, Movements, and Beliefs*. Scribner: New York, 1987.

Cohen, Norman, *Self-Struggle and Change: Family Conflict in Genesis*. Jewish Lights: Woodstock, 1995.

Cooper, David, *God Is a Verb: Kabbalah and the Practice of Mystical Judaism*. Riverhead Books: New York, 1997.

Davies, Paul, *God and New Physics*. Simon & Schuster: New York, 1983.

Dawidowicz, Lucy S., *The Jewish Presence: Essays on Identity and History*. Harcourt Brace Jovanovich: New York, 1960.

Dobrinsky, Herbert, *A Treasury of Sephardic Laws and Customs*. Yeshiva University Press: New York, 1988.

Dosick, Wayne, *Dancing With God: Everyday Steps to Jewish Spiritual Renewal*. Harper: San Francisco, 1997.

Elijah Meir Bloch, *Sefer Shiure Daat*. Philip Feldheim: Jerusalem, 1972.

Falk, Marcia, *The Book of Blessings: New Jewish Prayers for Daily Life, the Sabbath, and the New Moon Festival*. Harper: San Francisco, 1996.

Feinberg, Chaim, *Leaping Souls: Rabbi Menachem Mendel and the Spirit of Koktzk*. Ktav: Hoboken, 1993.

Fishbane, Michael, *Text and Texture: Close Readings of Selected Biblical Texts*. Schocken: New York, 1979.

Fox, Everett, trans., *The Five Books of Moses*. Schocken: New York, 1995.

Frankel, Ellen, *The Five Books of Miriam: A Woman's Commentary on the Torah*. G.P. Putnam's Sons: New York, 1996.

Friedman, Maurice, *Martin Buber's Life and Works*. 3 vols. Dutton: New York, 1981–1983.

Glatzer, Nahum, ed., *The Language of Faith*. Schocken: New York, 1975.

Goldhagen, Daniel Jonah, *Hitler's Willing Executioners: Ordinary Germans and the Holocaust*. Knopf: New York, 1996.

Gordis, David, *God Was Not in the Fire: The Search for a Spiritual Judaism*. Scribner: New York, 1995.

Green, Arthur, *Seek My Face, Speak My Name: A Contemporary Jewish Theology*. Jason Aronson: Northvale, 1992.

———, *Jewish Spirituality*. Crossroads: New York, 1978.

———, *Tormented Master: A Life of Rabbi Nahman of Bratslav*. University of Alabama: University, 1978.

Green, Arthur, and Holtz, Barry, *Your Word Is Fire: The Hasidic Masters on Contemplative Prayer*. Paulist Press: New York, 1977.

Gurary, Natan, *The Thirteen Articles of Faith: A Chasidic Viewpoint.* Jason Aronson: Northvale, 1996.

Hallie, Philip, *Tales of Good and Evil, Help and Harm.* Harper Collins: New York, 1997.

——, *Lest Innocent Blood Be Shed: The Story of the Village of Le Chambon and How Goodness Happened There.* Harper & Row: New York, 1979.

Hammer, Reuven, *Entering Jewish Prayer: A Guide to Personal Devotion and the Worship Service.* Schocken: New York, 1994.

Hayyim of Volozhin, *Nefesh Ha-Hayyim.* Jerusalem, 1973.

Heschel, Abraham Joshua, *The Insecurity of Freedom: Essays on Human Existence.* Jewish Publication Society: Philadelphia, 1966.

——, *God in Search of Man: A Philosophy of Judaism.* Harper & Row: New York, 1955.

——, *The Sabbath: Its Meaning for Modern Man.* Farrar, Straus, Young: New York, 1951.

Horowitz, Isaiah, *Shnei Luchot Habrit.* Haifa, 1992.

Howe, Irving, and Libo, Kenneth, *World of Our Fathers.* Harcourt Brace Jovanovich: New York, 1976.

Howe, Irving, Wisse, Ruth R., and Shmeruk, Khone, eds., *The Penguin Book of Modern Yiddish Verse.* Penguin Books: New York, 1988.

Hundert, Gershon, *Essential Papers on Hasidism.* New York University: New York, 1991.

Idel, Moshe, *Hasidism: Between Ecstasy and Magic.* SUNY Press: Albany, 1995.

Kafka, Franz, *Parables and Paradoxes.* Schocken: New York, 1961.

————, *Dearest Father, Stories, and Other Writings*, trans. Ernst Kaiser and Eithne Wilkins. Schocken: New York, 1954.

Kamenetz, Rodger, *Stalking Elijah: Adventures With Today's Jewish Mystical Masters*. Harper: San Francisco, 1997.

————, *The Jew in the Lotus*. Harper: San Francisco, 1994.

Kaplan, Aryeh, *Jewish Meditation*. Schocken: New York, 1985.

Kasher, Moshe Shlomo, *Or Ha-Hasidut*. P. Casher: Jerusalem, 1984.

Kass, Leon R., *The Hungry Soul*. Free Press: New York, 1994.

Kirzner, Yitzchok, *The Art of Jewish Prayer*. Jason Aronson: Northvale, 1991.

Klirs, Tracy Guren, *The Merit of Our Mothers: A Bilingual Anthology of Jewish Women's Prayers*. Hebrew Union College Press: Cincinnati, 1992.

Kook, Abraham Isaac, *The Lights of Penitence, the Moral Principles, Lights of Holiness, Essays, Letters, and Poems*, trans. Ben Zion Bokser. Paulist Press: Mahwah, NJ, 1978.

————, *Orot Hakodesh*. Mossad Harav Kook: Jerusalem, 1964.

Kushner, Lawrence, *God Was in This Place and I, I Did Not Know It: Finding My Self, Spirituality, and Ultimate Meaning*. Jewish Lights: Woodstock, 1993.

Lamm, Norman, *Torah Umadda: The Encounter of Religious Learning and Worldly Knowledge in the Jewish Tradition*. Jason Aronson: Northvale, 1990.

————, *Torah Lishmah: Torah for Torah's Sake in the Works of Rabbi Hayyim of Volozhin and His Contemporaries*. Ktav: Hoboken, 1988.

Leibowitz, Nehama, *Studies in Bereshit (Genesis)*. World Zionist Organization: Jerusalem, 1981.

Lerner, Michael, *Jewish Renewal: A Path to Healing and Transformation*. G.P. Putnam's Sons: New York, 1994.

Levin, Nora, *The Jews in the Soviet Union Since 1917*. 2 vols. New York University Press: New York, 1988.

Lipset, Seymour Martin, and Raab, Earl, *Jews and the New American Scene*. Harvard University Press: Cambridge, 1995.

Maimonides, *Mishneh Torah*. 14 vols. Jerusalem, 1964.

Matt, Daniel, *The Essential Kabbalah: The Heart of Jewish Mysticism*. Harper: San Francisco, 1995.

Meah Berachot. Amsterdam, 1687.

Menahem Mendel of Kotsk, *Emet mi-Kotsk Titsmach*. Netzach: Bnei Brak, 1960.

Mendes-Flohr, Paul, *Divided Passions: Jewish Intellectuals and the Experience of Modernity*. Wayne State University Press: Detroit, 1991.

Milgram, Stanley, *Obedience to Authority: An Experimental View*. Harper Colophon: New York, 1969.

Mitchell, Stephen, *Genesis: A New Translation of the Classical Biblical Stories*. Harper Collins: New York, 1996.

Nachman of Bratslav, *Likkutei Tefillot*, ed. Nathan Steinharz. Bratslav Press: Brooklyn, 1977.

Neumann, Erich. *The Mystic Man in Mystic Vision: Papers From the Eranos Yearbook*, ed. Joseph Campbell. Princeton University Press: Princeton, 1968.

——, *The Origins and History of Consciousness*, trans. Eugene Rolfe. Princeton University Press: Princeton, 1954.

Newman, Louis, *The Hasidic Anthology: Tales and Teachings of the Hasidim*. Schocken: New York, 1963.

Ochs, Carol, *The Noah Paradox: Time as Burden, Time as Blessing*. University of Notre Dame: Notre Dame, 1991.

Pardes, Ilana, *Countertraditions in the Bible: A Feminist Approach*. Harvard University Press: Cambridge, 1992.

Pitzele, Peter, *Our Fathers' Wells: A Personal Encounter With the Myths of Genesis*. Harper: San Francisco, 1994.

Przysucha, Jacob Isaac ben Asher, *Sefer Kedushat ha-Yehudi*. Machon Nachat Yehoshua: Bnei Brak, 1995.

Riemer, Jack, *Jewish Reflections on Death*. Schocken: New York, 1974.

Riemer, Jack, and Stampfer, Nathaniel, eds., *Ethical Wills: A Modern Treasury*. Schocken: New York, 1983.

Rosenberg, David, ed., *Genesis: As It Is Written*. Harper: San Francisco, 1996.

Rosenblatt, Naomi, and Horwitz, Joshua, *Wrestling With Angels*. Delacorte Press: New York, 1995.

Rosenzweig, Franz, *On Jewish Learning*. Schocken: New York, 1965.

Roth, Philip, *American Pastoral*. Houghton Mifflin: New York, 1997.

Sarna, Nahum, *Songs of the Heart: An Introduction to the Book of Psalms*. Schocken: New York, 1993.

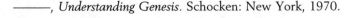

———, *Understanding Genesis*. Schocken: New York, 1970.

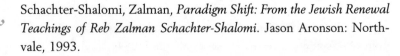

Schachter-Shalomi, Zalman, *Paradigm Shift: From the Jewish Renewal Teachings of Reb Zalman Schachter-Shalomi*. Jason Aronson: Northvale, 1993.

Scheindlin, Raymond, *The Gazelle: Medieval Hebrew Poems on God, Israel, and the Soul*. Jewish Publication Society: Philadelphia, 1991.

Schirmann, Yefim, *Hashirah ha-Ivrit be-Sefarad uve-Provence*. Mossad Bialik: Jerusalem, 1954–1956.

Scholem, Gershom, *Sabbatai Sevi: The Mystical Messiah*. Princeton University Press: Princeton, 1973.

Sefer Chasidim, ed. Reuven Margaliot. Jerusalem, 1957.

Sefer Siftei Kodesh. Jerusalem, 1968.

Shapiro, Edward, *The Jewish People in America: A Time for Healing. American Jewry Since World War. Vol. 2*. Johns Hopkins University Press: Baltimore, 1992.

Silberman, Charles, *A Certain People: American Jews and Their Lives Today*. Summit: New York, 1985.

Simon, Ernst, "Sigmund Freud, The Jew," *Leo Baeck Institutional Yearbook* 2, 1957.

Singer, Isaac Bashevis, *Nobel Lecture*. Farrar Straus Giroux: New York, 1978.

Staiman, Mordechai, *Niggun: Stories Behind the Chasidic Songs That Inspire Jews*. Jason Aronson: Northvale, 1994.

Sternberg, Meir, *The Poetics of Biblical Narrative: Ideological Literature and the Drama of Reading*. Indiana University Press: Bloomington, 1987.

Tanakh: A New Translation of the Holy Scriptures According to the Traditional Hebrew Text. Jewish Publication Society: Philadelphia, 1985.

Tarnor, Norman, *A Book of Jewish Women's Prayers*. Jason Aronson: Northvale, 1995.

Techinas: A Voice From the Heart. Aura Press: Brooklyn, 1992.

Verman, Mark, *The History and Varieties of Jewish Meditation*. Jason Aronson: Northvale, 1996.

Visotzky, Burton, *The Genesis of Ethics*. Crown: New York, 1996.

———, *Reading the Book: Making the Bible a Timeless Text*. Anchor: New York, 1991.

Waskow, Arthur, *These Holy Sparks: The Rebirth of the Jewish People*. Harper & Row: New York, 1983.

Weissler, Lenore E., *Traditional Yiddish Literature*. Harvard University Library: Cambridge, 1988.

Wertheim, Aaron, *Law and Custom in Hasidism*. Ktav: Hoboken, 1992.

Woocher, Jonathan, *Sacred Survival: The Civil Religion of American Jews*. Indiana University Press: Bloomington, 1986.

Yaakov Yosef of Polnoye, *Toledot Yaakov Yosef*. Jerusalem, 1965.

Yerushalmi, Yosef Hayim, *Freud's Moses*. Yale University Press: New Haven, 1991.

Zornburg, Avivah Gottlieb, *Genesis: The Beginning of Desire*. Jewish Publication Society: Philadelphia, 1995.

David S. Ariel, Ph.D., is president of the Cleveland College of Jewish Studies. During his sixteen years as its president, the college has become one of North America's leading institutions of higher Jewish education and adult learning. Dr. Ariel earned his bachelor's degree in Judaic Studies from the Hebrew University of Jerusalem, his master's degree in Near Eastern and Judaic Studies from Brandeis University, and his Ph.D. from Brandeis in Jewish Philosophy and Kabbalah. He has held research fellowships in Arabic, Hebrew, and Latin. He is a popular lecturer on Jewish beliefs, mysticism, and spirituality throughout the United States in a variety of venues, including universities, synagogues, churches, and community centers. Dr. Ariel established the first Jewish educator training program in Kiev, for which he received a Community Service Award from the National Conference on Soviet Jewry, and founded the National Jewish Videoconferencing Network. He has also served as a senior policy adviser to the North American Commission on Jewish Education. He lives in Shaker Heights, Ohio, with his wife and three children.

For more information about *Spiritual Judaism*, visit the author's web site at www.spiritualjudaism.com.